JERUSALEM ON THE AMSTEL

LIPIKA PELHAM

Jerusalem on the Amstel

The Quest for Zion in the Dutch Republic

HURST & COMPANY, LONDON

First published in the United Kingdom in 2019 by
C. Hurst & Co. (Publishers) Ltd.,
41 Great Russell Street, London, WC1B 3PL
© Lipika Pelham, 2019
All rights reserved.
Printed in the United Kingdom by Bell & Bain Ltd, Glasgow

Distributed in the United States, Canada and Latin America by
Oxford University Press, 198 Madison Avenue, New York, NY 10016,
United States of America.

A Cataloguing-in-Publication data record for this book
is available from the British Library.

ISBN: 9781787380080

This book is printed using paper from registered sustainable
and managed sources.

The chapter epigraphs from Philip Polack's verse translation of
Rehuel Jessurun's Diálogo dos Montes (Tamesis Books, 1975)
are reproduced with the kind permission of Michael Polack.

www.hurstpublishers.com

For Val

CONTENTS

CONTENTS

viii

LIST OF ILLUSTRATIONS

The author and the publisher thank Ets Haim Library (EH) and the Jewish Historical Museum (JHM) in Amsterdam for their help in reproducing many of the figures illustrating this book.

1. Title page of Rehuel Jessurun's *Dialogo dos Montes* (EH).
2. De Hooghe's *Hof van den Baron Belmonte* (JHM).
3. De Hooghe's *Jewish funeral near Amsterdam* (JHM).
4. Page from Saul Levi Morteira's sermons (EH).
5. and 6. Title pages showing Menasseh ben Israel's printing press stamp (EH).
7. Menasseh ben Israel's ceremonial pamphlet celebrating the royal visit to the Esnoga (EH).
8. Inaugural plaque of Amsterdam Town Hall. Public domain (Wikicommons).
9. *Letter by 24 members of Yeshuot Meshiho to hail Shabtai Tzvi as Messiah* (EH).
10. Berckheyde's *View of the Great and Portuguese Synagogues in Amsterdam* (JHM).
11. De Hooghe's "Glory of the Amstel and its Senate" (JHM).
12. De Hooghe's *Portuguese Synagogue in Amsterdam during the inauguration* (JHM).
13. Cohanim golden washbasin (JHM).

LIST OF ILLUSTRATIONS

ACKNOWLEDGEMENTS

In early 2017, Richard McIlroy from the BBC World Service's Heart and Soul asked me to look into a possible programme on 500 years of the Reformation, from a Jewish angle. I am grateful to Richard for inadvertently directing me to the realm of research that would consume me by the summer of that year, when I found myself renting a flat in Amsterdam with two of my children, close to the old Jodenbuurt (Jewish Quarter).

I would like first of all to thank Sara and Arun, for putting up with their mother pursuing a frenzied obsession with the incredible epoch of the birth of Sephardi Judaism in Amsterdam. I spent my time researching at Ets Haim, the oldest still-functioning Jewish library; it dates back to the seventeenth century, when Iberian New Christians arrived in Amsterdam and reclaimed their Jewish heritage. Their admission to the northern European city was a revolutionary by-product of the Protestant Reformation. But by now, I was working on a book, not a BBC programme.

Michael Dwyer of Hurst Publishers said he believed in the book idea, after I wrote to him with a synopsis and my enthusiasm. I was thrilled. When we finally met after he had read the first five or so chapters, he said, "It seems you've been ordained to write this book." The Judaism of the Sephardim has been very

ACKNOWLEDGEMENTS

close to my heart for most of my life, having first heard about their long odyssey from Val, my Cairo-born mother-in-law, who spent her childhood in Alexandria.

I cannot thank enough my husband, Nico, to whom I owe most of my natural induction to the world of Maimonides in Córdoba, Fez and Cairo. Since we met in our early twenties, I've been on an intoxicating journey with him, to retrace the old world where Sephardi Jews and Muslims lived in harmony for hundreds of years until the fall of Granada in 1492.

Somehow this search for the legacy of a centuries-old Arab–Jewish entente has linked me with Yossi Babila, the Iraqi-Jewish-origin security guard at Amsterdam's Portuguese Synagogue. On a Shabbat evening in August 2017, I arrived at the magnificent Esnoga with my children and asked in Hebrew if we could join the service. Yossi looked hesitantly at first at these unlikely guests for Friday night prayers, before opening the door. Soon Yossi was talking to me about his name's Arabic root—"Bab" means gate, and he was indeed the gatekeeper.

As luck would have it, I was invited to stay during my research trips to Amsterdam in Yossi Babila's converted attic flat inside one of the tall, narrow seventeenth-century houses that surround the synagogue. From my window, I watched 1,000 candles being lit in the Esnoga on the eve of Yom Kippur in 2017, a service that I joined, mesmerised by the power and beauty of the Portuguese Jewish liturgy. In 1603, it was the Yom Kippur service held in a harbourside house that marked the re-entry into Judaism of a group of Iberian Catholic immigrants.

I am immensely grateful to Bart Wallet for sharing his rich insight into the early days of the Portuguese Jewish community in Amsterdam as we sat in his office at the University of Amsterdam, near the historic waterfront. The research for this book also would not have been possible without the advice, contacts and enthusiasm of Heide Warncke, curator of Ets Haim

ACKNOWLEDGEMENTS

Library. Heide always left my requested manuscripts ready for me on the central desk whenever I wanted to visit.

Tirtsah Levie Bernfeld has been guiding me throughout the writing of the book, including going through fact-checking of certain passages during final edit. She was always available to talk; I even got replies late at night after I sent urgent queries. Tehila Joucovitzky first told me about the Sabbateans and the Turkish messiah Shabbatai Zvi, when I stayed at her Arlozorov flat in Tel Aviv. Hami Verbin, one of my oldest and dearest friends in Jerusalem, has given me invaluable research tips.

I am privileged to have known and spent time with Professor Ludo Abicht in Antwerp. Without his mugs of coffee during a jittery summer afternoon in 2017, I would not fully have been able to grasp the break-up of the Spanish Netherlands. I would also like to thank Abraham Palache, a descendant of the Portuguese Jews in Amsterdam, who was my first reader and who enthusiastically approved of my passion and efforts in an ambitious project to link the seventeenth century and the Portuguese Jewish presence in Amsterdam today.

Julie-Marthe Cohen from Amsterdam's Jewish Historical Museum offered important contacts and invited me to "Jews and the House of Orange: 400 years of history", a sumptuous gathering at the Portuguese Synagogue in Amsterdam in spring 2018, attended by the Dutch king. Her colleague Anton Kras sent me the beautiful images of engravings and paintings from the museum's collection. I was fascinated by my conversation with Mirjam Knotter, and the idea that Rembrandt might have been an ordinary artist who chanced upon his extraordinary, exotic neighbours in the Jodenbuurt.

Ian MacWilliam told me about the paradox of Dutch tolerance, and Bruno Jakić drew a mental map of the polders and dykes—the secrets of Amsterdam's stability. Olivia Buning, whom I met in the women's gallery at the Esnoga during Yom

ACKNOWLEDGEMENTS

Kippur 2017, gave me a taste of what life is like for today's descendants of the Portuguese Jews. David Cohen Paraira introduced me to the unimaginable wealth and success of his ancestors, the Suassos, one of whom features on the cover of this book. Rabbi Abraham Rosenberg directed me to the rich musical tradition of Amsterdam's Portuguese Jews.

I'm very grateful to Harrie and Frida Curiel for their hospitality and their patience as I researched the story of their family. The Dutch historian of slavery Okke ten Hove helped locate documents in Amsterdam's municipal archives, and even translated them for me. His research on Moses de Moses Curiel was crucial to my own. Ton Tielen, an expert on Sephardi Jews in Amsterdam, shared some important links. I am indebted to Michael Minco for the latest on Spinoza and other community news, shared over lunch at Waterlooplein, near where the first public synagogue of the 1640s once stood, on the Houtgracht.

The Jewish community in Fez gave me a very warm welcome during Hannukah 2017. I am grateful to André Azoulay, whom I first met in 1999 when I was living in Rabat, for my smooth re-entry into the country, among many other things. My eldest, film director son Rishi, despite working on his first major feature, helped with emergency babysitting. In that regard, I am also eternally indebted to Alix. Gayna's tours of the Rembrandt and Rubens rooms at the National Gallery in London were extremely enlightening. Hugh Fraser was always a good listener, whenever I had to clear my mind. Fuchsia Dunlop's tough regime of "no phone and no email until 4" during the writing of the book meant that I met all of my deadlines. I'm thankful to Daisy Leitch, Alison Alexanian, Ella Boldron and the production team at Hurst for their impeccable professionalism.

Finally, I have been so very pleased with the thorough, insightful editing of Lara Weisweiller-Wu. She has an ecumenical knowledge of history; with a forensic eye she combed through the book for anachronisms, and yet allowed me to digress when

ACKNOWLEDGEMENTS

it was needed to breathe life into an archaic tract. It has been a most harmonious process. Amid many editorial queries, comments and responses, we even managed to talk about picking berries in the Norwegian mountains and walking in the Cotswolds in the heatwave of 2018.

FOREWORD

In pre-modern times, a "nation" was primarily a religious identity that flourished within certain geographical boundaries. The religion adhered to by an overwhelming majority of any European nation was Catholicism—until the Protestant Reformation that began in 1517, when everything changed. The bifurcation of the faith was an almighty blow to European self-understanding: a visceral inter-clan warfare unfolded, with brothers killing brothers and the predominant faith wiping out all other persuasions. These wars would continue over the following 300 years to haunt the idea of European nationhood. Old nations would splinter, setting off mass exoduses of displaced people. Out of their plight and steadfastness, new nations and new communities would emerge, strikingly dissimilar to those of the old system. As religious refugees found themselves on distant, different shores, a new sense of "homeland"—a new idea of "nation" or national identity that was not based on the predominant religion—entered European thought. This notion would manifest itself in the first signs of tolerance—a pre-requisite of any modern society, where state is separate enough from house of worship that ethnic and religious minorities are left to be who they are, without fear of torture, expulsion or forced conversion.

Amsterdam of the seventeenth century was a breeding ground for such ideas. A large majority of its incoming refugees were

FOREWORD

Iberian New Christians, also known as *conversos*: a formerly Jewish community of Spain and Portugal that had been forced to convert to Catholicism and was now fleeing the Inquisition. The enduring mocking and suspicion toward these converts, the labelling of those accused of secret Jewish practice as "Marranos" (literally "swine"), had permanently instilled in the New Christians the fear of being outcasts—fears that had now been proven justified, a century after their official conversion. As refugees from the Inquisition and Europe's wider religious wars arrived in Amsterdam, the harbour looked like "a carnival of nations".[1] Then, "nation" was a word used to denote the ethno-religious identity of each group of new arrivals: French Protestant Huguenots, Sephardi merchants from North Africa, Spanish formerly-Muslim Moriscos, and New Christians from the Iberian Peninsula, among many others.

None of these groups taking refuge in Amsterdam in the late sixteenth and early seventeenth centuries attached this new concept of "nation" to their collective identity as decisively as the New Christians did. They started pouring into the Netherlands from about the 1590s, culminating in a substantial settlement by 1609, when the northern Netherlands signed a twelve-year truce with Spain during their Eighty Years' War (1568–1648).

Ever since they had begun wandering around the world for survival from the first century CE, the world's Jews had dreamt of messianic redemption and return to Israel. At every Passover—the meal to commemorate the Exodus—they prayed to spend the following year in Jerusalem. Jerusalem stretched far and beyond the ancient city's geographical scope; it became an idea, a spiritual garden of Eden in which every person of the Jewish faith wanted to ensure their place. Historians documenting this Jewish hope for a homeland, or the anticipation of an imminent miracle such as "Jerusalem", have seen the dreams of the Iberian New Christians as highly important. This is because they accomplished a tangible enactment of that dream, by coming to Amsterdam and establishing a Jewish community that would soon reflect the prototype of a Jewish nation—as one Dutch historian phrased it, "they achieved as good a nation as was possible, in a pre-messianic context."[2]

The Dutch regents of the seventeenth century soon became used to calling the Iberian settlers by their own description for the community: the Portuguese Nation. This term was used as an official label for the migrant business community from Iberia, but the *Nação* would become an imagined nation, denoting the entire Iberian Jewish community and, later, other Sephardi migrants to Amsterdam. These concepts, which often overlapped, will be further explored in this book. As an ethnic and religious identity, the *Nação* was instrumental in linking Iberia's "Old Jews", who had been forced out prior to the Inquisition, with the incoming New Christians. In other words, even when individual New Christians changed their religious adherences back and forth, most of them ultimately becoming New Jews, they remained within the *Nação*.

By the middle of the century, this community had grown to 400 families, or some 2,000 members—still small compared with the numbers in other places where Jews had enjoyed a medieval Golden Age, such as Salonica, Venice, Livorno, and the Iberian Peninsula itself prior to expulsion. In Amsterdam, a fully recognised Jewish settlement came into being with incredible speed; its growth and contribution to modernity are unmatched in history. And what made the Amsterdam New Christians' accomplishments in high Judaism all the more remarkable was that they were not even Jews to begin with. As converts, they had settled and lived in other parts of the world before, including in neighbouring Antwerp, and ran successful trade and diplomatic missions in the Muslim and Christian worlds. It was only when they arrived in Amsterdam that they decided to return to

Judaism, inviting fellow Sephardi Jews from elsewhere in the world to join their new community and strengthen the Jewish nation, their *Nação*.

By the 1640s, Judaism was fully recognised in the Dutch Republic, and the officially acknowledged "Hebrew Nation" enjoyed unprecedented liberty and high status. This prestige was illustrated in May 1642, when the Dutch *stadtholder*, Frederik Hendrik, visited the new public synagogue in Amsterdam with the queen of England, Charles I's wife Henrietta Maria. It was the first such high-profile official visit to a Jewish synagogue by Christian monarchs anywhere in the Christian world. In just four decades, the former Catholics from Iberia had created "a zealous Jewish community who would soon be a model for those of the Old and New Worlds alike."[3]

Even then, Spanish and Portuguese continued to be the key languages of its creative expression, in which the *Nação*, as it continued to call itself, wrote poetry, prayers and plays, registered trade deals with the Dutch and issued the decrees of the Sephardi governing body, the Mahamad. When I spoke to him as I began writing this book, the Dutch historian Bart Wallet mused enthusiastically that "they were mad about theatre". "They loved going ... both to public playhouses and to private homes of the Dutch elite. When they came to Amsterdam, the first thing the [New Christians] did [was], they got membership cards to the public theatre." Speaking in his room on the third floor of the university building, situated on one of the oldest streets near Dam Square, Wallet burst into a rapturous retelling of this golden age in the history of Dutch Jewry. "So when they became Jewish, they thought, 'Okay, we'll go to the synagogue, we're going to say the prayers, but the melodies of the prayers must emulate the opera!' That was a direct influence of their Catholic upbringing."

Indeed, the forced baptisms of the late fourteenth and fifteenth centuries had driven many Sephardi Jews of Iberia to

settle in Italy, particularly in Venice; in this way, Italy had maintained a continuous Jewish presence lost in 1492 to those who
had stayed behind. Somehow, these "Old Jews" and the Marranos
had maintained some contact. Those who left Spain following
the Inquisition tried their best to keep the strong Sephardi network functioning. When opera was born in Italy at the end of
the sixteenth century, its melodies soon spread far and wide, and
the musical tradition of southern Europe preferred the new
operatic form to the old Catholic polyphonic music. The first
opera, *La Favola d'Orfeo* (The Fable of Orpheus), was composed
by Monteverdi in 1607, around the time the New Christians
were leaving the Iberian Peninsula and arriving in Amsterdam.
Many of them would have passed through Venice, soon to
become the centre of the new musical tradition, with the first
commercial opera house opening in 1637. The opera quickly
spread to dominate popular culture throughout Europe. Some of
the first Sephardi Jewish theologians who came to northern
Europe to teach the New Christians proper Judaism were from
Venice. Might there also have been poets and songwriters, even
rabbis, whose creative imagination was influenced by Europe's
latest chart-toppers?

There was certainly at least one maverick rabbi, who was
thought to have been greatly influenced by the "Christian music",
and who transported it into the synagogue: Leon, or Yehudah
Arye, of Modena. Born in Venice in 1571, he became a top rabbi
in the Venetian ghetto after which the Amsterdam community
would later model itself. Leon of Modena is known to have
shown a deep interest in the musical tradition of Italian churches,
and arranged choral performances in the Venetian synagogue.[4]
Jointly with a local composer, he authored a book on music, at a
time when music in the orthodox Jewish world was associated
with Christian liturgy or secular songs. It is possible that he
incorporated some of the contemporary popular melodies into
special prayer services.

FOREWORD

"There, in the world's oldest Jewish library, Ets Haim, one would find the most beautiful operatic melodies that were reflected onto the first prayer books of the new Jews," Bart Wallet explained to me, trying to conjure up this young community straddling two worlds: their old tradition in Catholic Europe, and their new Jewish life on the banks of the Amstel. It was in Ets Haim, the Tree of Life, located adjacent to the Portuguese Synagogue in Amsterdam, that I came across a rare manuscript: a play, written by a former New Christian in the early seventeenth century, probably in 1616. The drama, which portrays the community's culture, was converted into a traditionally Jewish format before it was performed in 1624 by the students of the city's first Jewish congregation.

The enthusiasm of the theatre-loving New Jews of Amsterdam has prompted me to start Chapter 1 of this book with that remarkable day of 1624 in mind, to take readers on a dramatic journey with the extraordinary Portuguese Jews of the Dutch Republic, who began their lives as Christians.

INTRODUCTION

The Jewish life in Amsterdam had an unusual start. The New Christians came to the Netherlands not as Jews, but as Catholics. Around 1600, they arrived in the Dutch Republic, fleeing from the Inquisition in their Iberian home. For some years, many of them continued on as Christians. In Middelburg in the south-western Zeeland province, a well-known Portuguese Catholic priest worked with the new arrivals.

They had left because they felt persecuted, despite having lived in Spain and Portugal for over a century as Christian converts. They also left for economic and other reasons, the Portuguese merchants wanting to establish a network in all important port cities. But life had still been more comfortable in their ancestors' adopted homeland of Iberia, and travel for New Christians was not always easy. Some were suspected of being "Marranos"—secret, crypto-Jews, accused of judaising Christian converts since the introduction of forced baptism in the late fourteenth century. The decree to interrogate the sincerity of the New Christians' faith was issued in 1492 by *Los Reys*—Isabella of Castile and her husband, Ferdinand of Aragon, jointly known as "the Kings". That year, following their reconquest of Granada from Boabdil, the last Muslim ruler of Andalucía, they gave the Jews and Muslims there a choice: to convert or be expelled from the united Catholic Kingdoms.

Some Jews crossed the narrow channel of the Mediterranean to North Africa, some to Italy—in both places, the escapees could continue to live as Jews. Many went to Portugal, where the Spanish edict had a slightly delayed impact and the Jews still enjoyed limited freedom. But a great majority of the Sephardi Jews converted to Catholicism to remain in Spain and hold onto their properties, social positions and businesses, where they had thrived during the previous 800 years of Muslim rule. These *conversos*, or New Christians as they came to be known, would live like regular Catholics, going to Mass and baptising their children. But a small number among them—the Marranos—secretly practised Judaism, or a rudimentary, memorised version of it. If discovered by the Inquisition police, they knew full well that the punishment could be death at the burning stake. In Portugal, which formally came under the Inquisition in 1536, the last "public" Jews of Iberia were in turn forced to convert to Catholicism. The king of Portugal closed the borders at the order of the Spanish monarchs, making it impossible for the Jews to sail to North Africa, where many of their co-religionists had settled earlier following the Spanish expulsion.

A New Christian could not travel abroad without a special permit from the Catholic authorities, and since Spain was ruling a great swathe of Europe and the New World at this time, waging frequent wars against Muslim North Africa and the Ottoman Empire, it would be hard for the Marranos to leave the Peninsula for 100 years after the 1492 edict of expulsion. But they never gave up searching for a place where they could be free from persecution, enjoy better economic possibilities and have the freedom to practise Judaism.

The opportunity arrived after the Union of Utrecht treaty, signed in 1579 by the seven northern Dutch provinces to mark their sovereignty and union. This led to the Seven United Provinces' declaration of independence from Spain in 1581, opening the doors for the New Christians, among other immigrants, to settle in Amsterdam, Middelburg and other major cities of the new Protestant republic. The end of the sixteenth century marked Amsterdam's emergence as one of the more important commercial centres in the northern hemisphere, with the expansion of colonial networks and new trade links with the Dutch East Indies. The Dutch Republic, after it separated from the Catholic south, was on the verge of entering what would become known as the Dutch Golden Age.

The Union of Utrecht had decreed that "each person shall remain free in his religion and that no one shall be investigated or persecuted because of his religion."[1] The signatories to the treaty probably had the Catholics, and not the Jews, in mind under this code of religious tolerance, but when it came to its application to Amsterdam—the city that accepted most outsiders—they did not outright violate it. Besides, the New Christians who came to Amsterdam were not given entry as religious refugees like the French Huguenots; they were merchants setting up a business colony of the great Portuguese colonial empire. So, while each individual town could devise its own rules regarding admission of Jews, their residency in the Dutch Republic did not require the wearing of identifying marks or living in a designated ghetto—common practices in other parts of the world at this time. Opposition to this declaration of tolerance was strong, but the Dutch Republic strengthened the commitment with the introduction of hereditary rule by the principal stadtholders, the House of Orange, thus preventing dissenting voices from breaking up the young republic.

Over the next decades, as the doors of immigration opened wider, many more of Iberia's New Christians headed for the most promising city in northern Europe, along with other fortune-seekers from central and eastern Europe. Then they realised that, with independence from Spain, the city had just turned

Protestant. Now, from 1590 to 1650, a period of religious mobility thrived in Amsterdam, when it was possible to convert from Christianity to other religions—something that had been forbidden all over Europe. Everyone in sixteenth-century Europe was being forced to reconsider their religious affiliation. What had once been a Catholic destiny by divine decree was no longer necessarily the norm. The Pope was no longer the supreme authority in the life of an old Christian. The Lutheran Reformation that kicked off in 1517 with the publication of the *Ninety-five Theses* posed a difficult question to every European Christian: am I a Catholic or a Protestant?

This period of "Confessionalisation", as it is known in the academic literature, meant that people had to know why they were Catholic, Lutheran, Reformed, or Jewish. This phase broke with an earlier one in which the choice had been made for them by their rulers. The New Christians, therefore, were at a historic junction. They could decide if they wanted to remain Catholic, become Protestant, or return to Judaism. It was a very short window in post-Reformation European history, but the Marranos— those who had secretly remained true to a form of Judaism—made the most of this once-in-a-lifetime opportunity.

Many of the New Christians arrived determined to return to Judaism, or so the myth goes.[2] But even the many who lacked it or were indecisive about their faith wondered, as they found themselves in a Protestant city, whether their Catholic identity would jeopardise their chances of survival. Some reflected on becoming Protestant. This was a community used to adapting to new environments and new religions throughout its long history as wandering refugees. What difference would it make, if they were now to join the Protestant Reformation sweeping northern Europe? Of course, it would have been far easier to become Protestant in the Calvinist Dutch Republic, and a handful of Iberia's New Christians did choose that option. One such convert to the Protestant faith led John Calvin's *Institutes of the Christian Religion* in Middelburg, promoting his ideology.

But the Marranos among the new arrivals were not convinced by this offshoot of Christianity, however dynamic it claimed to be, with its concepts of iconoclasm and strong emphasis on the teachings of the Old Testament. Many had grown up with countless family legends of Christian oppression on the Iberian Peninsula; in such history, writes one of the most prolific historians of the Spanish Inquisition, one may trace

> the darkest page in the dark record of the Jewish people, one of the saddest episodes in the history of human thought, and the ultimate decline of Spain from the high status to which her achievements and her genius entitled her—everything, in a word, which is associated with the term "The Spanish Inquisition".[3]

Even if the first group of New Christians to emigrate to the Dutch Republic didn't consider becoming Jewish, over time they found that it might be permissible in Amsterdam to do the impossible. After 100–200 years as Christian converts, they wanted to give their ancestral faith a go. The Marranos among the New Christian merchants reminded their people of the extermination of the Iberian Jewish population "from the Atlantic to the Mediterranean and from the French frontier to the Straits of Gibraltar". The 1391 massacre in Seville, ignited by hateful sermons of the preacher Ferran Martínez, had become a contemporary legend that still induced shivers of terror among the New Christian population. The ancient Jewish quarters (*Judería*) of Moses Maimonides' hometown Córdoba, of Valencia, of Barcelona and elsewhere in Catalonia, had frequently been the scenes of mob violence and further massacre throughout the fifteenth century. The force of militant Christianity had wiped out the Jews from these places, 100 years before the official Inquisition began when the last Andalusian city fell to the Catholic Kings.

These memories of humiliation under the Inquisition formed the most powerful factor in choosing such an untested, challenging path. Without them, the New Christians would likely have resettled in Amsterdam as Christians. Many settled in Germany around the same time, and remained Christians; this rarely happened in Amsterdam. Perhaps they would have joined the clandestine Catholics there, forced underground by the Protestant Reformation. Or they could have entered the Reformed Church, which would have been easier, as the Protestants valued the Law of Moses and the universal wisdom of the Jewish Prophets. Yet they chose Judaism over Christianity, still haunted by their ill treatment in the Catholic world.

Even after most of the population had been forced to accept baptism and live as Catholics around 1492, these converts had never completely managed to lead a life without the stigma of being dirty "Marrano". They were always inferior to the "Old" Christians. Recollections of their people wearing the *sanbenito*, paraded in shackles through public squares before Inquisition trials that almost always sentenced the accused to the stake to prevent further secret "judaising"—these collective memories were still raw. They had remained marginalised, deprived of full citizens' rights in their Iberian home. The olive groves and blue sky, the gurgling rivers and almond blossoms were not, after all, symbols of Jerusalem. In fact, in spite of the Jews' continuous residency on the Peninsula for at least 1,000 years, they did not compare Iberia to Jerusalem. The elders of Amsterdam's New Christian community conjured up this grim history of persecution and decided: no more allegiance to Christianity, no matter the form in which the faith was presented to them. Instead, they sought Jerusalem in the most unlikely of places—in a cold and grey city of many canals, under a permanently overcast sky.

But the tricky question was: how does one return to Judaism? The community's conversion to Christianity had happened a long time ago, and Judaism was now a religion this community did not properly know. All it had were century-old memories kept alive by the families. The closest modern-day comparison to this extraordinary decision to "re-convert" or "un-convert" would be if Indian Muslims who fled to Pakistan in 1947 then "returned" to the faiths of their Hindu or Buddhist forbears who had been forced by Muslim rulers centuries earlier to convert to Islam.

That said, what happened to the Jews of Spain in the fifteenth century was unprecedented in their history of religious oppression. The Jews had not been new to persecution, but while many in the past had embraced death in the face of forced conversion, a great many had also fled and become wanderers. Often, after long and difficult voyages, they had found favourable spots somewhere in the globe where they could resume the practice of Judaism. In most of the Muslim and Christian worlds, therefore, the Jewish faith had never quite vanished completely.

It is true that England had been without Jews since 1290, and 100 years on France followed suit; in this sense, the Iberian purge fit into a larger, late medieval development. Still, it was different. As Cecil Roth put it, "in 1391 [with the Seville massacre], for some mysterious reason ... For the first and only time in the whole course of their long history, the morale of the Jewish people—or of a considerable portion of it—broke."[4] The reason, he wrote, is impossible to pinpoint. In terms of violence and militancy, it is thought that the Inquisition surpassed all past attempts by European kingdoms to de-judaise their populations. But in Spain, the Jews may not only have relented because they faced extreme violence. According to some early historians, they may also have given in because of their deep connection to the "soft, scented air of the Iberian Peninsula" after residing on the land since time immemorial.[5] After all, the green of the olive groves and the blue of the sky may have made them think of the Jerusalem from which they had been exiled, and which they kept alive in all their prayers. In their hearts, they thought of themselves as truly Iberian. In any case, in the face of extreme violence, the Jews of Iberia submitted to conversion.

Many of the converts were sincere, and adhered to the Catholic faith both outwardly and inwardly. But a significant number remained secretly Jewish, Marrano. They feared the wrath of the God of the Old Testament for their pronounced apostasy, and went on keeping the Hebrew traditions at home. Over time, however, their memories of Judaism faded, and traditions that became totally oral in the absence of any Hebrew books were often reinvented or rejigged to accommodate the Marranos' public identity as Christians. Keeping Jewish literature or prayer books was an offence punishable by burning at the stake, so the rituals were constantly being attached to similar Christian ceremonies behind which Marranos could hide: "they would form religious association with titularly Catholic objects, and under the patronage of some Catholic saint, [use] them as a cover for observing their ancestral rites."[6]

Because of this, what these secret Iberian Jews knew of Judaism could in no way be verified by any known religious authority—let alone by Rabbinical sources that could not enter the Peninsula, especially after the official declaration of the Inquisition in 1492. Over the next century, the Marranos may have known or learnt about Judaism from Christian polemical works on the Jews, with which both northern and southern Europe abounded. But they did not have links with living Judaism. They did not know what a synagogue was, nor were they acquainted with the quintessential Jewish Law, the *halacha*. Despite the clandestine practice of what they thought of as Judaism, they were mostly culturally and to some extent religiously Catholic. Many of them had even attended Jesuit schools.

So, how did it begin? How long would it take before the New Christians in Amsterdam would be certified as Jews by the rabbis of the older Sephardi diaspora, who had maintained a continuous Jewish life?

There was a curious twist to this process. The New Christians did not know Dutch, did not try to learn it, and would not speak the language until well into the eighteenth century. All this time, they would hang onto a very strong Iberian identity, although they had renounced Catholicism. It was hard to transport an identity born of a fragrant land of almond blossoms in the hills, of poetry recitals in church squares, to a strict, puritan, flat landscape with a Calvinist system of belief. The old faith from which the New Christians had been separated may have been closer to the outlook of the Calvinists than Catholicism, but the lives they had lived until recently, the languages they still communicated, read poetry and wrote love songs in, did not weave well into the Protestant culture. In a way, returning to Judaism was more like returning to the old Iberia, before they had been forcibly baptised.

This unique phase in the Iberian-Jewish-*converso*-Dutch-immigrant life is described by historians as one of a "patchwork culture",[7] or a "conflicted, split identity".[8] These are in fact two opposing interpretations: the former stresses how the Amsterdam Sephardim combined many different influences and wove these into a dynamic, integrated whole; the latter conforms to the idea that the Dutch Sephardim had a conflicted sense of who they were. It would be fair to say that, even if a great many New Christians came out as fully integrated, a sizeable number found it difficult to reconcile with the rapid pace of conversion.

This conflicted generation's inner dilemma nevertheless led to a productive quest for self-development within a soon-to-be autonomous community, a *Nação*. The challenges of combining the new Jewish identity with recent Iberian Catholic tendencies created conflict between the former Marranos and the rabbis they brought over from Venice and Morocco to lead them into a

Jewish life. These were real Jews, "Old Jews", who had left Iberia earlier on before forced conversion took place, thus preserving a Sephardi Jewish continuity from the dispersion from ancient Judea at the beginning of the first millennium CE. They were horrified to see the kind of Judaism that the Marranos had invented and practised.

It had become an oral religion, spiritualised by their avowal of loyalty under persecution to Judaism. The textual version of the religion, internalised from the Old Testament, had been available to the Marranos as part of the Christian Bible, but they had not known any other written form of the banned religion in Iberia. There had been no law books, no prayer books or pamphlets for rituals and rites. And yet, in Amsterdam, the determination to return to the ancestral religion manifested in a kind of steadfastness that the community had not experienced before. The rabbis who came over to guide them were perplexed by the former Marranos' spiritual orthodoxy—one devoid of the rituals that are an integral part of Judaism, and with no more than a rudimentary knowledge of the Old Testament. How, then, would the New Christians soon reinvent themselves as what historians have called "the First Modern Jews"?

Since the exodus from Judaea that had sent the faith's followers to all corners of the world, what was happening in Amsterdam in the early seventeenth century had not taken place anywhere before. Outside Europe, the continuity of the faith had not been interrupted, and in isolated cases of Jews converting to Islam or Christianity, the community had never re-entered Judaism at a later date. While conversion from Judaism to another monotheistic religion was more customary, the opposite hardly ever happened in the predominantly Muslim or Christian societies in which Jews lived. And in this period, everywhere else that Jews were accepted, they were weighed down by innumerable restrictions on their movements; they were confined to separate quarters, and in the Christian world—although they prospered in areas of trade and business—they were generally barred from governmental appointments. They were forbidden to shave their beards. In Europe and North Africa, the Jews wore badges showing their lower status among the "real" citizens. Forbidden to be styled as "Don", the Iberian Jews had instead worn "a badge of shame". In Amsterdam, however, the New Christians—now "New Jews"—wore no identifying marker to separate them from the rest of the population. Within the first half century of their arrival, they elevated themselves to become part of the high culture and the upper class—despite being barred by an old law from most of the Dutch trade guilds.

The swift rise of the Iberian Jews as a distinguished social class in seventeenth-century Amsterdam has challenged sociologists and historians. How did they do it? The key to their success had many dimensions, some of which they chanced upon in a city that was just emerging as a new power. Freed from papal restraints, Amsterdam offered a message of welcome to all new arrivals, in particular those who claimed to have been persecuted by the Papal Bull. The city's Calvinist rulers needed a workforce to help them lead world trade, and others in the Reform Church were curious: they were moved by the legend of the persecuted Jews from the Catholic south, by their search for a true Jerusalem, a homeland, in the liberal, Protestant north. The Dutch authorities were compelled to shelter this people that had been lost in the fog of anonymity, shame and secrecy.

This was determined as much by altruism as by the authorities' interest in a people who had skills with which no other immigrants to the Dutch Republic could compete. The Jews were welcomed in Amsterdam because they could operate an international business network. They kept close contact with the Iberian Peninsula, they had family members who were Catholic, and they had family and friends, also Catholic, in the Spanish and Portuguese colonies. They also had Jewish family members in Hamburg, North Africa, the Levant and the Holy Land—as far as the vast Sephardi diaspora extended—all of whom were a part of the *Nação*. Amsterdam's Calvinist ruling elite was keen to exploit this extraordinary network. When they arrived, the city was already thriving. Amsterdam was the financial capital of the world. London would take over in the ensuing century, but during a 100-year period of unbound, seaborne opportunities, Amsterdam was booming, and its Jews were very much part of the Dutch success. They quickly became involved in their new adoptive country's colonial enterprises in the Indies, making optimal use of their own past colonial expertise, earned from working with the Portuguese and the Spanish—many of whose colonies the Dutch would soon take over. The New Christian immigrants passed on—or, rather, traded in—their knowledge, ideas and networks. In return, they were offered a safe, permanent settlement in Amsterdam, a city that they would call their Dutch Jerusalem.

Another important aspect of the New Jews' success was that, as well as establishing contacts with the Sephardi diaspora, they also forged strong links with local business communities. Barred from most of the trade guilds, which were traditionally reserved for the native-born, many Jews entered into joint ventures with influential Dutch businessmen, stretching the Jewish-Dutch network well into Russia. Given this advantage, the Dutch authorities would often turn a blind eye to casual violations of the guild law.

Pulling together their resources in the greatest diplomatic and commercial venture of early modern European history, the Jews of Amsterdam made their presence indispensable to Dutch economic growth. Just seventy years after the arrival of the first Marranos, the New Jews occupied some of the flashier canal houses on the east bank of the Amstel, enticing famous Dutch artists and painters to move into the neighbourhood. This was the interesting paradox of Amsterdam's Jewish quarter, the Jodenbuurt, compared with Europe's other Jewish neighbourhoods at the time: instead of being a segregated island of impoverished refugees, it attracted respectable gentiles who were queuing up to become residents. All kinds of immigrant and religious groups lived there together. Far from being ghettoised and stigmatised for their race and religion, in Amsterdam the Jews formed a thriving community, well respected and even exoticised by the city's artists. At one point Rembrandt's neighbours on Jodenbreestraat included some of the richest, most flamboyant and influential Jews of the city.

In this fertile setting of prosperity and stability, a new phenomenon swept through the Jewish imagination. Messianism, the idea of a final redeemer at the end of history, became increasingly popular among both the Iberian Sephardim and the city's Ashkenazi Jews, who had also arrived in the Dutch Republic in great numbers as they fled central European pogroms, coming to bask in the success of the Sephardi community. This was an unprecedented occurrence in the pre-Zionist world: the Jews of the two main branches, separated in the diaspora since the destruction of the Temple in the first century, were now together in one city, living in the same neighbourhood and benefitting from the alliance. This would be of great significance in the further rise of messianism in the mid-seventeenth century.

The history books of the eighteenth century give detailed accounts of Amsterdam's special role in the united Jewish revival. The two streams of Judaism, Sephardi and Ashkenazi, were living side by side and got to know each other in a climate of tolerance, mutual empathy and economic solvency. There is another side of the story, though, which will be elaborated later: the Iberians also showed a patronising attitude toward the Ashkenazi Jews, whom they considered detrimental to their own superior

13

social status among the wider Dutch. The Sephardim advocated their own "*bom judesmo*". Their social welfare system, however, did not at first exclude the poor Ashkenazi refugees.

As the two denominations came together into one Jewish Nation, their co-existence in Amsterdam was seen as a precursor to the arrival of the Messiah. This hope was intertwined with the thinking of the time: that perhaps the Jewish wandering, the aspiration of the previous diasporas, had reached its completion. The next and final step would be the Jews' return to the land of their ancestors. In other words, Amsterdam was the penultimate stage in the fruition of the Jewish hope of Israel. But there were still one or two preconditions that must be met, before the Messiah could show up.

On Amsterdam's harbour, both Sephardi and Ashkenazi men would wait daily for the boats from the colonies to arrive. It was not always to receive their loved ones who had businesses in Brazil and the West Indies. They also believed that the sailors from the New World would come home carrying news of the Ten Lost Tribes, whose possible discovery obsessed the Sephardi and the Ashkenazi Jews of the mid-1600s. In the Talmud or the Jewish law books, the final redemption, the so-called "end of history", is predicted to come when the Ten Tribes are found and reunited with the rest of the Jewish diaspora. Every time ships from the colonies arrived with stories of Native Americans, of new exotic peoples, the Jews of Amsterdam would jump, thinking that perhaps, there in the wilderness of the New World, the sailors had found the missing link to the promised Jewish Kingdom.

One particular story was brought back by a certain sailor, Antonio de Montezinos, who declared after his return from the Americas that he had indeed met representatives of some tall and sun-scorched people across a fast river in Peru, who could be the ones they were looking for. "I was listening to them, they were speaking in Hebrew!" he reportedly said. This was a cause of huge excitement among the Dutch Jews, and in the Christian world. One of the city's most influential rabbis, Menasseh Ben Israel, would later expound on the incident in his book, *Mikve Israel*, (The Hope of Israel), to satisfy the Jewish as well as Christian interest that Montezinos' story generated. He celebrated the exultation of the known world around this messianic fervour: the ten tribes, the imminent future, and the arrival of the redeemer.

Ben Israel may have been a leading promoter of the idea that seventeenth-century Amsterdam held the key to the final messianic era. The freedom and security that the city offered was regarded by its Jews as the best they could get in the "Galut"— the stage of penance, as the diaspora was called. It wasn't the geographical Jerusalem that the New Jews pined for. And even if they did, most believed that Amsterdam was the precursor to Jerusalem. It was as good as home; a launch pad for the final lift-off. After all, until now, in the societies these Jews had lived in, the usual understanding was that the synagogues would not be visible to the public. This was part of a long list of security measures adopted by the long-persecuted people, and continued even when they lived in fairly moderate societies such as Venice, Fez and Salonica.

It would be in Amsterdam that the Jews would worship for the first time in a synagogue not only visible from the outside, but even modelled on the Jewish Temple, copied and built by a Dutch architect. The Jews' rebuilding of their Temple in exile— whose destruction sent them into that exile in the first place— was an important objective for the Calvinist rulers too. They strongly believed in the Second Coming of Jesus, which could only happen after all the Jews had returned to Jerusalem.

After the building permit for a public synagogue was granted, the community then had to come up with what it should look like. What is a synagogue, outside of Israel? The last time their ancestors had prayed in an ostentatious, public place of worship had been the Temple itself in Jerusalem. So, they decided, a temple they must build, completed in 1639. The architectural excellence achieved by the Dutch architect was based on a model and accompanying drawings and booklets of the Jewish Temple by a fanatical architect–rabbi, Jacob Judah Leon. Rabbi Leon travelled with his model all through Europe, and even visited the court of the *stadtholder*. So popular that he was nicknamed Templo, it made him something of a celebrity among both his city's Jews and those in the Protestant world who were preoccupied with messianic speculations and the Jews' return to Jerusalem.

Through its huge, two-storey windows, light poured into the first officially public Sephardi Jewish synagogue in Amsterdam, casting a diminutive effect on the worshippers, who had until now prayed in smaller, mostly private establishments, of which there had been many from the early 1600s on. It was to this imposing synagogue that the stadtholder Frederik Hendrik would pay his state visit in 1642. Three decades later, another Christian Dutch architect, Elias Bouman, would be shown the plan of Templo's "Solomon's Temple" and asked to copy it, in order to build what would become a most impressive building on the Amstel: a brand new, gigantic Portuguese Synagogue, completed in 1675. Its magnificence has been well documented by many travellers and social historians of the time. By building such a majestic public house of worship—one that would become a city landmark and remain so until this day—the Sephardi community was making an important statement: "We're not in Jerusalem, but we have Amsterdam. And in Amsterdam, we are free to build a temple."[9]

In old etchings and paintings of the seventeenth and eighteenth centuries, the Portuguese Synagogue towers over all other buildings in the city. Visitors from Italy, Spain and England wrote in their travelogues that they had seen this stunning building, and expressed their surprise that it was a synagogue. It was all the more remarkable because just opposite there was a Catholic church, nondescript, small and secret—no one could see it was a church, since Catholics were not permitted to hold services in public. Yet the Sephardim were allowed to show off both their wealth and their newly reinstated old religion. In Amsterdam, the former New Christians built a model Jewish community, self-governed with its own laws and institutions, and a synagogue that resembled the biblical Jewish Temple.

Every immigrant society in Amsterdam enjoyed a unique monopoly on a particular profession, authorised by the municipal authorities. The Scandinavians, the Huguenots, and of course the Jews were all given different religious and trade privileges. Throughout the seventeenth and eighteenth centuries, most of the major professions would be restricted to the native Christian Dutch population only—officially. "The newcomers could not belong to most of the guilds, true, but these regulations were not strictly observed," says Wallet. The city authority's main objective was to maximise profit from the various workforces that assembled in Amsterdam. The Sephardi Jews were the most influential and wealthiest among the immigrants, and as their influence grew in the city, the rules became more lax. One could find Jews in professions such as law, traditionally reserved for the natives. "A lot was possible in Amsterdam," adds Wallet, "thanks to the economic boom." The most fascinating of all was the new Jews' unbending determination to change the course of their fate. "Not only did the old Catholics become New Jews, they became the first modern Jews."

The following chapters will explore this theme: the formation in seventeenth-century Amsterdam of an autonomous Jewish congregation, consisting of former converts and their Sephardi Jewish teachers, amidst an unprecedented epoch of tolerance and a unique confluence of cultures. Among the Iberian Jewish settlers, there were writers, poets, singers and philosophers. With their sound knowledge in art, trade, diplomacy and navigation, they became a paradigm for reform and enlightenment for other Jewish and non-Jewish communities around the world.

The following pages will traverse the spectacular rise to stardom of a persecuted people, and then the tragic, abrupt end of that glorious chapter, ironically at a theatre. Amsterdam's Hollandsche Schouwburg theatre was where the 400 years of Dutch Jewish history suffered a devastating blow, when the Nazis and their collaborators assembled the Jews of the Netherlands before sending them away to death camps. The old Jewish theatre is now a memorial to the 107,000 Jews who were taken to camps, of whom only 5,500 returned after the war, with the 20,000 who had survived in hiding. The Amsterdam Jews, once 10 per cent of the city's population, have now been reduced to a community of 1,000.

But the legacy of the seventeenth-century Jews of Amsterdam lives on. It resonates through what the world has subsequently achieved. The Amsterdam Sephardim contributed to changing the history of European civilisation, by spearheading the Age of Enlightenment, the father of which was a young Iberian Jew. Baruch Spinoza grew up in the Jewish quarter in Amsterdam and, although his work on secularism, reason and rationalism cost him his membership of the synagogue, his thought was the product of one of the first modern societies, and he was one of its leading voices.

We shall look into how and why the Sephardi community in Amsterdam became a model for *haskalah*, the Jewish Enlightenment. This Enlightenment was in itself one of the primary sources of the later Zionist inspiration. The period between the formation of the first modern Jewish society in seventeenth-century Amsterdam and the birth of modern Zionism two centuries later in central Europe is not a topic for discussion here.

INTRODUCTION

But in the following chapters we shall see, through the lives and works of members of the *Nação*, that a great many "Zionist" goals were achieved in Amsterdam.

Theodor Herzl, the pioneer of Zionism, wrote in *Der Judenstaat* (The Jewish State) that the Jews must consider themselves not just a religious body, but also a nation capable of developing its own political institutions in a land of their own. Imagine a time capsule transports you back to Jewish Amsterdam in the 1600s. There you would meet the *parnassim*, the wardens or governors running the community as a political and social institution parallel to the Calvinist central government, with daily dealings and economic cooperation between the two. Applying the Jewish law, the *halacha*, these wardens are ruling a thriving "Nation", as successfully as ever before in the diaspora. The walls of a ghetto do not restrict their lives. They believe Amsterdam is the final act in the repertoire of Jewish diasporic life before the messianic era can begin. Their indomitable messianism is nothing less than a full-scale campaign for Zion, 200 years before Zionism was born. Amid this ancient yearning for a homeland, under the city's liberal awning and unprecedented economic prosperity, the *Nação* answers directly to its own leaders.

The following chapters will trace how this New Jewish community of Iberian descent changed the old idea of the Wandering Jew; how its members settled in Amsterdam and prospered beyond belief, becoming part and parcel of the Dutch economic miracle. We will see how the Iberian business diaspora, within the ideological confederation of the *Nação*, left an unprecedented legacy, expressing the "Hope of Israel" and establishing a prototype Jewish nation three centuries prior to the creation of the Jewish state of Israel, the modern world's first.

PART I

AN END TO WANDERING

1

TEMPEST-TOSSED AND FOUND

"What greater consolation could they see,
Those whom fate till now has forced to flee
The venomous barking dogs who, filled with rage,
Their thirst for Israel's blood can ne'er assuage,
Than, having issued from such narrow straits,
To enter freely, through these spacious gates,
This refuge for all souls in misery,
This resting place, this little sanctuary?"

Rehuel Jessurun, Prologue, *Diálogo dos Montes*, 1616[1]

In 1624, a remarkable thing happened in Amsterdam's Jodenbuurt: a play was performed in its first unofficial synagogue, Beth Jacob (House of Jacob), established at the beginning of the century by the Portuguese (Iberian) New Jews. The staging of a play in a synagogue was unusual enough, let alone what the play represented: humanised biblical mountains, each vying to prove themselves the greatest of them all. They put forward arguments before the King of Judah, Jehoshaphat, the judge at this compelling tournament.

Diálogo dos Montes (The Conversation of the Mountains), is written in a well-known one-act play form, the *auto*, that was popular in medieval Spain and Portugal. After forced baptism was introduced in the fourteenth century, the Jews had lived on the Iberian Peninsula as converts for some 200 years. The "little sanctuary" evoked in the play's Prologue is seventeenth-century Amsterdam, where they came to settle and began their lives as Jews. "The venomous barking dogs" are the Inquisitors, who came after the New Christians, centuries after their conversion to Catholicism. As we have seen, the Spanish and Portuguese Inquisitions drove the Marranos from the 1590s to north-western Europe, where the Protestant Reformation had opened a new era of tolerance.

The warmest welcome was offered by Amsterdam, a promising northern port in the great age of mercantilism, where the Iberian Sephardi traders' expertise was revered and received with open arms. Here, the New Christians were given refuge along with other religious minorities. The little sanctuary of Amsterdam began to grow into the most economically prosperous, cosmopolitan city in Europe, with "spacious gates" through which fortune-seekers, the persecuted, religious and political dissidents, vagabonds displaced by religious wars in central and eastern Europe, and others from the further shores of North Africa and the Caribbean entered freely. It became a "resting place" for these wandering communities, a respite from the woes they had suffered at the hands of religious fanaticism elsewhere.

The Iberian newcomers were reeling from this welcome reception in Amsterdam, a realm of toleration unimaginable since the beginning of their long exile, the great Jewish dispersion, in the first century CE, when diaspora Jews in the Roman Empire far outnumbered those in Palestine, even before the destruction of the Temple in 70 CE. While many Jews had enjoyed a somewhat Golden Age in Spain until the first round of forced baptism in the 1390s, or had enjoyed relative freedom to practise and prosper in Italy, their economic activity was confined to a handful of businesses. They wore identifying marks, and intermingling with the Christian majority was limited to business networking, financial transactions, and mediating diplomatic missions with the Muslim world.

In North Africa and the Ottoman Empire, the Jews had significantly more freedom and better status than in Christendom. Under Islamic law, Jews and Christians are considered fellow "People of the Book", entitled to certain rights and, more importantly, the freedom to practise their religion. But "alien" populations in the Muslim world at this time were also subject to a special super-tax. Tolerance was conditional on their acceptance of an inferior status, with restriction on movements. In both Christian and Islamic polities, Jews were generally confined to their designated area of residence, often the poorest part of the city: the *ghetto, judería, mellah*.

In Amsterdam, none of these constraints would be applied to the Iberian arrivals who would be known as the "Portuguese" community. The city was in a great flux, with Calvinism, the third wave of the Protestant Reformation, sweeping the country. It was the heyday of the Dutch moderates, with the Republic experiencing a percolation of religious ideas that resulted from, but also challenged, Luther's Reformation. Earlier in the sixteenth century, their own philosopher, Erasmus, had put forward a "middle way", countering the harsh Lutheran edict. He advocated a balance between respect for faith as in Protestant ideology, and making room for a splash of Catholic free will. The Dutch regents of the late sixteenth and early seventeenth centuries were much influenced by Erasmus' humanism and his life's work in favour of religious tolerance.

It was in this liberal climate that the New Christians found themselves musing over the choices laid before them. For the first time in centuries, they could envisage living openly as Jews. If there was any serious opposition within the community to the collective decision to return to its ancestral faith, this was not recorded. But in view of *Diálogo dos Montes'* likening of the Catholics to "venomous barking dogs", we can very well imagine how the New Christians felt about the "Old" Christians. The idea of belonging even to a reformed version of that faith must have appeared akin to self-flagellation. It was time to break free of the old terror of the south, and live with dignity in the new "true north".

The Jewish longing for a "little sanctuary", as they wandered through the world, goes back to the destruction of the Temple in the first century. The theme had been long ingrained in the imagination of the exiled, as their poetry vividly portrays, shown by *Diálogo dos Montes* and its "tempest-tossed" people seeking refuge from the Inquisition. Similarly, the Marrano poet, Samuel Usque, spoke of Catholic Europe as his "hell on earth", and he searched for a sanctuary elsewhere, in the Ottoman Empire: "There is a city in the Turkish kingdom, which formerly belonged to the Greeks, and in our days is a true mother-city in Judaism."[2]

That was Salonica, where he found himself along with other fellow Sephardim. The city was ruled by law, he wrote; the Sephardi Jews fleeing pogroms and discrimination, annihilation and forced conversion, came there to live in peace and liberty, turning the Ottoman city into a "new Jerusalem". To them, Salonica's lush and fertile land appeared to be "watered by an abundant stream of charities."[3] There were other such cities during the long exile where the Jews felt comfortable, thrived in businesses and even enjoyed government positions, as in the Iberian Peninsula under Muslim rule, and in North Africa.

The imagery of a "tempest-tossed" people looking for their "Jerusalem" is as old as the Jewish expulsion from Judea. The idea of a "storm", sometimes natural but most often a manmade turmoil of persecution, has also appeared frequently in Jewish writing through the ages. After surviving a storm, the Jews would pay homage to the welcoming land, comparing it to a "sanctuary". The great twelfth-century sage Moses Maimonides, who was born in Córdoba, wrote in his 1167 journal: "When storms threatened in the past, I wandered from place to place, but by now, by God's mercy, I have been enabled to find a sanctuary in Cairo."[4] This was from a tireless promoter of human endurance and wisdom, who had suffered multiple "storms" of persecution and expulsion: driven from his Spanish birthplace when he was only thirteen, Maimonides had fled to Fez, but was chased out by the advance of the Almohads; he finally found a safe haven in Cairo, where he became a private doctor to the vizir of Saladin. But Cairo of the twelfth century was not "Jerusalem". No literary term such as "Egyptian Jerusalem" was used in Jewish writing from that time and place. Instead, Egypt has been and will always be memorialised by the Jews as a place where they were slaves, until they were led across the Red Sea to freedom in the Judean hills.

The loss of the "mother-city" never left the diaspora's imagination, and the Jewish religious journey has been one of finding an alternative abode until the collective return to the biblical Jerusalem. For centuries, the devout waited for the arrival of the Messiah to signal the final return, while the sceptical and the pragmatic tried, over and over again, to carve out a Jerusalem in exile. They endowed their new places of residence with religious credentials. Over the millennia, many cities in the Iberian Peninsula and the Mediterranean belt achieved the status of Jerusalem in the lives of the exiled Jews. But in 1492, their "home in exile" came tumbling down, when they were told by Isabella and Ferdinand that they had three months to submit to baptism, or leave the territories of Spain, Sicily, Majorca and Sardinia.

Each of these places had been an alternative home for the Jews for many centuries. Life wasn't perfect, but it was good enough, glorious even, when they were favoured by a kind monarch impressed by their loyalty and trade skills. The exiled Jews had settled comfortably and led a good life in the haven of Spain and Portugal for over a millennium, despite the enduring ultimate Jewish aspiration to return to Israel proper. But this home away from home was snatched from the Iberian Jews by a savage force, sending them on a perilous journey. A Lisbon-born finance minister in Spain at the time of the expulsion, Don Isaac Abravanel (1437–1508)—who claimed direct descent from the biblical King David—described the tragic exodus as follows: "When the dreadful news reached the people, they mourned their fate; and wherever the report of the decree spread, Jews wept bitterly. The terror and lamentation were greater than at any time since the expulsion of our forefathers from their own soil in Judah to foreign strands."[5]

Abravanel wrote that a great many of the Jews had sworn not to break their Divine Covenant, facing the most unforgiving Christian enemies. Many had gone into hiding and would live the most dangerous and uncertain lives of Marranos for the next 100 years. The more courageous among them joined the exodus and dispersed, searching for a land that would accept them as Jews:

> the people, old and young, women and children, a multiple of 300,000 from every province, went forth on one day, unarmed and afoot. I was among them. They went whithersoever the wind carried them. Some fled to the kingdom of Portugal, others to the kingdom of Navarre. Many chose the way of the sea and were lost, drowned, burnt to death and sold into slavery.[6]

Abravanel himself went on a journey by sea, and ended up in Naples. In his case he survived well, for the time being, becoming finance minister there. For a few years he lived a calm, successful life as an advisor to the royal house, until the French invasion of 1495. Dispossessed once again, he left Naples, finally settling in Venice.

These voyages were an essential part of Jewish writing and reminiscences over more than 1,000 years. The recital of glories and misfortunes became part of the Jewish liturgy and literature. It was the only way for the perpetually shifting fate of the people to be remembered, and their collective hope renewed. No sooner had one Jerusalem vanished, than another journey into a different exile was set in motion, in search of another Jerusalem. This pattern tells the story of a people who never gave up; a people with tremendous faith in humanity and its continuity on Earth. It was this unequivocal faith in the scriptures that kept the Jewish diaspora going: the conviction that in the end they would be saved, after having fled "seven ways" (Deuteronomy 28:25), having been lost and tossed back and forth among all the nations of the world.

Each time, they made it work, with the much-tested versatility of one of the most exiled peoples in human history. It is said about Leon of Modena, the music-loving Venetian Jew born in the late sixteenth century, that "he could deal out a hand of cards with the same expertness as he composed in Italian and Hebrew."[7] This survival instinct became the exiled Jews' second nature, and so the search for a permanent home never left them, even when faced with enemies like the "venomous barking dogs" of the Inquisition.

When he wrote *Diálogo dos Montes*, the poet and playwright, Rehuel Jessurun, had it all in him: the history of his people, the stories of expulsion, exile, and the search for a Jerusalem. The play is an allegory of the Jews' physical and spiritual journeys, told in an esoteric language that would only be understood by his small audience, who had been on the same sea-voyage as him, and who had now arrived in what appeared to be a new promised land.

If standing here, I cast my eyes around
At all the beauteous adornment found
Within this House of God, this holy place,
Astounded and amazed I stand in face
Of such great beauty.[8]

These words were acted out in 1624 before the congregation of the first New Jews, Beth Jacob. The play attests, among other things, to the rediscovery of roots and of a second home by a lost generation. It is also an homage to the rulers of the land that had welcomed them, in the old Hebraic tradition of declaring loyalty to the land offering shelter. It is the betrayal of this loyalty by the Spanish Kings in 1492 that prompts an inconsolable Don Isaac Abravanel, at King Ferdinand's court, to cry out, "O King, save your loyal subjects. Why do you act so cruelly toward us? We have prospered in this land and we would gladly give all we possess for our country."[9]

Yet Abravanel and Jessurun, like others before them, were not dissuaded by the repeated violations of their allegiance to their rulers. Throughout the play, Jessurun eloquently expresses his people's gratitude for and excitement at the discovery of not just any scrap of land, but a thriving seaborne empire that welcomed them to live there. For the tempest-tossed Sephardim, it was like messianic salvation.

It would seem from the outset that Amsterdam was the journey's end for the Marranos, who chose to drop their cloak of secrecy. The law in the Dutch Republic, following its split from the Spanish Empire, was clearly defined: civil law, which decreed religious freedom for all. What protected the religious minority in Amsterdam and the rest of the United Provinces was a modern, manmade law enshrined in the Treaty of Utrecht, not the divine law that Salonica's sultans adhered to. While Islamic law provided only limited protection to the People of the Book, what was officially called "freedom of conscience" in the Dutch

Republic implied that the state was not concerned with how people perceived their identities.

Within a few years after their arrival in Amsterdam, almost all the New Christians became New Jews. The ambivalent—there were some, including Baruch Spinoza's grandfather—did not reveal their doubts to the leaders of a community that was fast becoming well-organised, with religious freedom and a welfare system to which everyone contributed, and to which needy new-comers or existing members could apply for financial support. This was like the ten-year tax relief that the current Israeli state offers to Jewish immigrants, as a practical incentive to make *aliya*—emigrate—to the Jewish homeland, boosting the popula-tion. The Portuguese *Nação* offered similar perks and benefits to the New Christians as well as to the "Old Jews" of the Sephardi diaspora—in short, whoever could prove their connection to this Iberian Jewish nation.

The few who were not forthcoming in joining Judaism after settling in Amsterdam would very soon change their minds, embrace their ancestral faith and benefit from the *Nação's* impec-cably run social welfare system. There were other issues to con-sider, too, such as the right to burial in western Europe's first public Jewish burial ground near a major city. Spinoza's grandfa-ther had to undergo post-mortem circumcision in order to qualify for burial in Beth Haim, the Jewish cemetery in Ouderkerk on the Amstel River. Spinoza historians believe that this had a profound impact on the philosopher's later intellectual leanings towards denial of the God of the Old Testament.

The *Nação* continued to use its well-established trade net-work with the former mother nations of Spain and Portugal. The New Jews drew on the Sephardi elders' knowledge of run-ning a community in Venice, from where some of the early founders of the Amsterdam *Nação* had come. Sephardi rabbis and educators—whom the New Christians needed, to teach them "true" Judaism—also came from North Africa, where many Spanish Jews had found refuge after the first wave of Iberian exodus in the fifteenth century.

Though there was an older Jewish presence in Hamburg, and Antwerp had a sizeable, thriving colony of New Christian merchants—some of them possibly secretly-worshipping Marranos—Amsterdam had no Jews until the end of the sixteenth century. Within the first years of arrival, the *Nação* established the Beth Jacob congregation in a private home. This was the venue for the 1624 performance of *Diálogo dos Montes*. Its author, Rehuel Jessurun, was a former monk from Lisbon, Paulo de Pina, who had embraced Judaism and assumed his new name shortly before moving to Amsterdam in 1604.

Jessurun's prologue is delivered by Earth, who introduces the seven biblical mountains and, as the competition's moderator, presents the contestants to an early modern audience. Earth enters the scene and tells those watching why the Jews' congregation in the city of Amsterdam had been such a different story, one of freedom previously unknown in their long history in exile. But the audience will have been well aware of the setting, and its history. They were the first generation of Portuguese New Jews, well acquainted with the legends of their ancestors; they knew that they descended from a long line of wanderers searching for identity. By reiterating the legends, Jessurun paid homage to the courage and conviction of these wanderers, who had carried the stories from Egypt to Jerusalem to Spain to Morocco to Italy to Iberia, and now to the northern harbour, where they had settled and assumed their lost identity.

Rehuel Jessurun was one of the founding members of Beth Jacob. He was its treasurer, *gabay*, when its various branches and institutions were being formed, regularly reporting to the congregation's first rabbi, Saul Levi Morteira, a Venetian Jew. It was to Venice that the Jewish institution-building in Amsterdam was owed. The Portuguese *Nação* was experimenting with an identical model, and it was proving to be more successful than it had been in the Venetian ghetto. Unmarked by any visible insignia, the Jews of Amsterdam were able at least externally to blend into the population, in their dress and the silky, shiny curls of their wigs. With their sun-kissed olive complexion, they were easy to distinguish from the pale northerners, but that was never a hindrance to where they could or could not go. They could walk in any part of the city and travel in and out of their neighbourhood whenever they wanted. Their movements were not monitored, and there was no "curfew" for Jews as was the case in the ghettoised life in southern Europe and North Africa.

The opening scene of the play expresses disbelief at this incredible privilege, and imagines the joy and bewilderment of *"dos filhos de Jaacob"*, the sons of Jacob, still being persecuted elsewhere in the world, could they see what Beth Jacob had achieved:

> What astonishment
> Will shine in the dark night of banishment
> Of the sons of Jacob, who by villainy
> Oppressed, come fleeing from the tyranny
> Of cruel Edom and his evil brood,
> Some with holy zeal alone imbued,
> Others driven by ignoble terror,
> Still others tortures suffering in horror,
> In dark and gloomy prisons locked away
> From where they never see the light of day.

The Jews of the world would be thrilled by the community's newfound home, after its members had been scattered across the globe by hostile forces, says Earth.

> Oh what astonishment there'll be, I say,
> To see that the tempest-tossed who've made their way
> To this true north, should find here sweet repose,

A haven to recover from their woes,
And in this holy house, the sacred name
Adonai, Adonai, may openly proclaim![10]

It would be another half a century before the Sephardim of Amsterdam would build their magnificent public synagogue, on Vlooienburg, a manmade island on the Amstel's east bank. The island would offer accommodation to seafaring Sephardim—merchants and negotiators with connections—as well as the poor and vagabond Ashkenazi Jews who would soon arrive from eastern Europe and Germany. This was where famous gentile resident artists such as Rembrandt Harmenszoon van Rijn would choose to live, drawing artistic inspiration from the neighbourhood's abundant "exotic" material.

In the early decades of the seventeenth century, Jews still prayed in private homes and Beth Jacob, although its existence was known to the authorities, was not a publicly visible congregation. But the Portuguese "New Jews", who for the first time could pronounce the euphemistic name of the Jewish God, Adonai, were satisfied. Adonai was the sweetest word. The generations of Marranos could not even whisper it for 200 years. Not yet having a public house of worship was hardly something that could dampen the sense of elation among the New Jews, who were still coming to terms with the trauma of the Inquisition. They were grateful to the city corporation, which allowed them to pray in the privacy of their home-synagogue while the Catholics were pushed underground. Dutch Catholics were praying in makeshift churches, in warehouses or cold, damp attics.

The Dutch rulers' liberal attitude toward the Jews was interlinked with Calvinist ideals, in which trade and profit were of paramount importance. The spirit of capitalism would not have anything to do with the hullabaloo over saints and heretics, and so Catholic churches were always hidden, careful not to be exposed to the ire of the authorities. But the Jews were allowed

TEMPEST-TOSSED AND FOUND

to be publicly identified as Jews. Their international knowledge and expertise as merchants in the far-off societies they came from were much sought after by the Protestant establishment. Within the first quarter of the seventeenth century, the *Nação* would establish two more congregations, Neve Shalom and Beth Israel. The three would eventually be united in 1639 into the congregation of Kahal Kadosh of Talmud Torah, the Holy Community of Law, by Saul Levi Morteira, Beth Jacob's Venetian rabbi.

Morteira was heavily involved in the New Christians' conversion to Judaism, their initiation into rituals of which they knew very little. Under his direction and governance, the Jews watched the biggest schism in Christianity with curiosity. The Dutch Catholics, far from "the venomous barking dogs" of their co-religionists in Iberia, were barely able to make a noise in Amsterdam, while the Calvinists officially allowed the *Nação* to grow into a strong community. The city authority did not preoccupy itself with the strange rituals of the ancient bearers of the Old Testament's message. The Calvinists had a more important mission to complete: rooting out the remnants of Catholicism.

Against this unimaginable backdrop of European religious regime change, even the most ambivalent New Christian took shelter under the umbrella of Beth Jacob and the two other congregations. Many rejoiced at seeing adherents to the faith of their former oppressors living in hiding. The trauma of the Inquisition and its aftermath was still so vivid for these people that a great many of them, though their ancestors originated in Spain, did not want to be associated with the country. They chose to be collectively known as Portuguese. This Portuguese identity would also be embraced by the Sephardi Jews who came from North Africa, the Ottoman Empire, Venice, Lombardy, Livorno and Modena. Some later historians believe that this was a myth, that the term "Portuguese" was chosen simply because the majority of the immigrants to Amsterdam hailed from Portugal. Only much later did some New Christians from Spain join the community. However, many of those who came to Amsterdam from Portugal were Spaniards by origin, who had fled across the border in the period before the Inquisition reached Portugal. In other words, most of the New Christian refugees arriving in the Dutch Republic had ample reason to distance themselves from Spain, author of their persecution.

But what the New Christians did not forsake, at least in the initial stage of the community's formation in Amsterdam, was the Iberian cultural legacy they had brought with them. Though Jessurun rediscovered himself as a Jew and settled in Amsterdam as an active member of the first Jewish congregation, he did not forget the Spanish one-act plays he had seen being performed in Portuguese churches during his youth in Lisbon. Jessurun projected onto that dramatic form, the *auto*, his newly acquired knowledge of Jewish stories from the Midrash, the rabbinical commentary on biblical texts. The play celebrated the still-close links between theatre and homily, a very Catholic tradition. The New Christians, born in Iberia and arriving in Amsterdam as adults, were very much inspired by that literary genre, which their Venetian rabbi strongly opposed—as we shall see, Saul Levi Morteira's lifelong mission as rabbi of the first Jewish community in Amsterdam was to exorcise the former New Christians of their Catholic leanings.

Jessurun incorporated into *Diálogo dos Montes* seven of Morteira's short sermons, delivered to the New Jewish community in its early days. The roles of the seven mountains, whose *diálogo* links together Morteira's seven sermons, were played by the students of his new yeshiva, the first Jewish seminary in western Europe: Ets Haim, or Tree of Life. It is interesting that Jessurun does not challenge his audience with deep theological, Talmudic disputations as the personified biblical mountains present their winning arguments. Having lived so long as Catholics or Marranos, most of the New Jews had never seen a Torah scroll before coming to Amsterdam. Still, the popular imagination must have abounded with the stories of the giving of the Torah on Mount Sinai. It was no coincidence that the performance of *Diálogo dos Montes* was scheduled during the week of Shavuot, the festival celebrating the bequeathing of the Law books to Moses. The audience could very well imagine which of the seven mountains would be the winner.

Traditionally, *autos*—derived from medieval shepherd's plays with a predominantly religious theme—combined the allegorical with the historical, in a contemporary setting. Jessurun's play picks out from the Midrash the biblical mountains and their known functions, and guides the audience to decide on Sinai as the winning mountain.

Though the competition is about merely choosing a favourite of the seven, in retelling the significance of each mountain Jessurun transmits to the audience an old, forgotten pride. He rekindles the special status of the Jews in God's eyes, as the chosen people to whom the Torah was given. The play celebrates God's Providence, which a majority of the New Jews believed was reserved for those with a Jewish connection, even after they had lived for many generations as converts. The overwhelming expression of gratitude to the *"piqueno santuario"*, the "little sanctuary" of Amsterdam, and the representation of this miracle as God-given, bear testament to that belief.

But Morteira was not in favour of this idea of universal salvation reserved for Old Jews and Marranos alike. He was a traditionalist who, to his mind, had been invited to teach Judaism to a bunch of former Catholics, and he did not want to encourage the salvation theory. The pragmatic rabbi believed this would "undermine the willingness of the *conversos* (who are still in Spain and Portugal) to leave the Iberian Peninsula and return to their Jewish roots."[11] Jessurun's attempt to incorporate the sermons of his rabbi, who was vehement in his antipathy toward an Iberian culture he believed tainted by Catholicism, was intended to convince Morteira, and reassure the congregation, that they were truly Jews, and proud of their mixed culture. The two traditions could learn from each other and find a fine balance. In Morteira's Old Jewish world, lived in ghettos, one did not make room for secular or Christian thoughts in the life led by the *halacha* (Jewish law). There had been more adventurous rabbis such as Leon of Modena, who was influenced by Christian choral music and opera, and had tried to reflect their melodies in Jewish prayer services, but *Diálogo dos Montes* probably was one of the first early modern Jewish plays to be performed before a Jewish audience.

It could not have been accidental that Jessurun's work played upon one of the most important Protestant beliefs of the time. The Reformation gave high importance to the Second Coming of the Messiah, which could only happen when the Jews had returned to the Promised Land. Overseeing the Jews' arrival and their settlement in Amsterdam must have appeared to the Dutch authorities as a godly duty, as this was one of the preconditions for ultimate salvation in the End of Days. The play is almost appealing to Amsterdam's sense of duty to take care of its Jews, since their prophet was the bringer of the Old Testament from God on Mount Sinai. After delivering a long eulogy to Sinai's key position among the mountains, Jessurun's Earth sings a hymn to Mount Zion, lamenting the destruction of the Temple. It then elaborates Zion's importance in encapsulating the hope of the wandering Jews' eventual return to Jerusalem.

Diálogo dos Montes remains a showcase of the renewal of Jewish faith among Amsterdam's first-generation Portuguese Jews. It was "a tract for its time",[12] a rapturous celebration of freedom by the new settlers. They could barely believe that once again God had chosen them,

from all peoples who upon me (Earth) dwell
With miracles no human tongue can tell;
Just as the faithful shepherd guides his sheep,
Leading you to possess again and keep
Your ancient heritage.[13]

Here Earth hints at what also became a signature trait of the time, the ultimate Jewish aspiration: redemption for the "long-afflicted sons of Jacob" with the arrival of the Messiah. "O may you see the Redeemer in your days/For which this House of Jacob daily prays."[14] Forty-two years after Jessurun's play was performed in the synagogue of Beth Jacob, a short-lived miracle would appear on the horizon of Jewish messianic hope. In 1666, twenty-four Dutch Jews would write a letter to the much-discussed "messiah" Shabbatai Zvi from Izmir, in modern day Turkey, asking him if the time was ripe for the community to join him on the march to Jerusalem. The debacle of this false messiah will be discussed in detail later in the book.

The messianic hope of *Diálogo dos Montes'* audience was very much tied to their general belief in eventual salvation. Jessurun addressed this prevailing thought in order to reiterate Amsterdam's importance in this period of stability and prosperity for the Jews, who within two decades after their conversion from Catholicism had managed to create a community where Moses' Law ruled. The *halacha* had been handed down directly from God to their ancestors, who had been redeemed by Him once and would be protected from harm again, with the same *"maravilhas grande"*, great wonders. This is exactly what Sinai wishes for, in his closing speech. In humble exaltation at winning the contest as the chosen mountain, he blesses the chosen congregation, *"congrega eleita"* of Beth Jacob, which will soon be "restored" to the *"patrios montes"*, Mountains of the Homeland:

Faithful community,
House of Jacob where my Law's adored,

Chosen to smooth the way for bringing home
The harvest, may you be
Speedily restored
To the mountains of the homeland, where you'll come
To dwell in *pas perfeita* [perfect peace], proud and free.[15]

This passage draws on the first memory of freedom, the exodus from Egypt to the Judean mountains. Jessurun, speaking through the voice of Sinai, praises Beth Jacob for upholding the Laws, because of which Beth Jacob has been "chosen" to bring home the "harvest" of freedom. This is where the sons of Jacob would find "perfect peace".

"Bring home the harvest" they certainly would. The following century would shower on Amsterdam's Portuguese Jewish community unparalleled success, stability and self-rule—strictly led all the while by the Law given to their people on Mount Sinai. The community would emerge as one that was deeply religious, but totally at ease with the Calvinist ideals of economic prosperity. The *Nação* would fully cooperate with and become part and parcel of the Dutch dream. In return, they would be rewarded with privileges akin to citizens' rights. By the time the grand Portuguese Synagogue was built in 1675, after Rabbi "Templo"'s old designs of what Solomon's Temple might have looked like, Amsterdam's place was well established in the Jewish imagination, both in the city itself and around the world, as the "New Jerusalem".

Diálogo dos Montes is the only known surviving play ever to have been staged in Amsterdam's Portuguese synagogue. The leadership, under Rabbi Saul Levi Morteira, banned further performances. Thirty years on, the same rabbi, as the head of the united Kahal Kadosh of Talmud Torah, would be at the forefront of the ruling to excommunicate Baruch Spinoza. Jessurun, while celebrating wholeheartedly the joy of those who had just escaped the Inquisition, also shows off his newly acquired knowledge of Judaism, borrowing a great deal of primary source material from

Morteira himself. By including the rabbi's sermons, he intended to add legitimacy and authority to the play, for it to be performed in a synagogue. It was a bold act so far as the Jewish tradition permitted, but Jessurun also did something that was unique—he adopted the Iberian literary form to voice a quintessentially Jewish conversation.

The presentation of a Jewish theme in the guise of an essentially Christian play-form might have been too much for the rabbi from Venice, whose predecessors had escaped Catholic persecution decades earlier. For Morteira, *Diálogo dos Montes* was far too reminiscent of the traumatising Inquisition. The liberated Jews of Amsterdam did not need to be reminded of the Catholic tradition of staging faith-based plays in public places on saints' birthdays and in Christmas markets, at which the New Christians were obliged to be present to avoid banishment or burning as "secret Jews". It would not be surprising if Beth Jacob's chief rabbi thought his congregation need not face something that could rekindle these nightmarish memories. He wanted to save his people from harking back to the cultural tradition of their oppressors. He was aware that a significant number among his congregation still held Catholic convictions and cherished Iberian culture, and he wanted to purge his people of such past cultural leanings.

Instead of allowing performances of *autos* that borrowed heavily from the Eucharistic storytelling during Mass or Corpus Christi, Morteira decided to divert his congregants' attention to Jewish rituals and ethics; Jewish orthodoxy. Throughout his time as chief rabbi of Amsterdam, he championed Judaism against Christianity in sermons and secret polemical writings, so that the doubting Portuguese Jews could be reassured and persuaded to remain true to the ancestral faith they had embraced. Morteira never gave up his conservative approach to guiding the community. It was a tough job—he had been assigned to dismantle the New Christians' religious identity and construct a new Jewish one. In order to reinstate and nurture "true faith" within the community, he became uncompromising. Under his rabbinical rule, there was no room for the slightest deviation from the Mosaic Law, and its literal interpretation permeated the daily lives of residents of Vlooienburg. Under his draconian leadership, for nearly half a century, the Kahal Kadosh of Talmud Torah would grow into an exemplary, orthodox Sephardi congregation.

Morteira's critics have spoken of his "mediocre talent"[16] and condemned his banning of the theatre and excommunication of free thinkers. But it is undeniable that his unification of the community was pivotal to the emergence of the *Nação* as an indispensable element in Dutch society and its collective prosperity. As the Israeli historian, Hyman Reuven Rabinowitz, has pointed out, Morteira's intention was not to innovate, but to fortify the new faith of the former converts, to help them detach from the European Christian culture that had always undermined the Jews. In Morteira's living memory, European theatre had often been used by popular Christian playwrights as a tool to demonise the Jew as a shrewd, diabolical monster. At a time when in England and Germany public sentiment was "roused to an outbreak of Jew-baiting", the *Nação* enjoyed its little sanctuary in Amsterdam, away from the public vilification of the Jew as "a greedy, inhuman pig", "bent on gratifying a satanic lust for Christian Flesh". Shakespeare's infamous Shylock is Morteira's co-religionist and a fellow Venetian. Why sully the experience of stability and peace in Amsterdam by transporting into the synagogue a tradition that he believed was linked to Christian oppression?

There were many in Morteira's congregation who disagreed with him about the place of Christian play-forms, but it was important to maintain a visibly Jewish identity to the community amidst Dutch Reformed society, and they rarely protested. We could very well imagine that, to Morteira, bringing into the Holy

Community an intrinsically Christian art—staging a spectacle in a place of worship—was an unholy deviation from the New Christians' return to Judaism. This kind of cultural expression would come under severe scrutiny during most of the seventeenth century, as the community's collective identity was given a more zealous, orthodox Jewish makeover.

Diálogo dos Montes was the Portuguese Jews of Amsterdam's first direct expression of the old Iberian artistic tradition that they had carried with them. Today, it stands out as a remarkable parable of the seafaring, wandering Jew's ordeal in hostile lands; his flight across oceans and continents in pursuit of the hope of Israel. This the Jews found in their adoptive homeland: in a Protestant city in the far north of Europe, where they felt so safe and settled that they called it their Dutch Jerusalem.

2

FROM ATONEMENT TO SALVATION

So, from very early on, the community was placed on a "broad, beaten path"[1] by Saul Levi Morteira, leading a strict rabbinical Jewish life. But Morteira was appointed rabbi of Beth Jacob only in 1616—what happened before that? What did the community look like until then, in the preceding two decades of its life in Amsterdam? The New Christians first started migrating in the 1590s. What hopes and dreams did they arrive with? How did they think they would emerge as a community in Amsterdam, a city that beaconed an unprecedented promise of freedom, a fear-free existence, for the first time in their history of exile?

The New Christians had been romantically connected to Judaism for as long as they could remember. Back in Spain and in Portugal, the Sephardi community—despite conversion and Catholic oppression—had preserved a handful of old Jewish customs, and a few, the Marranos, went on practising them in secret. This was extremely dangerous: being caught as a secret Jew sent one straight to death row. When they came to Amsterdam, to the land of religious freedom, some of them tried to revive and openly observe these rituals and rites that had lain dormant for two cen-

turies. But while many could be re-enacted, the theology behind
the rites was unchartered waters for the New Jews. Having lived
in isolation from an active Jewish life for so many generations,
most had forgotten how, for example, to prepare a Seder plate for
Passover; how to keep kosher when no ritual slaughterers were
available or when no one could explain its merits.

Many of Amsterdam's first-generation Jews were baffled at the
intricacies of the dietary regulations. Some, despite being deeply
committed to their new faith, found the kosher rules pointless,
claptrap of the rabbis. In fact, a few years on, breaking a particular dietary rule—mixing meat with milk—would lead to an
excommunication order against the first "heretic" in the community, Uriel Da Costa (see Chapter 6). However, the New Jews
all knew these rites were necessary to belong to a mainstream
Jewish life, and most set aside scepticism when faced with adapting to strict halachic codes of conduct prescribed by the Sephardi
rabbis brought over from the Old Jewish settlements beyond
Iberia. Since the rabbis' arrival in Amsterdam, the New Jews of
the Portuguese *Nação* had been leading a life according to whatever Jewish customs they could salvage from memory. Theirs was
not normative Judaism, but they wanted to learn, and to live
according to the strict Talmudic rules required to belong to the
Sephardi diaspora. At the very beginning, there was bafflement
but little opposition when the Old Jewish rabbis put forward
"enforceable boundaries of behaviour".[2]

Psychologically this was problematic for some, but they
needed the rabbinical stamp of approval on their new identity.
Initially, their main worry was what full integration into
Amsterdam's Sephardi community would do to their relationship
with family and friends back in Spain and Portugal who had not
been expelled because they had continued to practise as New
Christians, or were married to "Old" Christians. This, says historian Miriam Bodian, threatened to some extent the unity of

the New Christians in Amsterdam: "The emigres' encounter after they left the Peninsula with Jews whose links with rabbinic tradition were unbroken inevitably aroused conflicts, cultural as well as religious."[3]

But the New Jews also knew that failure to integrate into a mainstream Jewish life would throw their "return" to Judaism into jeopardy. They realised that they would have to relinquish the folkloric Judaism inherited by the Marranos under the Inquisition, and embrace without protest what the rabbis of the old world presented to them. There was no room for ambiguities. As soon as they arrived, they understood that they must have a bona fide Sephardi rabbinical authority to lead them: how does one keep Shabbat? How long should the Yom Kippur fast last in northern Europe? How does a ritual slaughterer work— now that they were allowed to keep a kosher slaughterhouse in Amsterdam? That profession had long been discontinued in their peninsular life. How does one take part in *mikveh*, the ritual bath for purity, and how can a submerge pool be created with rainwater that is not freezing cold? The "true north" had so far given them "sanctuary", but it had no previous Jewish presence as in Germany and central Europe, whose Jews were in any case of the Ashkenazi denomination. The legal–religious formula that dominated mainstream Sephardi Judaism was an unexplored concept for Amsterdam's New Jewish community.

The early émigrés invited rabbis from the Sephardi settlements in North Africa, Italy and Turkey to teach and guide them through Jewish rituals, services and ceremonies. Eager to understand the law books, they first hired an Ashkenazi rabbi from nearby Germany while waiting for suitable Sephardi teachers to take charge of the community. Rabbi Moses Uri Halevi arrived from Emden to guide them through the path of *halacha*. He was appointed as a ritual slaughterer and rabbi, to lead the first Jewish services held by the community. The men usually met in the house of Jacob Tirado, a Portuguese Marrano and a rich merchant—hence the first Jewish congregation in Amsterdam was named after him: "Beth Jacob", or House of Jacob.

Uri Halevi swiftly embarked on formally converting the New Christians to Judaism. He had brought with him and presented to them their first Torah. They had never seen Torah scrolls before. This earliest stage in the transformation of the New Christians into New Jews was laden with historic symbolism. A secret steadfastness in the face of systematic persecution—for both secretly practising Marranos and also some believing New Christians—finally turned to legal "judaisation", and a transition from folkloric to historic Judaism was set in motion. This time, the "judaising" was happening openly, in Amsterdam's freedom of faith, without the surveillance of the Inquisition police or fear of torture and expulsion.

* * *

Or was it? Paradoxically, the first documented gathering of "Jewish" worshippers in Amsterdam was in fact spied on and raided. Though the fracas over the incident was quickly resolved, and the detainees freed and allowed to practise as Jews, this episode resonated with haunting memories of a not-so-distant past.

It was Yom Kippur, and the year was 1603. Members of Beth Jacob gathered in the harbourside house of a Jewish Moroccan diplomat, Samuel Palache. Presiding over the service was the Ashkenazi rabbi, Moses Uri Halevi. Some accounts say it was actually in Uri Halevi's house where at least ten men—the number required to form the *minyan*, quorum, that validates a Jewish prayer—met on the eve of the Day of Atonement. Teaching the New Christians Judaism alongside Uri Halevi was Samuel Palache, an old Sephardi rabbi and diplomat from Fez, who happened to be in the city at the time on business. Palache had been deeply intrigued by the presence in Amsterdam of his old

Sephardi countrymen; his father, a rabbi in Córdoba, had fled Iberia with his family before settling in Morocco in the first half of the sixteenth century.

How Halevi and Palache, two religious leaders from Judaism's two opposing branches, came to be under the same roof appears to be undocumented, and has therefore been subject to various speculations. One explanation is that the Portuguese merchants were seeking to learn from the old masters, and wanted to have their reinitiation into Judaism sanctioned by both the Ashkenazi and Sephardi schools. Also, in those early days in the lives of the New Jews, the historic differences between the two denominations did not surface in the same way as they would in a few years' time, once the Sephardim had settled comfortably as a wealthy, well-connected and self-governed community, whereas the Ashkenazi arrivals from Poland and Germany remained impoverished and often dependent on Sephardi charity.

Sifting through various accounts of what happened on that Yom Kippur night, one could surmise that the neighbours had been suspicious for some time about several houses belonging to Portuguese immigrants. They had been watching strange olive-skinned men in exotic costumes going in and out, talking loudly in languages they did not understand. Rembrandt's famous painting *Man in Oriental Costume*, reportedly of Samuel Palache and featuring a bejewelled turban, tells us how exotic the Sephardim must have appeared against the pasty, pale Dutch population dressed in black and white, flitting about a flat, grey landscape under a Turneresque sky. Take a stroll along Amsterdam's well-preserved seventeenth-century canalside houses, and you can very well picture the setting on that day, 14 September 1603. The Yom Kippur service was being held in one of the grand gabled houses with a substantial attic space; a large iron hook adorned its protruding front beam, ready to lift the pulley with bulky merchandise from the waters below.

49

Judging by the names of the congregation mentioned in various records, including by the inhouse historian Miguel de Barrios or Daniel Levi de Barrios, who would document this incident later in the century, the men were wealthy. They had managed to smuggle out of Portugal a considerable amount of valuables, cash and family possessions. They would have been well dressed, like Rembrandt's "oriental" man—perhaps with the exception of the German rabbi, Uri Halevi. The *minyan* on that night exuded class, high culture and the newfound confidence of stowaways luxuriating in the sudden feeling of solid ground under their feet. The congregation did not arrive stealthily, but in full view of the neighbours. They greeted each other noisily, in Portuguese or Spanish.

On closer inspection, it would have been clear that they were conversing not just in the Iberian tongues, but also in Latin and perhaps French. They might even have exchanged a few greetings in Hebrew. In those days, with the Dutch Republic under strict Calvinism, Protestant vigilante groups were often on the lookout for clandestine Catholic gatherings. Catholic rituals and public meetings were banned in the Seven United Provinces that had broken away from Spanish rule in the late sixteenth century. Tonight, the Dutch vigilantes must have been watching the men for some time, before their suspicion grew deeper that the flamboyantly dressed merchants were none other than men from the enemy territory: Catholic Europe. Those gathered at the harbourside house must have appeared to the Dutch as Spanish informers. They mistook the closed-door meeting of the exotic congregation for a Catholic service, and called the police.

When the police came, all the men gathered were arrested and taken away for interrogation. As the story goes, the police then demanded that the men hand over their crucifixes, but the congregants said they had no such things in the house and were visibly perplexed by such an accusation. To make matters more exasperating for the authorities, the worshippers did not speak Dutch. The police searched the house and the detainees, but no crucifixes, rosaries or any other Catholic insignia were found. All that the search recovered were prayer books in Hebrew. They might also have found the Torah scroll that Rabbi Uri Halevi donated to the community.

Jacob Tirado—the wealthy merchant after whom the first congregation was named—knew Latin. He managed to convince the Dutch Reformed clergy that, far from being informers to the Spanish, the men present had in fact been persecuted by the Inquisition and had fled the Peninsula to come to Amsterdam. Before the clergymen could make sense of this information, the men of the *minyan* gave their religious identity as Jewish. Until that moment, there was no record of an organised Jewish presence in Amsterdam.

The Calvinist authorities reviewing the case did not know what to make of this group, who spoke the languages of Catholic Europe but professed their religious identity to be Jewish. The deliberations took up most of the night. The opinion of the Dutch regents differed from that of the Reformed clergy as to whether or not the Jews should be allowed to practise their religion publicly. In the end, what really persuaded the authorities and pastors to agree on letting the men live freely as Jews was not mercy, nor open-mindedness, but a fundamental tenet of the Protestant Reformation.

Liberated from Catholicism's intricate network of saints and priests, confession and absolution, the Protestant Reformation drew on Christianity's primary sources—the Old Testament and the biblical prophets—to find an alternative paradigm of social justice. The Portuguese Jews generated unfettered interest and enthusiasm among the Calvinists and other persuasions of the Reformation, because it was to their prophet, Moses, that God had revealed the Pentateuch. As we know, there was an older

New Christian presence in the south, in Antwerp, and it cannot be ruled out that some of its members were secretly practising Marranos, but Amsterdam was yet to see an organised Jewish community. After Antwerp fell to the Spanish in 1585, a handful of New Christians joined the Protestants fleeing to the northern cities to escape forced conversion. Some went to Hamburg and many moved back to the Iberian Peninsula. The Jews had never managed to emerge as a community, let alone form a congregation or synagogue, in the cities of Middelburg, The Hague or Amsterdam. The Marrano presence in Amsterdam had been scattered. As such, the regents had never come face to face with an organised prayer group such as this one. In municipal records, the Yom Kippur gathering is listed as the earliest Jewish service in Amsterdam, and Beth Jacob as the city's first congregation of Jews.

The Jewish poet and historian Daniel Levi de Barrios, however, recorded the first Yom Kippur in Amsterdam under a different date. In his late-seventeenth-century rhyming essay, this historic service of the Beth Jacob congregation was thought to have taken place eight years earlier, in 1595. This is debatable, according to modern historians, since the first documented New Christian presence in Amsterdam also dated to 1595. It is extremely unlikely that, in the very year of their arrival, the Portuguese converts formed a "Jewish" congregation and met for a Yom Kippur service, in the presence of an official rabbi. But memory can attach itself more readily to place than to time, as Halbwachs states in *The Collective Memory*.[4] A certain amount of anachronism is a historian's literary license, and Daniel Levi de Barrios, also known by his former Portuguese name, Miguel, made the most of it. In "Casa de Jacob", he described how, when the authorities realised they had come upon a group of Jews, they asked the people of the Old Testament to pray to the God of Israel on behalf of Amsterdam: "The Jews gladly consented through their representative, Jacob Tirado. When the incident was reported to the magistrate, the latter declared on the spot that Judaism could be practised openly."[5]

The night ended with all the arrestees being allowed to go home or return to their service, but the authorities and clergy remained perplexed for some time by the stories and etiquette of these people who claimed to be Jews. De Barrios portrayed an idealistic version of the actual event, but the details are the same: a congregation of former New Christians met in a house near the sea with a certain German rabbi called Uri Halevi, who led them in a Yom Kippur service. The presence and arrest of both Halevi and his son are firmly attested by Amsterdam's notarial records. But what de Barrios did not mention in his rhyming, romanticised version of the incident was that Halevi was actually charged by the authorities with receiving stolen goods—presumably as presents for his service—and with circumcising adults. Both charges seem totally plausible. Uri Halevi and his son, Aaron, were reported to have circumcised 2,500 New Jews.[6] However, the notarial records tell us that the father and his son were released along with the others, and "were allowed to continue their activity."

It is hard to tell how far this "activity" corroborated de Barrios' claim that the Dutch magistrate ruled "on the spot that Judaism could be practised openly". His depiction of the Portuguese New Christians' smooth transition to Judaism is idealised to mythical proportions, which was natural for a Marrano writer severed from his Catholic past. It was important for de Barrios to establish, in the imagination of the Marranos' descendants, the religiosity of their ancestors, their unconflicted ethnic Portuguese–Jewish identity, and their acceptance by a tolerant authority in a Protestant city. In the same way, Rehuel Jessurun portrayed Amsterdam as "the true north" to his people, the Sons of Jacob, "*dos filhos de Jaacob*", in *Diálogo dos Montes*.

JERUSALEM ON THE AMSTEL

The actual circumstances around the integration of the community in its early years were often more complex than the New Jewish writers mythologised them. Nowhere does de Barrios, writing in the 1670s and 1680s, mention that the authorities did not officially sanction Jewish practices in Amsterdam until 1614. There was no "on the spot" decision by a magistrate in that regard. De Barrios, like others before and after him who chronicled the forming of the New Jewish community in Amsterdam, did so with a strong, unwavering attachment to what Old and New Jews perceived as their common biblical heritage, with which they wanted to replace or obliterate the ignominy of the Christian past.

It is interesting that the Marrano literature does not say a great deal about the New Christians' Catholic life in Spain and Portugal. The New Jews' memoirs depict the Marranos' longing to return to true Judaism, and relate the elaborate stories of deception that these secret Jews devised in order to avoid the wrath of the Inquisition police. The philosopher, Uriel da Costa, writes about the questions and doubts he had when serving as a Church official in Porto, and how he found solace in the Old Testament. But none portrays what the New Christians' daily Catholic life looked like back on the Iberian Peninsula—how they joined Mass, celebrated Easter and Christmas, baptised their children and brought them up as obedient Catholics—nor how they felt about breaching the dietary laws that are of paramount importance in Judaism. What, for instance, it was like for them to eat pork—in fact to publicly gorge on pork, to evade the suspicion of Inquisition spies always on the lookout for the stray Jew or judaiser. Daniel Swetschinski's fascinating study, *Reluctant Cosmopolitans*, sheds light on this self-denial of the New Jews, the conscious erasing of their very recent Christian past:

> The Portuguese Jews of seventeenth-century Amsterdam concentrated their intellectual creativity principally in two distinct areas: in

the refutation of Christianity and in the elucidation of the Bible—areas in which they chose to define their identity as no longer being Christians and as descended from the deceptively familiar, yet entirely foreign, personages of the Bible.[7]

So although de Barrios' writing glorifies the new biblical identity of his former compatriots in a free Amsterdam, in reality, the path to Judaism for the New Christians in their northern sanctuary had not been uncomplicated; nor was the attitude of the hardline clergy toward the Jews, both New and Old.

Many in the Reformed Church may have been influenced by Martin Luther's later work, which vindicated the anti-Jewish sentiments prevalent in Germany. A section among the Calvinist clergy put forward strong arguments recommending that Jewish gatherings or practice of Judaism in public must be controlled, even banned, just as Catholic practices were. Jacob Tirado, Samuel Palache and other wealthy merchants tried to sway the opinion of the more secular city guardians in their favour, arguing that the Jews' commercial and language skills could be of enormous benefit to Amsterdam's growing economic and naval powers.

As we know, Palache happened already to be in the city, to set up a diplomatic mission on behalf of the Moroccan sultan. Previously there had been several diplomatic exchanges between the Dutch Republic and Morocco, as the sultan was keen on sweetening the then Anglo-Dutch alliance against the Spanish—the common enemy of all three. The Sultanate's mission, however, had been hampered by the Anglo-Spanish peace treaty in 1604, following which the Spanish Armada exercised a free rein, carrying out reinforced attacks on Morocco across the narrow Strait of Gibraltar. The Dutch, on the other hand, were still far from signing a truce with their Spanish foe—so the sultan's envoy was a welcome guest. At this stage Palache's negotiations with the Dutch authorities played a key part in securing considerable autonomy for the new Jewish community. Following the

Yom Kippur incident of 1603, an unwritten agreement based on mutual self-interest allowed the Jews to practise their religion. Soon, the new Sephardi congregation was saying to the Dutch, "Give us autonomy, accept us fully as Jews, and we'll give you trade connections with North Africa," and also the New World, where Marranos had settled as Spain and Portugal spread their colonial power.

This had instant appeal to the city authorities. The burgomasters believed the Sephardi merchants were agents of the world of international commerce and diplomacy. Early historians, such as Max Weber, put this Calvinist zeal for commerce into their interpretations of what the Protestant work ethic stood for: salvation is rooted in the spirit of capitalism. This has since been classified as a myth by leading contemporary historians, who assert that many early "capitalists" happened to be from the pre-Reformation Catholic empires. However, it could be said that, since pre-destination was one of the major pillars of the Protestant faith, and one could only be saved by *sola gratia*— God's grace alone—worldly work was seen as a duty. In the Calvinist Dutch Republic, salvation and material gain were equally sought after. Since you cannot determine your "election" by divine grace, you might as well live a life of hard work and thrift to prosper in this world, which may in turn demonstrate your worthiness of salvation.

The authorities paid little or no attention to the handful of clergymen in the Dutch Reformed Church who were opposed to public Jewish religious practices. Just then, another significant advocacy by an influential jurist and humanist, Hugo Grotius or Hugo de Groot, propelled the community forward. The urban magistrates of Amsterdam had turned to him and another lawyer—whose recommendations are lost—for legal advice on how to deal with, or think of, the growing number of Iberian Jewish merchants in the city. De Groot returned a passionate and moral appeal to the burgomasters and the clergy that the people of the Old Testament must be permitted freedom of worship. De Groot had his own reservations about Judaism's rejection of the Christian revelation, and had written polemical articles about Jews, but it is said that his humanist belief won out over his religious misgivings.

De Groot used many Protestant theological considerations to support his argument that the Jews should be allowed to settle in Amsterdam, the most important being the Calvinist belief that they were closer to the "true religion" than the Catholics—a bunch of idolators. He also argued that "states have an obligation under natural law to offer hospitality to strangers."[8] His draft resolution, written around 1616 and entitled *Remonstrance*, recommended no restrictions on the number of new arrivals from Iberia, nor on private worship, so long as the Jews abided by the city's regulations. It endorsed clear segregation, prohibiting sexual relations with Christian women, including prostitutes. It also forbade spoken or written attacks against the Christian religion and any attempt to convert Christians to Judaism.[9] According to contemporary historians, the importance of de Groot's proposals—which weren't even accepted—has been much overstated in popular literature. Yet this was the first extensive proposal for legalising the rights of Dutch Jews, and "the fundamental issue was made clear, i.e., the settled Jews would in fact be tolerated."[10] Their full civic participation would be authorised within the next decade.

In other words, though it did not immediately herald full religious freedom, the Yom Kippur of 1603 marked a watershed moment in the life of Amsterdam's first Jewish congregation. And De Groot's advocacy for granting legal status to the Jews of the Dutch Republic, giving them specific autonomy and freedom to be Jewish within their own community, "prevented the integration of Jews in Christian republican society", thus cementing their separate identity.[11] Having been served the States General's regulations in 1616, the *parnassim*—the community wardens—knew their legal position, and turned to the question of how to develop and self-govern in line with them. This was a moment of major awakening for the community. How should it want to be seen by the Dutch Republic, which was at war with Spain—the New Jews' former homeland? Would they hide their Iberian heritage, or play up its strategic significance in the new world order that was fast unfolding?

Although most of the new arrivals spoke Portuguese at home, they still wrote verses in Spanish and were avid readers of Spanish literature. The wealthier merchants took certain pride in showing off the legacy of the old Spanish aristocracy in their lifestyle and dress. They spoke Portuguese in their day-to-day dealings, but their artistic and linguistic connections with Spain remained strong, even when they were in full denial of their Christian past. In Amsterdam, they would produce volumes of literature and Jewish theological books in Spanish, and even have the Quran translated into Spanish on pure Dutch paper, with an Amsterdam watermark. This seventeenth-century Spanish Quran is one the oldest surviving translations of the Holy Book of Islam into a modern European language. During the heyday of commercial and diplomatic possibilities between the Arab world and the Sephardi diaspora, it is perhaps not surprising that the Iberian Jewish merchants, whose lingua franca was Spanish, wanted to learn the Quran to improve relations with the Muslims.

The origin of the term "Sephardi" is *Sepharad*, Hebrew for the Iberian Peninsula. So in a way, their very identity was determined by their geographical origin. The old Sephardi population that had dispersed around Italy, North Africa and the Ottoman Empire in the fourteenth and fifteenth centuries had kept Spanish alive, as had the New Christians who had settled in Portugal. It was their private language, with which they could communicate with the Sephardi network across the globe, from North Africa to the Ottoman Empire to Cochin to the New World, as well as with those New Christians back in Iberia who hadn't been lucky enough to escape. Thus Spanish, as well as Portuguese, served as a language of communication in Amsterdam between the New Jews and the Sephardi Jews from elsewhere, such as Samuel Palache of Fez. It was the language that the early Jews might have used to speak to the Venetian rabbi, Saul Levi Morteira.

However, the old Sephardim and the New Christians may have transported both Iberian languages to all corners of the world, to express their artistic skills and religious fervour—but the Yom Kippur incident posed an important dilemma for the first congregation, Beth Jacob: was it Spanish, or was it Portuguese? That night, Jacob Tirado had explained in Latin to the Dutch clergy that, far from being Spanish, they were in Amsterdam because of the Spanish oppression. How important, then, should the Spanish links be? Should the community want to be associated with the country that had subjected it to unimaginable woes, leading to the expulsion and near extinction of their people?

These questions had a profound impression on the emergence of the community in its early days as "the Portuguese Nation". These, and the Netherlands' continuing Eighty Years' War of independence against Spain (1568–1648), may have influenced the New Jews in their dissociation from Spain when they came to establish their national identity in the calm northern city of Amsterdam, away from the trauma of the Inquisition. They decided that they wanted collectively to be known as "Portuguese", even though many of their early religious leaders, including Moses Uri Halevi, Saul Levi Morteira and Samuel Palache, had nothing to do with Portugal. As a community, Amsterdam's Sephardim became the "Hebrews of the Portuguese Nation", the *Nação*.[12]

But this phrase denotes an array of parallel identities. In Amsterdam, the modern era was dawning. There was an explosion of identities, nationalities and other complex ways in which the city's residents, a carnival of peoples, wanted to describe themselves. These identities were also fluid; alongside those New Christians converting to Judaism from the first quarter of the seventeenth century, there were former Catholics redefining their newfound, Protestant faith, and a smaller number continuing to affirm their Catholic origins. There were also a handful of Moriscos—Muslims of Spain who had been forced to convert to Catholicism, who had also fled the Inquisition and found themselves in Amsterdam. Some tried to convert to Judaism along with their former compatriots, while others moved on to Muslim North Africa or the colonies.

Within this "melting pot" atmosphere, a new movement began to take root: religious tolerance, or social justice as promoted by humanists such as Hugo de Groot. This wasn't necessarily a conscious or conscience-driven stance by the Protestant authorities; toleration was the only logical state of being in the world's most promising international trade centre. From the ashes of the old, despotic Catholic Church, and amid bitter disputes between various Protestant groups born of the Reformation, grew a strong, unified Sephardi community in Amsterdam. The more the Protestant sects fought amongst themselves and with the Catholics, the stronger the *Nação* appeared to become. What seemed like an epoch of historic religious tolerance was in fact a no-man's-land in the sectarian battle for supremacy.

The New Jews kept a low profile as they evolved into a Sephardi nation of solid conviction, at the same time as the Dutch Golden Age was indulging in international commerce and high art with a strong biblical theme. The painters of this era filled their canvasses with scenes from the Old Testament. Cosmopolitanism was not yet an idea for distribution, but the

FROM ATONEMENT TO SALVATION

Dutch Protestants and the Portuguese Jews in Amsterdam became its early subscribers. The seventeenth century was a time of opportunities, created by multi-religious encounters and political restlessness. The arrival of another belief system in the multitude of faiths that filled post-Reformation Amsterdam was simply not a big deal. It seemed that the burgomasters had first to put its own, still fragmenting house in order, before meddling in the affairs of some 200 wealthy merchants from Iberia who wanted to live as Jews.

3

A SEA-CHANGE IN SEAFARING

"Nothing of him that doth fade
But doth suffer a sea-change
Into something rich and strange"

Ariel's song, *The Tempest* (1.1)[1]

The Old and New Sephardi Jews uniting under the umbrella of the *Nação* was greatly owed to the unique leadership of the community's founding rabbis, in particular Saul Levi Morteira, who came to Amsterdam in 1616 and took over from Uri Halevi as chief rabbi of the original Beth Jacob congregation in 1618. At one point, barely two decades after the community had first settled in Amsterdam, there were three congregations. Morteira would unite these as the Kahal Kadosh of Talmud Torah, the Holy Community of Talmud Torah, in 1639—a very important year that would mark the community's full institutionalisation. But the preceding four decades were also of immense significance.

Parallel to the "native" Dutch society, redefining itself with a Protestant identity amid the Eighty Years' War with Catholic Spain, the new Sephardi immigrants persevered in finding a common Jewish identity. This idea presented itself as a unifying bond for the entire Sephardi diaspora—both New Christians who had recently fled the Inquisition and the Old Jews from Fez, Italy, the Ottoman Empire, Hamburg and so on—and even a handful of Ashkenazim. The rabbis and other leaders did not want the great schism in Christianity to seep into the city's young Jewish community, which had already been encountering worrying differences of its own within the first years of its formation.

The emergence of three congregations shortly after the first Jews' arrival could not have been easy for that community's leaders to handle. They wanted to present a united front, both to the Dutch authorities and to the more recent New Christian arrivals, whose immigration to the Dutch Republic increased significantly after the Seven United Provinces signed a ceasefire agreement with Spain in 1609, known as the Twelve Years' Truce. The second congregation, Neve Shalom, was born around this time, partly due to the greater influx of Jewish immigrants as the New Christians arrived from Spain and Portugal. It might also have been a case of migrants assembling in synagogues defined by congregants' region of origin within the Iberian Peninsula, as had been practised in Venice. But it is equally believed that internal conflicts might have contributed to the need for a separate, second synagogue. According to the historian, Miriam Bodian, Neve Shalom owes its birth to the Sephardi brothers, Samuel and Joseph Palache, who did not get along with the German rabbi of the Beth Jacob congregation, Moses Uri Halevi: "It has been argued, convincingly in my view that as a learned Jew, Samuel Palache would not have been happy with the Beth Jacob group under Uri Halevi, presumably conducted according to Ashkenazi rite."[2]

While Halevi, the founding rabbi of the "Jewish institution" in Amsterdam,[3] led the New Christians through their religious reincarnation as New Jews, the Sephardi mediator from Fez ran the institution's diplomatic wing. Samuel Palache was an Old Jew like Halevi and Morteira, but had had a flamboyant career. He had risen to prominence defying all odds, among the Muslim, Catholic and Protestant societies he lived in. He became a mythical figure, with his stories of adventure as a wandering diplomat–rabbi–pirate, who straddled the Old and New Worlds that stretched from the Mediterranean to the Atlantic.

In Fez, his family had long enjoyed privileged positions as rabbis and emissaries of the Royal Palace. Their ancestors having fled the first wave of Inquisitorial persecution, the Palaches lived in Fez's Jewish ghetto, *mellah*, as traders, moneylenders and dealers of precious stones. The Jews, who had been in the region long before the Arab conquest in the seventh century, were protected, and many were held in great esteem by the successive Muslim rulers. But they were still required to wear a black cloth that marked them out as Jews and they had to return to the *mellah* before the nightly curfew. They were frequently subjected to hate crime because of the Jewish community's relative wealth.

It is understood that, as seafaring traders, and being among the sultan's inner circle, the Palache brothers were able to bend the curfew rules and other discriminatory laws. They had special permits to go in and out of the *mellah* as and when their globe-trotting businesses permitted. But, despite these personal privileges, Samuel Palache was unhappy with the institutional and general public oppression, the humiliation of the compulsory insignia denoting the Jews' lowly status, which Sephardim of older residence in Fez had become used to over many centuries since the institution of the first *mellah*, to protect the Jews from frequent pogroms. It was hardly surprising that Palache, who had long fought for the freedom of his people and studied the scriptures to become a rabbi as well as a merchant, would look for better opportunities elsewhere—not just for himself and his extended family, but also for the community as a whole. During a visit to Spain as a Moroccan businessman at the end of the sixteenth century, he heard extraordinary stories of the religious freedom that the Iberian New Christians were enjoying in the Dutch Republic, having reincarnated as Jews.

One day early in the seventeenth century, Samuel and his brother Joseph arrived in Middelburg, a thriving Dutch port and capital of the south-western Zeeland province. They settled there briefly. After a few years, Joseph moved to Hamburg, where many Jewish merchants—mostly Ashkenazi but also a handful of Sephardim—had already settled. Samuel decided to go up north to Amsterdam and check out the Beth Jacob congregation. He was intrigued by the Iberian converts and their anomalous "Jewish" rituals—a blend of folkloric Sephardi and rigid Ashkenazi rites, heavily tinged with the Catholic lore they still hankered after. Before long, he took it upon himself to teach them appropriate rites, to bring the Iberian men and women into the true Sephardi fold. The second Jewish congregation, Neve Shalom, was born before the end of the first decade of the seventeenth century, with Samuel Palache as its rabbi.

This was ten years before Morteira would take over from Uri Halevi as rabbi of Beth Jacob. The two congregations operated side by side for a considerable time, almost three decades, with an Ashkenazi rabbi running the first, and an Old Sephardi at the helm of the second. Palache had only one goal—something he probably delegated to his fellow Sephardi Morteira, when the latter arrived in Amsterdam in 1616: to align the New Jewish community with the age-old Sephardi way of life, which could be redeemed from Venice, Fez, Izmir, Livorno and Salonica, and from Andalucía before it fell to the Catholics.

The history of this very early period in the shaping of the community's Sephardi identity is sketchy. But, given the tension that may have existed between Sephardi and Ashkenazi rabbis who had found themselves in the shared role of educating and re-converting the New Christians, we can see that a definitive and unifying position was necessary. The emerging *Nação* needed a strong leader to forge unity. Despite being its first rabbi, Uri Halevi lacked Iberian origins, and Samuel Palache, though of old Iberian heritage, had an important day job. He must have spent more time on this than on the New Jews. He had an unequivocal interest in his old countrymen's return to Judaism, in the world's most promising commercial centre, but he was in Amsterdam primarily as the head of an important diplomatic mission. Around 1609, just a year after becoming rabbi of Neve Shalom, he secured the post of Moroccan ambassador; soon after, he journeyed back to Fez. When he returned to Amsterdam, it was with a personal letter from Sultan Mulay Zidan, to be delivered to Prince Maurice of Orange.

Palache had made a crucial decision very early on, it seems: to remain first and foremost a diplomat linking the many worlds he lived in, rather than holding a full-time position as rabbi in Amsterdam. Within a few years, he would hand over most of his rabbinical duties for Neve Shalom to a younger, more theologically-minded rabbi, Menasseh Ben Israel. This allowed Palache to engage more in Dutch–Moroccan trade, diplomacy and, most intriguingly, piracy in the Atlantic and the Mediterranean, against the Spanish Armada. During the extraordinary first two decades of the seventeenth century, a lot had happened both in Palache's home country, Morocco, and in his adoptive home, the Dutch Republic. A young sultan, Mulay Zidan, had succeeded the throne in 1603 after the death of his father, Ahmad al-Mansur, while the Dutch Republic, further united by Prince Maurice, had passed a strict form of Calvinism, the House of Orange having won out over other Protestant factions at the Synod of Dordrecht (1618–19).[4]

Meanwhile, Palache had been going back and forth between the two countries, bringing over more members of his family to the new settlement on the Amstel River. He was now the official head of the diplomatic mission created by Mulay Zidan to take advantage of Dutch–Spanish hostilities—the Twelve Years' Truce signed in 1609 was rejected by a large section of the Calvinist ruling elite. The Moroccan sultan could think of no better way to fight off the Spanish Armada, constantly encroaching on the Strait of Gibraltar, than to move closer to Spain's enemies. After his short visit home to receive his new credentials, Palache was back in Amsterdam, negotiating deals under a Treaty of Friendship and Free Commerce (1610) with the House of Orange as Zidan's official envoy, as well as performing his duties as a rabbi.

By then it was becoming evident from the New Jews' contributions to Amsterdam's prosperous global trade and networking that the Dutch Jewish settlement would not be dismantled by any immediate adversaries. There were still a handful of hardline Reformed clergymen, *predikanten*, who were suspicious of the Iberians, but any such protests at the New Jews' fast integration into the Dutch socio-economic milieu were cast aside. With ships coming and going to and from the Americas, North Africa, the Ottoman Empire, India, Indonesia and the Hanseatic belt, Amsterdam was transforming rapidly into a storehouse for the world's merchandise.

Samuel Palache was not only a spokesperson for Mulay Zidan on matters of bilateral trade, but also for his fellow Sephardi Jews, who were striving for more concessions from the Dutch authorities, in return for their unequivocal allegiance to the Republic that had given them sanctuary from their Spanish persecutors. A dealmaker by profession, Palache petitioned the Amsterdam City Authority to allow further immigration from the Sephardi diaspora. He assured the burgomasters that the new arrivals would bring with them personal savings and valuables, as well as a wealth of knowledge of the Spanish Empire's colonial enterprises in the Americas. The Sephardim, he convinced the City Authority, were masters of both navigation and financial speculation, and familiar with the hazards of the sea traffic. In the great age of maritime mercantilism, these were the most highly prized skills of all. Right across northern and north-western Europe, the Jews were depicted—though more often than not negatively—as a people well-versed in these matters. The names of international ports and trading centres would roll off the tongue of a Jewish merchant as if they were his familiar neighbourhoods:

> He hath an argosy bound to Tripolis,
> Another to the Indies.
> I understand moreover, upon the Rialto,
> he hath a third at Mexico,
> a fourth for England
> and other ventures he hath squandered abroad.[5]

The seafaring Jews knew the "peril of waters, winds and rocks", having braved it throughout their long history of perse-cution, dispersal and search for refuge.

Among the notable concessions negotiated by Palache was the purchase of a plot of land in 1614, for a Jewish cemetery in Ouderkerk aan de Amstel, one of the oldest villages on the Amstel River, 8 kilometres from the Jewish quarter, the Jodenbuurt. From Jodenbreestraat (Jewish Broad Street), mourners could now walk along the Amstel and reach the cemetery in two and a half hours. The first Jewish burial at the cemetery took place in 1615. It was important for the plot to be close to the Jodenbuurt, as Jewish burial must take place immediately after death. Obtaining permis-sion to build a cemetery so close to Amsterdam was an extraordi-nary achievement for the *Nação*. It assured the completion of another key commandment of Judaism and reaffirmed the ortho-doxy of the community. The cemetery, Beth Haim, which para-doxically means "House of Life", claims to be the oldest Jewish cemetery in the world that is still in use.[6]

Palache, with his fellow religious leaders of both Neve Shalom and Beth Jacob, had also been lobbying for a public synagogue.

As we know, the *Nação* had so far been holding prayers in private home-synagogues. This petition "led to strenuous Calvinist protests." But the hardliners relented, and some historical accounts point to a building at the top of Jodenbreestraat—close to where the Church of Moses and Aaron stands today—that was semi-officially used as the Neve Shalom congregation's synagogue after 1612.[7]

But the wandering Jew in Samuel Palache was trying to break out of the constraints of the communal life. Once he had negotiated important concessions toward establishing permanent rights for the Jews in Amsterdam, he turned to the New World. The lull in the Eighty Years' War with Spain brought by the Twelve Years' Truce meant that he could represent Dutch interests at the Spanish court without being hounded by the Inquisition. He liaised between the two old foes, as well as between the Dutch Republic and the Spanish and Portuguese colonies.

At the dawn of discoveries, the Dutch Republic was not only emerging as one of the world's greatest seaborne empires, but soon started superseding older colonial powers such as Portugal and Spain, seizing their territories in the New World. The port of Amsterdam had an advantageous position on the North Sea, but its ships had until now traded mostly in bulky merchandise such as timber for shipbuilding, iron, salt, grain, or handicrafts. The Sephardi merchants offered their expertise in trading lighter, more profitable commodities: sugar, precious stones, spices, and, very soon—once the Dutch position in the Americas was firmly secured—tobacco. The Iberian merchants, with their Sephardi and Marrano contacts in the Mediterranean and the New World colonies, gave fresh impetus to the activities of the Amsterdam harbour. The hooks high up on the canalside houses' exterior walls now hauled and stored much lighter and more precious goods.

Both sides grew rich as days, months and years went by, and the Dutch—even the more conservative, intolerant section of

Calvinist regents—became accustomed to seeing the Portuguese Jews help them build an empire in the West and East Indies, pushing the Spanish out. During the Dutch war of independence from Spain in the 1570s, which the seven northern provinces had won, Amsterdam had already deprived Antwerp—the old trade mart—of its former glory by cutting it off from the sea with a blockade of the River Scheldt, and by luring both New Christian and Protestant intellectuals to the north with the offer of safe harbour from the Inquisition. Enjoying excellent relationships with the Hanseatic Empire and the Muslim world, as well as newly secured trade arrangements with the known world outside of Europe, the Dutch Republic's growth was unstoppable.

Against this prosperous backdrop, Amsterdam's Sephardi *Nação*, which was playing a pivotal role in its host country's unimaginable maritime rise, became an increasingly self-contained community, yet more adventurous. Risk-taking never dissuaded the Jews, who had survived harsh indictments by so many nations for millennia and established themselves wherever they settled. The synagogue board, the Mahamad, offered personal protection to individuals who ventured out with their Dutch partners to form business and diplomatic alliances in all corners of the world. The only remaining constraint on the *Nação*'s considerable autonomy and religious freedom was the Jews' continued exclusion from most of the trade guilds. Even then, by about the second quarter of the seventeenth century the Dutch regents were often choosing not to take action against those who broke the rules.

In any case, the wealthier Jews had turned to international commerce, which was not part of the guilds. Nor was piracy in the Mediterranean, Atlantic and Caribbean. The Old Sephardi or Marrano naval presence across the New World dated to the time of Christopher Columbus, who set sail with the blessing of Queen Isabella, pitiless executor of the 1492 Inquisition. The explorer wrote in his diary, "In the same month during which their Majesties decreed that all Jews should be driven out of the Kingdom and its territories, they gave me the commission to undertake with sufficient men my expedition of discovery to the Indies."[8] Thus Columbus had taken along a large contingent of New Christian sailors and settled in Jamaica. More than a century later, Jewish ships belonging to the Dutch Navy, with predominantly Jewish sailors and Jewish commanders, were engaged in intercepting Spanish merchant ships loaded with loot and purchases from the colonies. This Dutch–Jewish Navy was supported by the descendants of the New Christians, who had already been living in the Spanish colonies and knew how to navigate the seas around them.

The Palache brothers were both involved in piracy and, with the covert support of the Dutch, would often come home with stray enemy ships. Inland, the Dutch–Jewish business transactions would meet the usual, legally required trade conditions administered by the City Authorities and the States General in The Hague. But once at sea, business ventures had a free rein. The merchant–sailors would improvise rules as they went along. The regents and the States General would turn a blind eye, so long as the actions of these "Jewish pirates" bolstered the Dutch Republic's overall profit.

Bound by the Twelve Years' Truce, the Dutch could not do anything publicly that might sabotage the break in hostilities. But the stadtholders were keenly following the advance of the Ottoman Army and the Moorish Sultans. Prince Maurice had already enthusiastically accepted the friendship of Sultan Mulay Zidan by allowing his emissary, Samuel Palache, into the heart of the Republic. This welcome, which was self-interested to the core, was duly paid off: "Palache had opened up North African trade as a gateway to the Ottoman Empire, and early émigrés had capital and access to trading partners in the New World, the

Levant and the Iberian Peninsula, all areas the Dutch had not (yet) penetrated."[9]

Having achieved such a remarkable status so soon after settling in Amsterdam, the Portuguese Jews were overcome with high emotions. They started calling Amsterdam their only home, their "Jerusalem on the Amstel". Many more Sephardim from other parts of Europe and the Middle East started pouring into the city, joining and strengthening the *Nação* in both size and influence. Even Joseph Palache left Germany where he had settled and joined his brother Samuel in Amsterdam, where the Jews unequivocally enjoyed more freedom and security than anywhere else in Europe or in the North African *mellahs*. Here, they became members of the Dutch bourgeoisie, hobnobbing with the burgomasters and having their portraits painted by Rembrandt.

This rapid entry of the first-generation Dutch Jews into a superior social class, with tremendous privileges and access to Amsterdam's high society, was owed to the early Sephardi merchants' careful deal-making skills. They traded in their versatile business network not only for greater freedom, but also for unprecedented security and their community's smooth transition into a proto-state, within a Protestant land where they would exude self-confidence, pride and class. This was not the everyday story of an immigrant community, of a sea-wandering people whose feet had just found firm ground. What the Sephardim achieved in Amsterdam—or rather, what they managed to revive, reinstate and grow within—was the old nobility to which they had once belonged on the Iberian Peninsula before the Inquisition, or even after that, for the few lucky Marranos who managed to evade suspicion.

The Jewish caballeros of Amsterdam strutted about in Jewelled garments of golden threads adorned with pearls and precious stones, and rode about in fancy coaches emblazoned with their coat of arms. Even the cases of their prayer shawls were decorated with coats of arms. Their spice boxes were of ivory, their wives' bonnets of Brabant lace.[10]

Samuel Palache, in his famous Rembrandt portrait, exhibits all of the above: jewelled garments in golden thread, pearls, precious stones. When Palache was rabbi of Neve Shalom, in the *Nação*'s very early days, Jewish merchants moved to large canalside mansions, held musical soirées, and staged theatre and literary competitions, despite the reservations of the community's hardliners. So long as they did not break Shabbat or the dietary laws, and so long as they did not question rabbinical authority and paid regularly and heftily to the Mahamad, they were mostly left to their social activities. Dutch legal restrictions meant that sexual relations between Jews and Christians, even Christian prostitutes, were prohibited, though records show that some in the Sephardi elite did defy the laws and have relationships with Christian women. The rabbis, however, fully supported the Dutch laws, which they considered to serve the community's interests. They allowed even the most conservative rabbis to look the other way as rich merchants indulged in lavish parties and sumptuous entertainment, mingling with Christian high society—because there the chances of non-Jewish offspring were limited, and so the community's Jewish identity was not under threat.

The *Nação* was strong, its foundation rock solid. The New Sephardim of Amsterdam walked about Jodenbreestraat with an opulent self-assurance and contemporaneity. They enjoyed a mainstream social life with the Christian Dutch, but remained deeply loyal to their religious conviction within the community. They were Europe's first modern Jews. And no artist left a more realistic image of them than Rembrandt Harmenszoon van Rijn, who lived on Jodenbreestraat himself. Long gone were the times when Moses was painted with two horns, and Jews were caricatured as hook-nosed aliens. Rembrandt's Sephardim had Van Dyke beards, wore broad-brim hats and crisped, white, millwheel-collared shirts—in line with the "native" Dutch style of the time.

It was not difficult for Palache and his congregation to mingle gracefully with the societies around them. What made this qualified integration really effortless was their centuries-long experience of dealing with Christian and Muslim elites elsewhere. Samuel Palache and others like him could take part in a Muslim breaking of the Ramadan fast at the sultan's court in Fez, dine with Prince Maurice of Orange in one of his palaces and then, thanks to the truce, take Dutch business interests to the Catholic king of Spain. The Sephardi merchants often made the triangular journey between these three worlds, strengthening their old knowledge with renewed access to these trade centres, and making themselves indispensable to the rulers of each empire and beyond. This was the beginning of the Dutch Golden Age, not just in mercantilism, but also in freedom of movement, freedom of expression and human rights.

To Amsterdam's Jews, who were free after centuries of secrecy to pray, form a congregation, build a synagogue and establish a burial ground, the United Provinces' edict of tolerance resonated strongly with a much earlier decree, by an ancient king. In popular history from this time, the Amsterdam golden age was considered to be as grandiose and epochal as when the Hebrews had been saved from Babylonian captivity in 539 BCE. As in Babylon, the New Christians had nearly been extinguished in Catholic Iberia, until the hope of Israel had appeared in the form of Amsterdam. The municipal authorities had offered them religious freedom and eventually the right to build a "temple", or at least a *Jodenkerk* (Jewish Church). This salvation echoed the conquest of Babylon by the Achaemenid Persian monarch, Cyrus the Great, who freed its captives to return to their homeland and ordered the restoration of the Jewish Temple and other houses of worship for formerly oppressed minorities.

The message of reconciliation and restoration of minority faiths inscribed on the famous Cyrus Cylinder[11] was a far cry from medieval Europe, ruled by Christian zealots bent on religious supremacy and ethnic cleansing. The Dutch Republic was born at a moment when the Jews of Europe were facing an ordeal worse than their ancient Babylonian captivity. And, like Cyrus the Great, Prince Maurice's father William of Orange (1544–84) had attempted to establish a state of different nationalities and faiths, approved by manmade resolution, rather than divine decrees that protected only Christians, in the case of Catholic Europe, or only "People of the Book", in the case of Islamic law.

There were, of course, limits to the Republic's foundational values of tolerance. No further act would come to repeal the old law regarding the trade guilds; for another century, the Jews would not be legally permitted to open high street or retail businesses, nor to run for political office. So, although they thrived on their new religious freedom and social status, the community's leaders remained sceptical of total assimilation. Maintaining a strong Sephardi identity, as standardised by the elders of Beth Jacob, would continue to be an important obligation for the leaders and members of the second congregation, Neve Shalom. Whether they were from Iberia or elsewhere in the Sephardi diaspora, all carried within them the spirit of the *Nação*. The rabbis and *parnassim* tirelessly impressed on the Portuguese Jews this need for community belonging. The creation of powerful charitable networks to help out the Hebrews of the Portuguese Nation helped induce everyone to sign up to the "Portuguese" identity. The early-seventeenth-century establishment across Europe of the Dotar—the Santa Companhia de dotar órphās e donzelas pobres, or Holy Society for Aiding Orphans and Poor Young Brides—played a vital role in forging this identity wherever people of the *Nação* were found.

A SEA-CHANGE IN SEAFARING

The term *La Nación* was first coined by Spanish Inquisitors to classify any group—in this case the New Christians—displaying "genuine collective traits". The *Portuguese de la Nación de Heberea* became an official term of reference in Spain for the Jews who had moved to Portugal after the expulsion. But before this—before the New Christians collectively came to be known as "the Nation"—the term was frequently used elsewhere in Europe to describe a specific ethno-religious group. Some historians believe the Dutch authorities borrowed the concept in order to categorise the new immigrants from Portugal in the late sixteenth and early seventeenth centuries.

What had started as a codifying terminology separating them as "foreigners" from the rest of Iberian society began to grow on the New Christians. They too adopted the term and, despite its ambiguous and often negative connotations, felt a romantic affinity with it. They came up with the idea of attaching the *Nação* to their biblical identity as the "Hebrews", in the same way as the word "Marrano", which literally means "pig", was adopted and reclaimed by the crypto-Jews. Several centuries in the future, the term "Negro"—originally a tool of white European racism—would enter African American popular culture to inform black identity. It could be argued that the New Jewish association with "the Nation" was also such a statement, rooted in their history of wandering and persecution, sealed by their attachment to a unified religious identity. In the sixteenth and seventeenth centuries, a "nation" was a people sharing a strong affiliation with a common religion. Very often it also included a common language.

The Jews of the world were yet to become a people, and were yet to have a common language. But there was one thing that was sacred to the scattered diasporas of New Christians and Old Jews: their romantic connection to the ancient heritage of their ancestors, before dispersion and forced conversion. The idea of

the Jewish people as a "nation" appeared often in the contemporary European Judeo-Christian discourse and literature. The
theme was popular, for example, in the Elizabethan drama. In
The Merchant of Venice, Shylock talks to himself and expresses
his dislike of Antonio because "he hates our sacred nation ...
Cursed be my tribe if I forgive him."[12]

The "sacred nation", *am kadosh* in Hebrew, was the Jewish
diaspora's common link. Concepts of *Nación*, *Nação*, "Nation",
became a rubberstamp for the specific identity of the Hebrews
amid a non-Jewish population. The Jews of sixteenth- and seventeenth-century Europe were also brought together, and conditioned to think of their people as a collective nation, by their
common suffering. Nowhere was that suffering more gut-
wrenching than in Catholic Europe. So when a large group of
Jews escaped from tyranny and arrived in Amsterdam, the historic and folkloric "nationhood" in their hearts leapt out—it
started taking discernible shape amid the relative tolerance of
that northern Protestant city.

* * *

Samuel Palache spent his rabbinical years in Amsterdam consolidating scattered practices of Judaism under a uniform Sephardi
umbrella. In 1603, at the time of the Yom Kippur arrests,
Amsterdam had fifty merchant families from the Iberian
Peninsula. Within the next five years, they had grown to 1,000.
And by the end of the first quarter of the seventeenth century,
1 per cent of Amsterdam's Jews reportedly controlled 10 per cent
of the city's trade. More immigration followed, not just from the
Peninsula, but also from the rest of Europe. There was a rush
even among the privileged, those with royal connections, to leave
everything behind and join the *Nação*. Amsterdam's role was
akin to that of an industrialised nation 300 years into the future:
it was a magnet for migrants, both economic and intellectual.

A SEA-CHANGE IN SEAFARING

Don Manuel Pimentel or Isaac Ibn Jakar, an Iberian New Jew and member of Neve Shalom, was one of the wealthiest men among the early pioneers in Amsterdam. It was he who bought the first patch of land for the cemetery in Ouderkerk aan de Amstel, in 1614. He had converted to Judaism early in the century and secured a prominent presence at the French court of King Henry IV, until the king was assassinated in 1610 by a Catholic fanatic, who feared that the Church would be weakened by the former Huguenot king's Protestant leanings and his excesses—gambling, womanising and befriending judaisers such as Pimentel. After the assassination, which followed several previous attempts by Catholic zealots, Pimentel had been forced to leave France. He went to Venice first, but as the once thriving trading port was fast decaying with the emergence of new sea powers, he moved to Amsterdam and joined Neve Shalom under Rabbi Samuel Palache in 1613.

Pimentel died in 1615, a year after he bought the land in Ouderkerk, and was the first Jew to be buried there.[13] It was as though he had known this was where his colourful life would end, and had negotiated its resting place just in time. Like Pimentel's, the lives of the Jewish people had been about seizing chances, in whatever shape they came. They had embraced chance to ensure a secure future and posterity, journeying across four continents in search of a home where it would be safe to live and to die. In Amsterdam, the Jewish search for a safe haven was completed with the establishment of a final resting place. The beautiful setting of Ouderkerk on the banks of the Amstel provided the perfect end to a life's journey.

Meanwhile, Samuel Palache, a wanderer at heart, was beginning to get restless as rabbi of Neve Shalom. He had always been a seafarer, a traveller, and to sea and travels he wanted to return. In 1614, in his seventies, he handed over responsibilities to Isaac Uziel, who continued to train his young and ambitious chosen successor, Menasseh ben Israel. Palache set sail for Morocco to see his old employer and friend, Mulay Zidan. Soon after his arrival, the sultan reportedly issued his most celebrated Jewish emissary with a privateers' licence to drive the Spanish off the Moroccan coast. Palache was already in possession of two ships, captained by Dutch mercenaries who had come with him to Fez.

But before long, Palache would once again say goodbye to his birthplace. His ships were bound for Holland. He instructed the captains to make a detour in the Atlantic. During the voyage, they attacked a Portuguese and a Spanish ship coming from the colonies, captured their cargo—which contained sugar, 'white gold'—and sent it to the Dutch Republic. This incident took place during the Twelve Years' Truce, and the Portuguese and Spanish authorities vehemently protested the rabbi's alleged piracy against Iberian vessels coming from the New World. The Dutch authorities replied that they had nothing to do with Palache's privateering licence, which had been acquired in his home country, Morocco, and authorised by the sultan.

There remained a large section in the Dutch political establishment that did not accept the peace treaty with Spain. These dissenters were joined by the so-called Sea Beggars, *Watergeuzen*—Dutch naval mercenaries, who resented the truce so strongly that they would have been thrilled by any force or individuals to succeed in harming Spanish sea power. The *Geuzen* were excited by the advance of the Ottoman Army through the Spanish Habsburg Empire. Their hatred for Catholic Spain was uncompromising: one of the Sea Beggars' medals famously read "*Liever Turks dan Paaps*"—"Rather Turkish than Papist". The "pirate rabbi", Samuel Palache, was hugely popular among them.

On his way back to the Dutch Republic from Morocco, Palache's ships were caught in a storm and made an emergency landing at Plymouth, England. There, the Spanish ambassador sued him for piracy and for harming Spanish naval interests.

Palache was arrested. While he was awaiting trial, Prince Maurice heard about it, and personally asked King James I of England, Scotland and Ireland to release the rabbi, whom he referred to as his friend. London kept him under house arrest in the lord mayor's home, where Palache more or less led the life of a free man, wandering about the city, which still upheld the thirteenth-century law forbidding Jews from settling in England. The Spanish ambassador's lawsuit was eventually dismissed, mainly because England did not want to lose its important Protestant ally. Besides, when accused by the Spanish ambassador of favouring a Jew over Spain, with which England had recently signed a peace agreement, London apparently replied that, if the treaty were to collapse, the "Inquisitors would burn both the English Protestants and the Jews."

Palache returned to Amsterdam victorious, but would soon fall ill and spend the last six months of his life bedridden. He died on 6 February 1616, at the end of a spectacular, adventure-filled life lived in many worlds. Prince Maurice and the city magistrates joined the funeral cortege, along with more than 1,000 men, women and children from Amsterdam's Jewish community, to which the deceased rabbi had been a guiding light. The day after his funeral, the States General from The Hague reported that "His Excellency [Prince Maurice] and the State Council accompanied the body of Señor Samuel Palache, Agent of the King of Barbary, as far as the bridge at the Houtmarkt."[14]

Houtstraat bordered the edge of the Jodenbuurt. Palache's coffin was transferred from a bridge to a traditional narrow boat to ferry him along the tributary of the Amstel River to Ouderkerk. "The community's youngsters ran along the riverbank following the barges that carried the mourners to the cemetery."[15]

Samuel Palache's contribution to the formation of the Sephardi Jewish community in Amsterdam was mythologised by later generations of the *Nação* and other Jewish historians, who looked on him in admiration and awe. Daniel Levi de Barrios, the "Marrano" historian, made numerous references in his *Triumpho del Gobierno Popular* (1683) to the New Jews' use of the Palache house for prayer meetings; other historians, too, have since memorialised Palache's role in forging the community's early identity. Their accounts unanimously agree that, without Palache's founding of Neve Shalom, it would have taken much longer for the *Naçāo* to be initiated into true Sephardi ways. After all, it would not be for another decade that the Sephardi Venetian rabbi, Saul Levi Morteira, would take over Beth Jacob from the Ashkenazi, Uri Halevi. Morteira would continue Palache's legacy, reaffirming the community's Sephardi orientation. It would be only a matter of years before Morteira united its three congregations under one roof, with the distinct Iberian Sephardi identity that Palache had fought to establish after relocating from Fez to Amsterdam.

Samuel Palache's unconventional and bold personality still inspires generations of Jews. The descendants of the Portuguese Jews in today's Amsterdam remember him as a pioneer who oversaw a nation of tempest-tossed, demoralised former Catholics transforming into an exemplary Jewish institution, at the heart of the Christian world's most prosperous city.

* * *

The commitment to return to Judaism was so strong among most of the early New Christian settlers, and the New Jewish community was so strictly guided, that the intensity of this conviction can only be understood against the ferocity of the persecution suffered back on the Iberian Peninsula. There were of course pockets of doubting individuals, but on the whole the community remained collectively committed to observing Jewish rites in private and public life. They agreed with the rabbis that dietary and other requirements were essential for creating a truly orthodox Jewish nation.

A SEA-CHANGE IN SEAFARING

This commitment of the Iberian exiles to their new syna-gogue-community was not formed overnight. The process was long, fraught with questions and sheer despair at losing posses-sions and social standing in leaving the Peninsula that they had considered their homeland for centuries. In Italian towns, the Ottoman Empire and North Africa, Sephardim fleeing the Peninsula had attached themselves to the existing Jewish ghettos or communities, and so had come immediately under an estab-lished rabbinical authority. These opportunities were not readily available in Amsterdam when the first New Christian refugees arrived at its harbour. The Netherlands had been under Spanish rule since the mid sixteenth century, and the Inquisition was operational there until the seven northern provinces broke away to create the Dutch Republic in 1581. The handful of Iberian refugees who had previously reached the Low Countries—some of whom even managed to live quite successfully in Antwerp as merchants—had not been able to shed their public appearance as New Christians.

In the early seventeenth century, under the rabbinical author-ity imported from the Old Sephardi world, the New Christians were publicly re-educating themselves into Jewish rites and Jewish law, the *halacha*. But many still remained deeply influ-enced by the memories of their former lives. The conflict was both internal and external. There was a constant need among the New Jews to create and clarify their positions first and foremost in their own minds, then within their community, and lastly in the context of the Dutch Republic and its relationship with the wider mercantile world. This act of introspection helped the early New Jews to produce an outstanding line of authors, poets, philosophers and historians, who would leave a powerful impact on Dutch thought in the Age of Enlightenment.

Torn by these inner and outer conflicts of displacement from home and rehabilitation in a safe haven, early historians such as de Barrios tried to paint an idealistic picture of the community, by "embroidering" a narrative that spoke highly of the Marranos' resilience in the face of brutal adversity. They were joined by poets and writers of memoirs and other prose, who left behind heartrending accounts of the New Christians' suffering and survival, which shed light on how and why they had made the unprecedented collective journey into Judaism. An early-seventeenth-century poem found in a manuscript in Amsterdam, written by an anonymous Portuguese Jew, conjures up the trauma he had witnessed at home, and how that had turned a New Christian into a most unlikely New Jew:

> In this appalling, dour and doleful
> Tribunal, which the people call Holy,
> The brave at once turn cowards,
> Ignorant the well-informed.
> Here the righteous are criminalised,
> Swearing things unseen undreamt.
> Here such conjuring, such legerdemain
> Christians into Jews transmogrified.[16]

Still, the *Nação*'s affiliation with the congregation in Amsterdam was not indicative of a total initiation into or acquaintance with Judaism. The first congregation was loosely formed in the spirit of what most had been accused of back in Portugal: judaising, even when many of them were devout Catholics. As the New Christian exiles settled in Amsterdam, some might still in fact have been crypto-Catholics, until spiritual leaders and rabbis were recruited from Emden, Fez, the Ottoman Empire, Salonica and Venice to direct them into the true Jewish path. In addition to Saul Levi Morteira and Samuel Palache, the community brought over notable theologians from the Sephardi diaspora, among whom were Rabbi Joseph Pardo of Salonica and Rabbi Isaac Uziel of Fez.

A SEA-CHANGE IN SEAFARING

Isaac Uziel took over Neve Shalom's rabbinical duties from his cousin Samuel Palache's departure in 1614 until the privateer's death two years later, when Uziel handed over to Palache's chosen successor, ben Israel. In 1616, deeply moved by the unique tolerance of Jews by the city regents and the contrast with what he had experienced in his hometown, Fez, he wrote, "people live peacefully in Amsterdam. The inhabitants of the city, mindful of the increase in population, make laws and ordinances whereby the freedom of religions may be upheld."[17] In the context of the early seventeenth century, Amsterdam's burgomasters must have been perceived by the formerly persecuted as saviours. It is worth exploring in some detail how great this contrast would have been for the incoming Rabbi Uziel and others from North Africa.

In Fez, the apparent religious co-existence wasn't necessarily born of tolerance, but of Islamic law, requiring the sultans to allow the Jews to live in their realm, with limited opportunities and imposition of high taxes. It is true that the Jews, with their unwavering loyalty to the ruling house, were also the sultans' more trusted servants during centuries of bloody interdynastic power struggles in the North African empire governed out of Fez. The Jews had had a strong political presence in the region long before the Arab conquest in the eighth century. After five centuries of various transfers of power between Arab and Berber sultans, which sidelined the once influential Jews of Morocco from political life, they turned to trade, commerce, jewellery, and intellectual development, creating a Jewish golden age. The eleventh-century philosopher-rabbi-physician, Maimonides, stayed between 1166 and 1168 in Fez el Bali, the old city of Fez, attracted by its long, continuous rabbinical culture. This is where he wrote his commentary on the *mishna*, the Oral Torah. His work is regarded as the first major rabbinical literature, and in fact has "come to be regarded by some as a primary source in its own right."[18] At one point, the Jews held the most important financial positions at the royal court.

However, sporadic pogroms and persecution had continued since the Arab conquest, and the Jews ultimately required "protection" by the fourteenth-century Merenid sultans. The first walled Jewish *mellah* was created next to the new Royal Palace, in the new, defensible royal city of Fez Jdid. The Merenids preferred to reside here rather than in the *medina*, the old city, due to fear of rebellion and lack of security. The *mellah* also allowed the sultans to carry out efficient taxation of the wealthy Jewish community. It is said that the word *mellah*, which means salt, derived from the predominant trade of the time, which the Jews had monopolised; others say it is because they were entrusted by the Berber sultans with preserving in salt the severed heads of executed Arab rebels, for display on the palace gates. In order to keep popular resistance at bay, the sultan's loyal followers were subjected to humiliating restrictions on their movements. The gates of the *mellah* would be locked during the night, and the Jews were required to take their shoes off every time they passed a Muslim graveyard or a saint's tomb. They were required to wear black cloaks and tie black cloths around their arms. Some lucky ones, such as Samuel and Joseph Palache, were given special permits by the sultan thanks to their maritime trade links, but most Jews lived in a closed community, reminded daily of their inferior status.

This may have been one of the reasons why the Palache brothers brought their extended families, friends and acquaintances to Amsterdam. Two of Amsterdam's founding rabbis came from Fez. This was a giant step in the Jewish aspiration for sovereignty. If one visits the old Fez *mellah*'s tiny seventeenth-century synagogue, at the end of a dead-end road, one understands how important the sudden gain of power must have been for Moroccan Jews who arrived in the Dutch Republic. The synagogue is inconspicuous, its entrance dwarfed by many neighbouring houses, almost hidden in the honeycombed architecture of the *mellah*. The streets are so narrow and overhung by houses that a visitor's overwhelming feeling is of claustrophobia. The *mellah* was almost completely destroyed during a pogrom in 1912, but its rebuilding complied with some of the original plans, although greatly improved with modern sanitation. One could very well imagine how stagnant and malodorous these alleyways must once have been.

Edith Wharton, travelling to Fez, Sefrou and other Moroccan towns in the early twentieth century, gave a moving account in her book, *In Morocco*, of the closed neighbourhoods that were home to the country's Jews for six centuries. Sitting in a pew in the tiny synagogue in Fez,, now a museum, I myself could imagine her description of dark figures wearing black gabardines flitting in and out of the wonky building, of black-cloaked women descending down the steps into the subterranean *mikveh*, the ritual submerge pool.[19] Compare this with the manmade Vlooienburg peninsula in Amsterdam, with its open streets and picturesque bridges over the canals. Even the earlier synagogues—or "temples", as they were referred to in Dutch records and paintings—stood as major landmarks on the Houtgracht (today's Waterlooplein), long before the grand Portuguese Synagogue was built in 1675.

We can see, then, why it did not take much persuasion to get Rabbi Isaac Uziel to transfer his position from the *mellah* of Fez to the Dutch Jerusalem. From what Wharton described as the damp and dark "rabbit-warren" alleys of the *mellah*, from that "buried city", "lit by oil lamps" and under the archways of the "black and reeking staircases", Uziel would transport himself to Jodenbreestraat. Its name—Jewish Broad Street—speaks for itself. Here, manmade canals zigzagged through the neighbourhood, ships laden with merchandise arrived from all over the world, Jewish printing presses published Hebrew textbooks, and former Marrano philosophers and playwrights wrote treatises and dramas for mass circulation.

In Amsterdam, by the time Uziel arrived from Fez, the community had already established their mini-state within a state, and everyone was allowed to roam freely in and out of the Jodenbuurt. There was no nightly curfew. Some wealthier Jews soon started moving upriver to areas where rich Dutch merchants lived, while Dutch civilians, painters and artists moved into the Jewish quarter. The *Nação* was fast becoming more confident, and its affluent members started mingling with the Dutch bourgeoisie, considerable exceptions being made in the guilds. The Portuguese émigrés would find themselves in trades such as printing, bookselling, and the kosher meat business, which stretched to poultry farming and groceries. On a Shabbat morning, the Jews of Amsterdam would pass in their finest clothes through the canal streets lined with reformed churches to go to synagogue. It was coexistence of a kind one would find in future democratic societies, three centuries on. The fear of pogroms was a relic of the past; the Jews lit their Hanukkah candles in the menorah on their windowsill in full public view and celebrated the harvest festival of Succoth with flamboyance and confidence, decorating the bridges over the canals with foliage and fruit.

In their fashion, posture and visible affluence, portraits of Jewish merchants and socialites from this era do not look very different from those of their "native" Dutch compatriots. A large painting in Amsterdam's Jewish Historical Museum in Amsterdam of the Suassos—a Marrano banking family—shows its members flaunting the finest jewellery and cloth of the time; the children's rosy cheeks exude health, wealth and confidence. Membership of the Jewish congregation in Amsterdam was synonymous with belonging to a powerful "commercial consortium".[20] Even those who had lost all their assets in fleeing the Inquisition had a chance at a new life, in the most financially thriving city in Europe. Just as the Jews had traditionally thrust themselves into business and commerce in the old ghetto, in Amsterdam they embraced whatever local opportunities or colonial ventures were available to them, practising old skills and gaining new ones, and entering into joint ventures with native Dutch merchants where trade was barred to them by law. Within the first decades of their settlement, some of the Portuguese Jews had become so wealthy that they could almost pass as real burghers.

They managed to avoid attracting the Dutch-born merchants' envy, as had been the case in Morocco and Iberia, where professional and material jealousy had led to daily taunts and periodic persecution. Even if such hostilities did creep in, the situation remained under control in Amsterdam, thanks to the *Nação*'s protection by the synagogue and its charity network, and the absence of overt prejudice necessary for a trading empire, which depended on stability and cooperation. Had the regents had to spend their time containing a public hate campaign against new immigrants, the Dutch Republic's international trade would have suffered greatly. Burgomasters and traders alike recognised the need to accept the clash of cultures. From this point of view, the Dutch were one of the first Western nations to promote the modern concept of "live and let live".[21]

4

THE WAR OF THE RABBIS

As the merchants became richer, they strengthened their membership of their congregation with large donations, both toward improving the living conditions of the *Nação*'s poor, and for its artistic and theological development. Young boys were given exclusive religious education in Hebrew, in parallel to their schooling in Portuguese, Spanish, and also some Dutch, German and Latin. They studied law and medicine, and some even went to university for higher degrees, though they were still not allowed to become professors. A trend grew of finding ways to bypass the guild restrictions. Attracted to this haven of intellectual and trade opportunities, Marranos and Sephardi Old Jews were constantly arriving in Amsterdam's harbour from the Iberian Peninsula via other escape routes such as France, and from North Africa and the Ottoman Empire. The community always made room for everyone. The city was bursting at the seams with skilled professionals.

Very quickly, religious learning within the *Nação* reached a high level of erudition and sophistication, and the first theological seminary—or the modern-day yeshiva—was established in

1616.[1] Ets Haim, The Tree of Life, was where a number of Dutch rabbis would be trained and come to prominence in the international diplomatic circle still dominated by Sephardi Jews. Rabbi Isaac Uziel of Fez was among the first teachers at Ets Haim; following in the footsteps of his predecessor and fellow Fez native, Samuel Palache, he made sure that the community followed the right Sephardi path, kept alive in Moroccan exile by their forefathers. Uziel taught the first batch of students who had enrolled to study the Torah and the Talmud at Ets Haim, Western Europe's first yeshiva.

Menasseh ben Israel was among these first Talmudic scholars to be trained at Ets Haim, under Isaac Uziel's direct guidance. A young Menasseh must have been among the mourners who had followed Palache's grand funeral procession to Ouderkerk cemetery. He is best known as the pioneer who negotiated with Cromwell's England for readmission of the Jews, after 350 years. Born in Portugal in 1604 to a Marrano family recently forcibly converted, by his late teens ben Israel had grown into a fine Dutch-bred—though not Dutch-born—theologian, becoming rabbi of Neve Shalom at the age of eighteen.

The place of ben Israel's birth, however, is subject to speculation. It is said that he may have been born during the family's flight from Portugal, in the Madeira Islands, or on the escape route to France. At birth he was named Manoel Dias Soeiro. His father was suspected of judaising and was tortured in Lisbon, paraded into the city square in a *sanbenito*, publicly shamed. His property was confiscated by the Inquisition. In broken health and a penniless state, he seized the first opportunity to flee with his family to Madeira off the coast of Morocco, about 1,000 kilometres from Lisbon. But since the islands belonged to Portugal, the Soeiro family was soon on the move again, settling in the French port of La Rochelle. Manoel could very well have been born here. The family spent a few years in La Rochelle, which was one of the transit points to which French Protestant Huguenots also escaped after the Reformation.

All who sought religious sanctuary in La Rochelle—Huguenots, Marranos and Old Sephardim—were soon hunted down by the Inquisition, and this strategically important seaport in the Bay of Biscay came under siege. Economic and food blockades led to famine. The Soeiro family was once again forced to leave, with Manoel and two other children. They arrived in Amsterdam around 1610, and Joseph Soeiro, who had been a merchant, found his skills useful at last. He joined the Beth Jacob congregation and officially converted to Judaism, along with his whole family. Young Manoel became Menasseh ben Israel and was admitted to the religious seminary, Ets Haim. He was too young when Samuel Palache was handing over the rabbinical duties of Neve Shalom to Isaac Uziel, but he would become Rabbi Uziel's chosen student and successor. He was groomed to take over from his master while still a boy. The great rabbi from Fez died in 1622, leaving his teenage protégé at the helm of a congregation and a community that still needed direction towards normative Judaism.

But by then, it was clear to the members of the Portuguese Jewish community that they had come to stay in Amsterdam. It was not a transit point like the other places where they had stopped over. Ben Israel married a woman with a connection to the noble Abravanel family, who claimed descent from the biblical King David. This would play an important part in his career as rabbi. Ben Israel would devote his life to the search for a Jewish homeland, wherever in the world that was possible, and laid the groundwork to bring this goal closer, both through diplomacy with notable Christian statesmen and monarchs of his time, and by venturing out to the New World and following up leads in the search for the Lost Tribes—without whom Jewish salvation could not happen.

One of the most prolific scholars that Ets Haim would ever produce, Menasseh did not stop at becoming a rabbi and a theologian; he also explored ways to test the countries around him, in case the *Nação* ever needed another place to accommodate them, for the influx of the Iberian New Christians into the Dutch Republic was continuing at a steady pace. In addition to his knowledge of Latin, classical Greek, Arabic and biblical Hebrew, ben Israel taught himself most of the European languages needed to communicate with the known world. He tirelessly wrote Talmudic tracts and exegeses for his congregation. He also wrote to the monarchs of the surrounding European countries and the Muslim world, to develop closer diplomatic relations and coax them into accepting the settlement of Jews in their realms.

Ben Israel's writing was much influenced by the cultural interaction between Christianity and Judaism. Although one would not call it a harmonious confluence of Judeo-Christian ideas, there existed in seventeenth-century Amsterdam, among the Protestant clergy and statesmen alike, a genuine interest in the language of the Bible. Ben Israel wanted to make sure the Jews presented a positive image of their culture and religion, challenged the centuries-old prejudice and gained the endorsement and admiration of their host society. He established himself as one of the most eloquent representatives of the Judeo-Christian "special relationship", loyal expression of which would become an underlying theme in Dutch Jewish interaction with the Calvinist authorities. With echoes of *Diálogo dos Montes*, ben Israel's mid-century book, *Hope of Israel*, explains Amsterdam's acceptance and tolerance of the Jewish community as part of the divine providence in which the exiled communities believed, carrying it with them to every new country of refuge: "So, at this day we see many [Christians] desirous to learn the Hebrew tongue of our men. Hence may be seen that God has not left us; for if one persecutes us, another receives us civilly and courteously."[2]

THE WAR OF THE RABBIS

As a Hebrew scholar, Menasseh ben Israel was naturally excited by the increasing interest that the Calvinist clergy, intelligentsia and artists were showing in the Old Testament and its prophets, and by extension in their Jewish neighbours. Ben Israel's erudition in this area was sought after and he soon found friendship in high and influential places, where he regularly provided commentaries on Hebrew texts and passages from the Bible. Of particular interest to the theologians of Ets Haim was the fact that, with the arrival of Calvinism, over-reliance of the laity on saints and confessions receded dramatically—and in its place came an ideal of universal literacy, no longer restricted to the upper classes as had been the norm under Catholicism. Everyone had to be able to read the Bible themselves, no longer relying on the intercession of priests. Art, literature, science and international law flourished in Amsterdam, and access to knowledge had been greatly facilitated by the introduction of the printing press. Ben Israel became one of the first men in the city to own a printing press in 1616, and his business would thrive throughout his life.

This set such a trend that one of his successors in the printing business, Joseph Athias, would break all records in the area of Bible printing—both Old and New Testaments—not only in the Dutch Republic, but for the whole of Christian Europe. In the introduction to a Hebrew-Yiddish Bible printed in his press in Amsterdam in 1686, he wrote, "For Several years I myself printed more than a million Bibles for distribution in England and Scotland, and in those countries, there is not a plowboy or a servant girl who does not possess one."[3] Athias, a Jew, would later be admitted to the booksellers' guild, an illustration of just how far the Calvinist authorities were prepared to relax the rules when such modifications were deemed beneficial to Amsterdam society.

A teacher of theology and a promoter of the "primary sources", as the Old Testament teachings came to be known to Protestant northern Europe, Menasseh ben Israel would seize upon the opportunity presented by the new Calvinist interest, happily coinciding with the flourishing of Amsterdam's printing industry. In the first quarter of the seventeenth century, he established a virtual monopoly on printing religious and philosophical treatises—his own and those of others, both Jewish and Christian. In 1627, the first Hebrew prayer books for the *Nação* were printed on ben Israel's press. This allowed him to meet Dutch society's need for a Hebrew scholar to expound for the Calvinist establishment on the *halacha* and the teachings of the biblical prophets. From this advantageous position, he started extending his diplomatic skills to England and Sweden, among other countries.

Ben Israel became intrepid enough to publish important works in the vein of the humanism and freedom of conscience that flourished in the Dutch Republic at this time. In his book *De la Fragilidad Humana*, he appealed to the Protestant world with the tradition of Jewish universalism, as coded in Leviticus 19:18, "Thou shalt love thy neighbour as yourself." He elaborated his faith in salvation for all, not just the Jews, extending God's Providence to all people in the Amsterdam Jews' great humanism and readiness for integration. Ben Israel was almost pre-empting "the accusations of egoism and xenophobia" that Spinoza was to make against the Jews in his *Tractatus Theologico-Politicus*.[4]

Rabbi ben Israel's promotion of Jewish humanism, and his enthusiastic entente with the Christian world—which had ostracised and persecuted the "Jewish nation" all over Europe for millennia—generated discomfort among his colleagues and congregation in Amsterdam. At first he was in denial about the community's view of his exchanges with the Calvinist establishment. As his tireless pursuit of knowledge produced book after book on the human condition and man's propensity for greater good than evil, important transformations were taking place within the *Nação*. There were by now three congregations, illustrating the considerable differences in approach and ideology among the Portuguese Jews.

This second split had come about when a prominent member accused the Beth Jacob congregation of "homiletic interpretations of Scripture",[5] and those who opposed this view decided to leave under Rabbi Joseph Pardo, who formed the third congregation, Beth Israel, after 1619. The dispute became so huge that the rabbinical courts, the Bet Din, of Venice and Salonica became involved in resolving it. To the *Nação's* founding members, this was not good news. Menasseh ben Israel's intellectual fascination with the salvation of all men—rather than only saving and uniting his own divided people—began to create quite a few dissenters against his principles, including the powerful rabbi of Beth Jacob, Saul Levi Morteira.

The *Nação*, having abandoned an oppressively Christian society in Iberia, was itself turning to orthodoxy. It was becoming a deeply religious, passionately Jewish society, under the watchful eyes of the influential Morteira. With his knowledge of Venetian Jewish organisation and his zealous insistence on the 613 precepts of the Talmudic law, Morteira took on the role of containing the community's orthodox Jewish ways and convincing fresh New Christian arrivals of the importance of the *halacha* and its application to every aspect of life. Grown men willingly submitted themselves to the knife of the *mohel* for circumcision to renew the Abrahamic covenant with God; strict kosher rules were imposed on the community's diet; and all boys were required to enrol in religious seminaries at the age of five. With a few exceptions, the *Nação's* members had agreed to lead the truly traditional Jewish life that their Venetian, German or Moroccan teachers presented to them. It was religion, after all, that had saved and united the community in Amsterdam, so to religious orthodoxies the Dutch New Jews succumbed.

Menasseh ben Israel was himself deeply religious, but unlike most of his congregation, his understanding of the *halacha* transcended the literal and verged on the universal. In 1639 he published *De Termino Vitae*, which advocated, even more emphatically, salvation for all men. As if to answer this appeal to the whole Judeo-Christian world, in the same year Rabbi Morteira turned solely to his community, to unite its three congregations into one body. With firm leadership he shook awake the *Nação*, which he felt was becoming complacent as it grew richer and more established. Thus, in 1639, Morteira created a single *kehillah* (congregation), and became its chief rabbi. This, of course, put Menasseh ben Israel's career in jeopardy. Neve Shalom, along with Beth Israel, was disbanded by Morteira, who now claimed to be the sole guardian of the *Nação*. Ben Israel became poor overnight, and his self-esteem suffered a great blow when Morteira appointed ben Israel's rival, Isaac Aboab da Fonseca, as his assistant.

Kahal Kadosh of Talmud Torah, the United Congregation of Talmud Torah, heralded a well-organised community as the Jews had never before experienced. The old Jewish communities in Italian cities such as Venice and Livorno, as well as in the Ottoman Empire, had enjoyed glory and status, wealth and high position, but the Amsterdam *Nação*'s success story was markedly different. Its already unique character was set in stone by Morteira's act: the united synagogue would be recorded as the first "purpose-built Jewish House of Worship in the Atlantic world".[6]

The newcomers had already settled comfortably under the common identity of the Portuguese *Nação*. And now, under Morteira's rigid leadership, it emerged as an exemplary political, legal and social institution. The Venetian rabbi's uncompromising orthodoxy had paid off. He had always believed that the New Jews' practices were fragile, and that the only way to maintain a homogeneous, successful community was through a strict observance of Jewish rites and laws. Before long, the *Nação* managed to create a paragon Sephardi Jewish centre that would become so successful that its members would increasingly see their city as the New Jerusalem.

This remains one of the greatest paradoxes in Jewish history: how, in an age of religious conflict, did a Portuguese Jewish nation made primarily of former Catholics come to thrive in an orthodox Calvinist society? The *Nação* of Amsterdam became a beacon for the Sephardi diaspora and a template for other Jewish settlements in the West and even the East Indies, as Dutch colonial power spread. Extraordinarily, the New World started to receive a steady Jewish migration from the Dutch Republic—a new diaspora produced not by Christian persecution, but by the pursuit of wealth.

This new opportunity would change the life of Menasseh ben Israel, who had been finding it hard to make ends meet following his exclusion from rabbinical position following the 1639 unification of the congregations. He turned to commerce and the Americas posed a tantalising enterprise. He sent his brother, Ephraim, to Brazil to look for lucrative trades, which he soon found. Subsequently, ben Israel became very involved in the family business in the Americas. But his spiritual and intellectual yearnings remained unfulfilled. He missed his family and his "Jerusalem of the North".

When an interesting possibility for return to Amsterdam appeared on the horizon, ben Israel welcomed it. The newly Jewish community in Recife, Brazil, invited Isaac Aboab da Fonseca—Morteira's assistant rabbi—to lead their synagogue, and he accepted. It was an agonising decision, but ben Israel decided to swallow his pride, applied for the job vacated by his rival, and got it. Chief Rabbi Morteira, one would assume, accepted ben Israel's application for the sake of unity in the congregation, and the two men would work together over the next decade to shape the *Nação*'s development, ensuring its full acceptance by the Dutch mainstream while maintaining a strong Jewish identity.

Surprisingly, the two rabbis' work was even complimentary. Morteira held the community together with a strong emphasis on religiosity—there was no room for secular thoughts, or ideas that would challenge rabbinical authority. He frequently carried out investigations into heresy within the community. Ben Israel, in moderation, continued his diplomatic efforts on the community's behalf while remaining deeply orthodox. He met regularly with Christian Hebraists from all over Europe and advised them on matters relating to the Old Testament. His printing press started publishing books on Hebrew language and grammar. They were hugely popular among the Calvinists, who considered a good understanding of Hebrew an attestation of their knowledge of the Old Testament. Hebrew letters and words for God replaced the Catholic graven images that had once adorned the churches of Europe. The Reformed Church replaced the image of God with the Hebrew transliteration—YHVH—that denoted His unutterable name. The four letters, Yud, Hei, Vav, Hei, jointly known as the tetragrammaton, began to appear in governmental and religious texts.

Ben Israel found various ways to prove that there were closer ties between Jews and Protestants than between Jews and Catholics. He became more vocal in his own theological views, amid the continuing iconoclastic militancy that had broken out in Protestant Europe toward the end of the sixteenth century. It was then that knowing how to write and read Hebrew correctly appeared to be of paramount importance among the iconoclasts. By the mid-seventeenth century, ben Israel was held by the Dutch establishment in such high esteem, and his books of philosophical exegesis were so widely read by the Protestant Hebraists, that he could cautiously present his own theory on predestination, the doctrine to which Orthodox Calvinism and the House of Orange scrupulously adhered. His religious polemic *De Termino Vitae*, aimed at Calvinism's obsession with predestination and again published by his own press, proved that by the mid-century Amsterdam's Jews were seen as intellectual equals. Ben Israel's revolutionary theory was a testament to the unparalleled freedom of speech enjoyed by the *Nação*: "All Jews without exception admit that the date of death is modifiable."[7]

Ben Israel argued with his Protestant friends that, if the span of life was predetermined by God, why then do we call the doctor? He argued that the God of the Old Testament knows the order of the world, but His knowledge still leaves man free to plan his own conduct. God's foreknowledge is fully compatible with man's free will. "A man does not act this way or that because God knows in advance that he will so act, but on the contrary, it is because a man acts according to his own will that God knows his actions for all time ... I support this solution unconditionally."[8] Ben Israel further explained man's free will by comparing God's foreknowledge with that of a man's view of the world from atop a tower: he can see the coming and going of the people below, but he only knows their actions—he doesn't tell them which direction to follow.

What was the source of this intellectual courage to question the predominant thought of the time? Historians argue that the culture of questioning, and the conflict between the individual and divinity, could have been imported by the New Jews from their long history in exile, when they were forced to internalise doubt about other religions they had been made to embrace. In Amsterdam's intellectual freedom, they were finally able to vocalise their questioning minds without fear of being burnt alive. Ben Israel was also clearly influenced by the great philosophical trends of the age: humanism, and challenges to divine authority. When the Jews embarked on the Age of Enlightenment in the West, they arrived from a society in which old understandings of community and authority had already broken down. Ideas of the primacy of the self, taught by both Enlightenment philosophy and late Reformation theology, fitted precisely into this intellectual predisposition.[9] One of ben Israel's young students, Baruch Spinoza (1632–77), would soon explore the area of free will much more boldly in his own work, upsetting the religious orthodoxy that Morteira had been trying so rigorously to uphold in Amsterdam. Orobio de Castro (c. 1617–87), was another writer in Amsterdam's Portuguese Jewish community, who explained ever so clearly that all former New Christians who had received a university education back in Iberia had been filled with doubts—doubts passed on to their offspring, who grew up in a functioning Jewish society in Amsterdam.

This was exactly that Morteira had been fearful of. While, on the one hand, this doubting mind contributed to the development of modern thought in Enlightenment society, it also deeply threatened the Jewishness of the *Nação*. Ben Israel, despite his piety, churned this questioning into groundbreaking, scholarly disputations with Christian and Jewish philosophers. But Morteira's strong commitment to an Orthodox Portuguese Sephardi identity for the community would not be swayed. The wise and experienced chief rabbi, with his exemplary organisational skills, stepped in when he felt his intervention was needed to keep the balance. Morteira did not forget that, throughout the community's formation and settlement in Amsterdam, the Calvinist authorities had remained strongly in favour of near-complete autonomy for the Jews. He did not want the *Nação*'s gratitude for this support to go unnoticed. He authorised a special prayer for the city of Amsterdam: "Blessed art thou O Lord our God, who has shown us your wonderful mercy in the city of Amsterdam, the Praiseworthy."

Morteira, just like other founders and leaders of the community, saw in the inimitable tolerance of the Dutch city authorities a God-given chance for the community to live a Jewish life. For him, this meant he must exercise full rabbinical control so as not to let heresy creep in and destroy this chance. The force of the old Marrano scepticism was still in the air and Morteira did his best to uproot the seed of doubt before it could germinate. As if to prove him right, the rich merchant Abraham Pereyra, who would play an important role in saving ben Israel from perpetual poverty, published this on coming to Amsterdam from Portugal: "Shall I escape from the falsehoods into which I sank? But woe to me! They are so deeply submerged within me that only with difficulty shall I be able to free myself from the false news that dominated me."[10]

Morteira and, to some extent, ben Israel were careful that the community did not indulge too much in what they considered "false news" from around the Christian world. But while ben Israel was an advocate for acceptance and integration, Morteira insisted on just tolerance by the mainstream Dutch society. The Reformed Dutch Christians and the Jews must not mix at a social level. The chief rabbi, having united the Jewish Nation of the Portuguese exile in Amsterdam, would not let his congregation forget the brutal rejection they had faced in their Catholic homeland. They must always remember the story of their recent exodus from the lands of the Old Christians: not to trust the Calvinists, no matter how enthusiastically they tolerated their city's Jewish immigrants.

As time went by, Menasseh ben Israel, through personal conduct with the western European Christian world, began to realise that tolerance and acceptance were not quite the same thing. Acceptance, in another word, integration, required interchange of ideas, debate and intellectual engagement. And only through intellectual cooperation could he offer the Republic of Letters—which would later be known as Protestant Enlightenment—Jewish universalism. This was what he sought to spread through his writing, and this was what Morteira tried to keep from entering the Holy Congregation of Kahal Kadosh. There were already mild doubters like Abraham Pereyra, and others with more extreme views like Uriel da Costa and his infamous cousin, Baruch Spinoza. Morteira's policy for the community was to develop in parallel with Dutch society, but as a semi-sovereign Jewish nation, without full integration. This proved to be so effective that, until the nineteenth century, the Jews of Amsterdam did not speak Dutch as their first language. Even Spinoza was thought to have a strong accent when he spoke Dutch, and all his work was written in Portuguese, Spanish or Latin.

Menasseh ben Israel did not outwardly protest his superior's policy, despite their personal conflict; perhaps the diplomat in ben Israel deferred to the chief rabbi for the greater good. After all, it was Morteira who remained firmly rooted in the *Nação*'s day-to-day running, overseeing its smooth governance and reinforcing its orthodox identity. Ben Israel, like his spiritual predecessor Samuel Palache, would often set off for other parts of the world, either on business or on intellectual pursuits. The two men gradually learnt to give each other space to flourish in their preferred endeavours: the older man would continue doing what he was good at, while his younger assistant was allowed to roam the world and promote his writing, as well as pursuing his mystical quest: to find the Ten Lost Tribes.

* * *

The central Dutch government more or less left the rabbis and the administrative board, the Mahamad, to run and control their own affairs. It is interesting to think that the *halacha*, the Jewish law, was much more prominent in the lives of Amsterdam's seventeenth-century Jews than it is in modern Israel.[11] The rabbis in Amsterdam could enforce *halacha* in almost every aspect of Jewish life, both individual and collective. If one Jew was stealing from another, the victim would not go to the Dutch court—the rabbi could convict anyone deemed to have broken the law, and the city police would act on this decision. The two authorities worked together. This reduced the need for extra money and resources to police the Jewish areas—in an age when more than 10 per cent of the city's population was of foreign origin, this must have satisfied the Dutch authorities. Thrift was the secret of steady progress in an early capitalist society. In fact, from time to time the city police would carry out investigations into the Mahamad's effectiveness in enforcing the *halacha* against Jewish criminals.

In other words, Kahal Kadosh ran a parallel law-enforcing authority and governed its people independently of Dutch state interference. The Jewish wardens rewarded the community's best citizens and punished its renegades as the *halacha* directed. This system of self-government had previously been in practice in one form or another in Jewish ghettos and quarters around the world, but the Mahamad in Amsterdam exercised freedom of a totally different kind. This ruling committee was not strictly required to report to a higher authority of the host state, nor were they serving as mere tax collectors delivering inferior citizens' money to a superior "mother" command.

Some criminal and other complex cases did end up at Amsterdam's central court, if the Mahamad could not reach unanimity. But before seeking assistance from the Dutch judge, which was the last resort, these cases would first be sent to prominent Jewish rabbinical judges in Venice, Salonica or another old Sephardi centre for resolution.

For the seventeenth-century Dutch Jews, Judaism was everything in their social identity: it was ethnicity, religiosity, culture; it was what held together the *Nação* in Amsterdam. Though there were odd protests or traces of scepticism, its members generally chose to abide by the rules, most of them enthusiastically—some for financial reasons, others because it was empowering for a historically persecuted generation to belong to a powerful body of their own people. Even the most despised offender must have felt before a Jewish judge that he was lucky it was not the Inquisition court presiding, and he was not wearing the *sanbenito* with the stake being prepared nearby.

The community's charitable network was proving to be immensely beneficial for those individuals who had no means to support themselves or who had fallen on hard times. As the scale of Jewish immigration grew with the prosperity of the community, so did the new arrivals' dependency on the Mahamad's coffers. While the first settlers had been businessmen or political and religious refugees, the later generations consisted mostly of economic and religious migrants. So long as one could prove one's Old Sephardi or Marrano credentials, one was entitled to benefits. The New Christian settlers in Amsterdam felt blessed by the *Nação* system: the protection of the *parnassim*, the liberty to roam everywhere, the freedom to practise their religion in public while living by their own law. It would seem, from this picture, that Chief Rabbi Morteira had won. He achieved in all practical and religious terms the self-government that he had championed. For most ordinary members of his congregation, there was no need to step outside the community's invisible boundaries. There was no ghetto wall, but the *halacha* separated the Portuguese Nation from the Dutch Reformed Church.

In Israel the *halacha* is used as family law; in Amsterdam at this time it worked as a civil legal code. There was no question of a power struggle between the religious and the secular—the latter was an anathema in Jewish Amsterdam. The rabbis had absolute power, often brutally, to get rid of elements that they believed might threaten the *Nação's* unity and religious identity. The two famous cases of excommunication, Uriel da Costa and Baruch Spinoza—which we will revisit later—prove the kind of power that the rabbis were able to exercise over dissenting voices within the community. The outcome of such a strictly controlled society was that the Jews could focus on advancing their position both within the community and in mainstream Dutch society, as well as in the mercantile communities of the Indies.

The rabbis and the Mahamad as a joint, autonomous law-enforcing body, also controlled the community's finances. The have-nots and the newcomers remained well cared and provided for. This welfare system was efficiently maintained, with regular fundraising charity efforts that also helped to settle the poorer arrivals from central and eastern Europe, the Ashkenazi refugees. Fleeing pogroms in Poland and Germany, they arrived in Amsterdam in great numbers very soon after the Sephardim had established themselves as a distinct group favoured by the Dutch regents early in the century.

Many wealthy Portuguese Jews may not have visited the synagogue, which, by the time the three congregations were united in 1639, had become a source of Jewish pride worldwide. The rich merchants had to pay to belong to the *kehillah*. Sometimes, it was not piety, but how much one paid, that determined one's place as a warden of the Mahamad. Most of the wealthiest Jews were such *parnassim* helping to run the community, some on multiple appointments. It was important to belong, because although the early merchants brought with them wealth, a strong business sense and extensive trade networks, their knowledge of Judaism was still not up to standard. They needed the rabbis to rubberstamp their Jewish credentials, and the *parnassim* needed their income to maintain a successful community with a high-quality welfare system.

The *Nação* became a model society to which the Dutch central government would sometimes refer when dealing with other immigrants: Lutherans, mostly from the southern Netherlands, Germany and the Scandinavian countries; clandestine Roman Catholics; Huguenots; and even some Moriscos—Spanish Muslims who, like the New Christians, had been forced to convert to Catholicism. They too were now crowding into the unique cosmopolitan city on the Amstel River. Amongst the volumes of documents in Amsterdam's Ets Haim library, we find early references to halachic resolutions of disputes over fatherhood, marriage, divorce and property. Consultation of halachic references vindicated specific rabbinical judgments. From policing to bar mitzvah to marriage, divorce and funerals—all remained in the hands of the Mahamad, which gave unprecedented powers to the rabbis, who ruled over all public and private matters in the community. Together, they established a strong socio-political institution alongside the Dutch Reformed Church.

As well as maintaining a well-run community in education, trade, and intercommunal relations with the Dutch and the outside world, the Jews also had their own gambling houses, run by two wealthy Portuguese merchants, Samuel Pereira and Abraham Mendes Vasques. And, in the presence of a Dutch law that banned sexual relations between Jews and Christians, they even had their own brothel, staffed by Jewish prostitutes from Germany who arrived with the Ashkenazi immigrants. The Ashkenazim lived a marginal life and did not have their own independent congregation until the mid-1630s. By then, the Amsterdam Sephardim had already established themselves as a well-connected, self-contained mini-state.

By contrast, Dutch etchings and paintings from this time portrayed the new Ashkenazi arrivals as beggars, peddlers and vagabonds. They were not at first accepted favourably by the Sephardi elite. These men and women, with their pale, middle European complexion, were often ridiculed by the rich, olive-skinned Portuguese Jews, as well as by Dutch gentiles, who saw them as archetypal conmen and crooks who tried to sell eye-glasses to blind gentiles—as shown in a Rembrandt engraving. The master frequently used scruffy wanderers passing through Jodenbreestraat as his models and "tronies". However, despite the general contempt that the Ashkenazi poor suffered after their arrival in

Amsterdam, the *Nação* acted quickly enough to take care of its co-religionists, with rabbis arguing that the influx of more Jews, regardless of denomination, strengthened their presence and enriched the Jewish demography. This would increase the likelihood of the Jews becoming a fixed feature in Amsterdam's multicultural social fabric.

Despite the inequality between Sephardi and Ashkenazi, the Jews of Amsterdam were experiencing an anachronistic fulfilment of the quintessential Zionist aspiration that would be laid out in the twentieth century. David Ben Gurion, one of the movements pre-eminent leaders, made this famous, albeit frivolous statement on the must-haves of a modern Jewish state: "When Israel has prostitutes and thieves, we'll be a state just like any other." As we have seen, the Amsterdam *Nação* had both. One of Zionism's preconditions for the creation of a Jewish state was the normalisation of the Jews in all spheres of society within that state. Three hundred years before the birth of modern Zionism, the Sephardim and Ashkenazim of Amsterdam aspired to and succeeded in achieving a greater normalisation than ever before, albeit within a parent body of state.

The constitution of the Dutch Republic's Seven United Provinces had already proved itself to be an anomaly in a generally imperial Europe. The idea of Dutch tolerance is rooted in the seventeenth century, when the regents and the House of Orange had to live with the Dutch Catholics, the New Jews, and other nations arriving at the harbour fleeing religious and political persecution. This circumstantial amalgamation of nations created in Amsterdam the first truly multi-cultural society in Europe. The Jews still faced limitations, but in comparison with what they had experienced until then in the diaspora, Amsterdam heralded a total sea change, even a miracle: an early taste of statehood. For the first time since Antiquity, Jewish political and social institutions could be taken for a test drive, and they passed with flying colours. Amsterdam was truly becoming the Dutch Jerusalem.

5

JUDAISM AS NATIONALITY

With miracles no human tongue can tell;
Just as the faithful shepherd guides his sheep,
Leading you to possess again and keep
Your ancient heritage.

Rehuel Jessurun, *Diálogo dos Montes*[1]

The idea of "Judaism" as "nationality" went from strength to strength, almost at the same speed as Amsterdam's growth. In spite of the advent of humanist trends in Dutch thought, everyone was still very much expected, as in the early modern period, to have a religion that one observed and which lent to one's national identity. Religion, nation and ethnicity were connected in a homogeneous unit. Because of this, in the lives of the Portuguese Jewish business community, the theme of "people versus nationality" that would become popular in post-Enlightenment Europe was yet to take discernible form. The *Nação's* "nationality" was still the great Portuguese identity, with a greater attachment to the east bank of the Amstel and the man-made island of Vlooienburg, in a friendly Protestant city. That attachment was sealed by a bond of gratitude to this land where a tempest-tossed generation became a liberated people—where they became "Jews" and ran their own affairs.

The community's position was further elevated—and its confidence boosted beyond the first generation's expectations—after the 1645–54 rebellion of the Portuguese in Dutch Brazil. Despite their cultural and linguistic affinity with Portugal, the Jews of the *Nação* in Amsterdam remained vehemently loyal to the Dutch, and it paid off. Amsterdam was growing into a fine, well organised, clean and almost crime-free city. More and more swamps were filled in, new canals were dug or rerouted for easy passage of the narrowboats of goods flowing between the merchants' houses and the harbour. Amid the greatly increased wealth stemming from its domination of New World trade, the city was also becoming an architectural phenomenon. Amsterdam is considered the first town in history to be built on a preconceived plan. Finally, its influential, outward-looking merchants insisted on introducing unprecedented democratic traditions.

These traditions would continue throughout the seventeenth century to attract foreigners who had been thwarted religiously, politically or even intellectually in their home countries. To Amsterdam they came and settled, some permanently such as the Jews, others for long sojourns. While in the city, they were more or less left alone to practise their faiths openly and publish their philosophical and political works, which would have been considered treasonous in their own countries. The French philosopher Descartes, who, like other seekers of spiritual and material fortunes, arrived in Amsterdam early in the century, left an accurate chronicle of the city in his day: "In this vast city, where I am the only man not engaged in trade, everyone is so actively occupied in money-making, that I might spend my whole life in complete solitude."[2]

For the first time in the history of their wandering, the Jews could buy properties, and they could do so anywhere in the city,

and live like their Dutch merchant neighbours. Their sumptuous, double-fronted houses lined the Nieuwe Herengracht, where
wealthy and aristocratic Jews entertained princes and fellow merchants, foreign traders and art dealers. The women wore clothes
in the latest trend from Paris. They went to *mikvehs*, ritual baths,
accompanied by their Ashkenazi and sometimes black servants,
brought over from the Dutch colonies, where the Jewish merchants owned coffee and sugar plantations. As a result of the
United Provinces' extensive mercantile network, the lifestyle of
the merchants—both native Dutch and Jewish—was becoming
increasingly ostentatious. So long as the Portuguese merchants
paid their membership fee to the Mahamad, it seemed they could
do anything they liked, in the privacy of their multi-storey
homes. The Jews were also investing heavily in the Dutch East
and West India Companies, and became army contractors to the
stadtholder. This was in stark contrast to the conditions that
blighted the Jews in the rest of Europe before and during the
seventeenth century.

At this time of great synergy between the *Nação* and the
Dutch in the world's most prosperous city, religion continued to
be a distinctive feature for both communities. Since the mid-
sixteenth century, the Netherlands had been engaged in a protracted war of division into a Protestant north and a Roman
Catholic south. When William of Orange began the Eighty
Years' War for the freedom of the Spanish Habsburg Empire's
Seventeen Provinces, he "visualised a state in which Protestants
and Roman Catholics would live on terms of mutual respect and
equality, or at least of mutual toleration."[3] This was also the
vision of the philosopher Erasmus, whose "middle way" offered
religious freedom to both denominations of Christianity. But the
hardcore Calvinists would not have anything to do with the
Catholics, who were supposed to have been given liberty of conscience under the 1579 Union of Utrecht that founded the

Dutch Republic. The Calvinists' militant wing, which had appointed like-minded Protestants as heads of all the town councils after driving out the Catholic clergy in the Dutch Revolt of 1572, would soon withdraw that clause of tolerance, forcing them underground or into exile. All municipal and state government offices would be reserved for those who publicly accepted Calvinism. A great many among the early republican rulers—and in particular the Sea Beggars, the firebrand Dutch mercenaries whom we met earlier—viewed the Twelve Years' Truce of 1609 with suspicion.

On the one hand, there was no stopping the Dutch Republic's rise from the late sixteenth century as the greatest sea power; but, on the other, the religious conflict involving various denominations of Christianity remained a niggling issue for the Republic. The truce with the Spaniards was vital for its success, allowing the influx of Jews and other immigrants from France and Germany, and with them manpower and money. However, the paragon Dutch prosperity was sporadically threatened by the wars of religion; even when the battle between Catholics and Protestants was tackled and won, the resultant infighting between various Protestant sects hit at the heart of Dutch stability. The religious-political tension reached a breaking point in 1616–18 during the Synod of Dordrecht, when hardline Calvinists, supported by the House of Orange, won out and rejected the Provinces' sovereignty over the Church. For the zealots, who celebrated raucously, any concession to the Spanish Crown was a sign of weakness, and they now resented the Truce even more fiercely. They called for "the complete elimination of Roman Catholics and of Protestant dissenters from any position of authority in Church or State."[4]

While the Christians were at loggerheads over whose revelation was greater, the Jews of Amsterdam were enjoying halcyon days. They had just returned to their true, ancestral faith, and they had found a spot on the western shores of the Atlantic where they were left alone to grow as Jews, within an independent, wealthy and well-organised institution. Luck could not have been more in the Jews' favour. With the 1619 public execution of the leading Calvinist moderate, Johan van Oldenbarnevelt, Prince Maurice decisively won the Calvinist sectarian war. Van Oldenbarnevelt's Remonstrants, with their liberal views of Protestantism and their advocacy of greater civil power, were declared heretics. Dissenters—Roman Catholics as well as others such as the Lutherans and Mennonites, who did not adhere to the Synod's declaration of what constituted true Reformed Christianity—were reduced to second-class status. This cleared the path for the orthodox Calvinists to impose on the population a stricter, more abstract version of the Protestant doctrine, one that despised iconography. *Beeldenstorm*, iconoclasm, became synonymous with the Dutch Reformation. Though the Synod also marked the end of state religion for the Republic, and the Reformed Church was not a formally established Church like the Church of England, its zealots were still able to tighten existing regulations on the Catholics, and to purge the churches of any remaining icons, statues or decorations that were in the way of reaching the true, abstract God of the Old Testament.

That omnipresent, abstract God was increasingly being established as a common thread in the new entente between the Jews, the Protestants, and the Muslims. The common enemy was the Holy Roman Empire of the Habsburgs, and the common credence was this faith in an abstract God. The House of Orange watched favourably the advances of the Ottoman army into Habsburg territory, and the Calvinists made a real case out of this foundation of their faith, advocating a kind of puritanical militancy akin to the doctrines propagated by today's jihadists. Earlier in the sixteenth century, they had burned churches and smashed idols. Now, claiming a metaphysical link to God, they replaced graven images in holy places with abstract symbols including the Hebrew tetragrammaton. In their iconoclastic beliefs, the Calvinists were in some sense the Islamic State of the seventeenth century.

The Mahamad's severe emphasis on instilling a strict Talmudic way of life in its former New Christians could very well have been influenced by the Protestant orthodoxy of the time. Despite the prosperity of the rich Jewish merchants, the Mahamad grew inward-looking. The stricter the rules became, the more authoritatively the rabbis could maintain what they considered "order". In the first quarter of the seventeenth century, the *Nação* mirrored the Dutch state, ruled by diehard Calvinists. Around the same time as the Calvinist *predikanten* (ministers) were banning theatres and dancehalls around the Dutch Republic—though never successfully in Amsterdam—the Jewish leadership decided, after the 1624 staging of *Diálogo dos Montes*, against future performances in the synagogue. Was Chief Rabbi Morteira influenced by the Calvinists' aversion to celebration of "Papist festivals"? Like the Calvinists, the Mahamad suppressed any voice of dissent or debate in the community that threatened the normative Judaic order it had established, as the excommunications of da Costa and Spinoza would soon demonstrate.

The rabbis' and wardens' strict policies could also have been directed by pragmatism—survival tactics. They felt extremely lucky that the ban against Catholics and Protestant dissenters introduced following the Synod of Dordrecht did not extend to the Jews. If they celebrated their exclusion, and even the brutal crackdown on Christian dissenters, they did so quietly, diplomatically, while maintaining regular interactions with the States General in matters concerning bilateral trade, community policing and good citizenry. They also responded, cautiously at first, to the interests of Calvinist intellectuals advocating limited state protection for the Hebrew masters of the Old Testament, among them Hugo de Groot.

JUDAISM AS NATIONALITY

Over the next 150 years, while the law did not permit Roman Catholics to worship in public or be christened and married by their priests, the Jews would enjoy not only public worship, building several synagogues, but would buy land—including their own cemetery—conduct public marriages and bar mitzvah ceremonies. Learned Hebrew scholars including Menasseh ben Israel would continue to engage in theological discussions with humanists like de Groot and professors at the prestigious new University of Leiden.

By now, the *Nação* was well aware of the opinion the Protestant authorities held of the "Hebrews": that they were a medium for attaining the wisdom of the Old Testament prophets. They had kept alive through the generations both the old traditions and cultural beginnings of Christianity and the stories of the giving of the Law to Moses. They had remained the preservers of history—the source of Christian history, for that matter—despite persecution and exile. The place of Jesus' resurrection was evoked in the Jews' daily prayers and their collective memories. Some within the Calvinist leadership believed that the key to final salvation was tied to the hope in the Second Coming of Jesus, which could only happen when the Jews returned to Jerusalem. By nurturing the Hebrew nation, they believed, they could hasten this Second Coming.

The hope in messianism would prove to be mutual, and its nurturing mutually beneficial. Accepting and granting considerable autonomy to Amsterdam's Jewish migrants was a considered decision on the part of Protestant ministers and lawmakers. The seventeenth century was a period when mysticism and messianism, both Christian and Jewish, joined hands and flourished. Scholars of the Old Testament were in great demand. Who better to teach the artists, academics and stadtholders to understand the Hebrew Bible and Hebrew language than the Jewish rabbis and theologians from Italy and North Africa? The era's overwhelming obsession with portrayal of biblical stories in paintings also informed the authorities' hunger for Hebrew knowledge. Vast canvasses by Rubens, Rembrandt and Ferdinand Bol, depicting scenes from the Old Testament, adorned the reception halls of the House of Orange, the Town Hall and rich merchants' private galleries. The Jews were part of young Protestantism's search for origins; mastering Hebrew was an integral component of the Protestant Reformation, and the Torah's teachings were accepted paradigms for ideal Christian societies, the building blocks of true Christian reform. This interest in the Jewish prophets began to develop into an intellectual, artistic and political curiosity about the Jews of the present.

The *Nação* must have observed closely this Protestant aspiration to enter the Jewish world of the Old Testament, to reconnect with pre-Catholic identity. Interestingly, the Portuguese Jews of Amsterdam were much more fascinated by the Hebrew Bible than by rabbinical literature, because the Old Testament was what, back home, they had been able to read openly without raising the suspicion of Inquisition spies. Also, as New Jews, they were seeing the Hebrew Bible from a very fresh angle; like the Protestants, they too were discovering "the original source".

Natural diplomats, both New and Old Jews jumped on the bandwagon. They took pride in identifying themselves with the biblical name for the Jewish people, the Hebrews. This is significant, because during the years in the ghetto they had been and were still, elsewhere, stigmatised for that very identity. Liberated from secrecy, the *Nação* was imbued with a new sense of dignity, and wanted to flaunt its ancient heritage, with all its orthodoxies, rites and rituals: Shabbat, circumcision, bar mitzvah, kosher, *mikveh*, festivals and fasts. By the mid-seventeenth century, the Jews of Amsterdam were celebrating Succoth, the festival of the Tabernacles, on Jodenbreestraat, decorating the footbridges with imported palm fronds. Only a self-confident community could do that.

JUDAISM AS NATIONALITY

The secret of a self-confident, self-contained community lay in its strong leadership, inter-faith diplomacy and, most importantly, exemplary wealth management. The Hebrews of the *Nação* mastered all three. The community's official acceptance into Dutch society was complete when, in 1642, the Portuguese synagogue was visited by the Prince of Orange, his wife, and the Queen of England, Henrietta Maria. Chief Rabbi Morteira's deputy, the Dutch-bred theologian, printer and negotiator Menasseh ben Israel, was there. He published through his own press a ceremonial pamphlet, eulogising the arrival of the royals. This was ben Israel's great opportunity to memorialise this most remarkable day in the history of the Jews in western Europe, with a fitting address to the congregation and the visiting dignitaries. One of the few extant copies of this pamphlet, which I was fortunate to hold in Amsterdam's Ets Haim library, consists of eight pages. The first bears the announcement of the event. The second contains his congratulatory address in Portuguese, in the name of his "Nation", to the Prince of Orange and his royal companion, Queen Henrietta Maria. In uncharacteristically flowery language, ben Israel dedicates his pamphlet to the six wardens of the Mahamad of the united synagogue, Kahal Kadosh of Talmud Torah.

He first addresses the queen—this is very significant, given that in just under a decade and a half ben Israel would embark on a historic campaign at Oliver Cromwell's court for the resettlement of the Jews in the British Isles. Ben Israel then enthusiastically praises the Prince of Orange for capturing a large swathe of the New World, including Brazil. He pays elaborate homage to the flourishing Dutch Empire. Of the Jewish Nation, he says that the Jews of Amsterdam no longer recognise Spain or Portugal, but Holland, as their true homeland. This was an important statement, but not the first such that had been made by the *Nação*. In *Diálogo dos Montes*, Rehuel Jessurun's Earth calls Amsterdam "a little sanctuary", where "in his compassion", God resettles the Jews for "a third time",

> ... and takes
> You from all peoples who upon me dwell
> With miracles no human tongue can tell;
> Just as the faithful shepherd guides his sheep,
> Leading you to possess again and keep
> Your ancient heritage.[5]

The sense of a world to come, and faith in the imminent arrival of the messiah, preoccupied the resettled Jews in Amsterdam. And these sentiments inspired ben Israel and others to think of similar settlements around the world. To have faith in miracles was a product of the time, described by both Jewish and non-Jewish thinkers as an age of mysticism and messianism. *Piedra gloriosa* (The Glorious Stone), an important work by Menasseh ben Israel, lent enormous faith to the Jewish diaspora, which the rabbi said must be stretched to all corners of the Earth, for the final salvation must be shared by all peoples. In his address to the royals, ben Israel praised the Dutch city authorities for protecting the Jews. He revisited this in *Piedra gloriosa*, saying, those who welcome the Jews will be rewarded by the messiah: "the Hebrews pray to God every day for the preservation of the princes who protect and shelter Jews in their kingdoms."[6]

As we know, Menasseh ben Israel's forte was his skill in international relations, and as a rabbi he had the erudition to substantiate this religious mission. His superior, Saul Levi Morteira, continued to turn a blind eye to his assistant's roaming Europe and the New World in pursuit of business and a messianic goal. It could be that the two men were getting on badly, and that for the sake of community harmony Morteira the sage did not oppose ben Israel's grand mission—to settle Jews in the remaining Christian world where there was no Jewish presence. By reaching out to that world, by seeking to have Jews accepted in all four corners of the Earth, he was trying to bring closer the advent of the Messiah.

Morteira might also have had to restrain himself from interfering in his assistant's travels because he needed first to deal with members of the united congregation who were openly challenging rabbinical—that is, his—control, and bringing into the community ideas verging heresy. Morteira gave his full attention to rooting out dissent and doubt; he turned to writing, producing manuscript after manuscript reprimanding heretics, in his distinctive Sephardi cursive. Interestingly, given his refusal to allow play performances in the synagogue, one of Morteira's tracts took the form of an imaginary dialogue, between two Portuguese *conversos*, "one of whom has just travelled to Rome to receive a Papal dispensation to join the Jesuits, since Jews were proscribed from membership in the order. The work is fictionalised, but Morteira must have met such *conversos* or [known of them]."[7]

From the moment he arrived in Amsterdam in 1616, through his takeover of Beth Jacob in 1618, to the eventual unification of the three synagogues in 1639, Morteira's main goal had been to gather the different stripes of the Sephardi community—New Jews, Marranos and the Old Sephardim—under a quintessentially rabbinical Jewish cloak. He was suspicious of any transgression, be it cultural or theological. A draconian promoter of normative Judaism, Morteira, after the incidents of "Jesuit Jews", oversaw the leaders of the Mahamad, the *parnassim*, in passing a law to discourage Jews without prior permission from visiting the lands of "idolatry", as Catholic Europe was known to the Jews and the Protestants; this included the southern Netherlands. Anyone who breached this ban was summoned to the synagogue and asked to read from a standard scroll, words that Morteira must have helped compose, pleading for forgiveness of the community. They also had to pay a fine.

The earliest record of such public apologies is found in a much later work of the in-house historian, Daniel Levi de Barrios.

According to Amsterdam's Portuguese Synagogue records, de Barrios documented a standard declaration, but in this instance, he himself was "the penitent", who mounted the designated platform inside the synagogue, the *teva*, and read from it. His offence was to have visited his ancestral Spain.

> I mounted this *teva* at the order of the Gentlemen of the Mahamad [Board of Governors] in order to ask of the Lord of the World and His sacred Law forgiveness for the wrong that I have done in going to a land of idolatry. And of this entire congregation, people of God, I also beg forgiveness for the scandal that I have caused, for which I am very sorry, with all my heart. And I will fulfil the penance they will impose, obeying in everything and asking that God forgive us. May there be peace on Israel.[8]

The law banning the *Nação* from visiting Catholic Europe was passed in 1644, and de Barrios read the above declaration in 1665, five years after Morteira died—this proves his legacy, the longest serving rabbi there had been in Amsterdam.

If Uri Halevi was "the first Jewish institution in the Netherlands" (Bodian), Morteira was its foundation stone. The three congregations that were unified by him in 1639, listened to his sermons for four decades, relied on his strict organisation, and his ability to shelter the community from adverse pressure. By 1640, in his heyday as chief rabbi as he oversaw the completion of the first public synagogue designed after Solomon's Temple, Amsterdam's Jewish model had been transported to other Sephardi settlements in the New World and in Europe, where active Jewish presence had ceased long ago or had never existed: "for all practical purposes, the synagogue community established circa 1636 by the Sephardi Jews of Amsterdam disseminated across the Sephardic communities of the Netherlands, Great Britain and their respective empires, lasting for two centuries (until c. 1825)."[9]

JUDAISM AS NATIONALITY

This remarkable achievement, by a community whose return to Judaism was barely half a century old, would not have been possible without Morteira's heavy-handed management, which kept the New Jews' old Catholic leanings at bay. He tirelessly guided the former New Christians into normative Judaism, plucking out or purging old Catholic memories and ritual tendencies. He even helped them to "invent" memories, "Jewish" memories, of how they had kept alive their biblical heritage when living under the Inquisition—even though the Catholic Church had been the only religious institution in the lives of many New Christians. Through numerous sermons and treaties, Morteira devoted his life to teaching these lay returnees to Judaism that they had to learn a different, Jewish interpretation of the Hebrew Bible, which the Catholic Church had said was anticipatory of Christian revelation. He wrote apologetics of Judaism for the wealthier and more educated members of his congregation, many of whom had been in Jesuit schools back in Portugal and had been given extensive instruction in Catholic doctrine.

Morteira's was a job that required prophetic levels of self-sacrifice and assiduousness. While the Portuguese Jews must accept Amsterdam as their "rightful, natural home", they should not buy into the contemporary, humanistic temptations of secularism. They must not forget that they belonged to the *Nação* of the Iberian Sephardim, and that their "little sanctuary", though centred in Amsterdam, was actually rather vast, because it offered a unique "nationality" to the entire Sephardi diaspora—from Europe to the Americas, the Mediterranean, North Africa and the Middle East, and all the way to Cochin, and the East Asian coasts. Morteira's sermons repeatedly reminded his congregants that, in spite of the kindness of their host country and the tolerance that had allowed the development of a common Sephardi Nation, their true identity belonged to that *Nação* only. Assimilation into the Protestant society would be akin to returning to the New Christian past.

123

Under his term as chief rabbi—a very long one, spanning the lives of all the Portuguese Jews who entered Amsterdam in the third quarter of the seventeenth century—the congregation never lost its orthodox character. The Sephardi institution was so strongly ingrained in communal life that the residents of the Jodenbuurt were under immense rabbinical pressure to ignore the surrounding Christian world. In fact, those members of the community who were not merchants would live their whole lives without coming into intellectual interaction with the Christians, although they of course had day-to-day contact with non-Jews in this dynamic city of people from all over the world. As a result, the explosion of ideas that swept post-Reformation Christian Europe—in particular, humanism and freedom of thought—generally passed them by. Even when a handful of tortured souls did challenge this exclusivism—the rabbis' inward-looking policies and the weight of rituals—they did not usually become Christians.

The following chapters explore the lives of two of the most (in)famous members of Morteira's congregation, who questioned the ethics of Judaism. They were Uriel da Costa, who was born to a Marrano family in Porto in 1590 and came to Amsterdam in 1618; and Morteira's most renowned student, Baruch Spinoza, who was born in Amsterdam in 1632. There were others, like Juan de Prado, who was born in Spain in 1612 and received a medical degree from Toledo University before settling in Amsterdam in 1655. De Prado apparently started, and incited others in the community to join, a "riot against the rabbis".[10] The *parnassim* believed that these "heretics" threatened to bring down the reputation and foundations of the community. The rabbis likewise believed that the key to the messianic hope, the Hope of Israel, was a fanatically controlled religious orthodoxy.

Often the product of fanatical orthodoxy is heresy. The ideas of the *Nação*'s first "heretic", Uriel da Costa, were censured brutally by at least seven excommunications, leading to his tragic demise in 1640. By the time his successor in this quest, Baruch Spinoza, was excommunicated in 1656, the relationship between mainstream Dutch society and the Jews had advanced at a phenomenal pace. From the mere tolerance of the previous decades, the talk of the town now revolved around full acceptance. This was what Menasseh ben Israel and others had hoped for—except that neither he nor Morteira believed in full assimilation. They undoubtedly never wanted to see their community undergoing acculturation, towards which Spinoza was accused of veering. When he was expelled, unlike da Costa, he left willingly, never turning back or applying for readmission into the synagogue. De Prado, who was officially excommunicated in 1658, also left the city, around 1660, and went to live in Antwerp.

In 1657, the States General recognised the Republic's resident Jews as Dutch nationals, although their "Emancipation", meaning full citizens' rights, would not be legally granted until 1796. That may partly have been due to the community leadership's reluctance to accept full citizenship, fearing that it would take away the rabbinical authority, the *halacha* and the rituals that ruled daily life in the *Nação*. The rabbis and governors of the Mahamad would continue to use them to crush heresy, without the Dutch state's interference, for another 140 years after gaining Dutch nationality.

6

THE DOUBLE LIFE OF URIEL DA COSTA

Exemplar Humanae Vitae (Examination of a Human Life) is the title of the short autobiography that Uriel da Costa left behind.[1] It is mainly through this that we learn about his sad and brief life in Amsterdam.

Da Costa was born in Porto, Portugal in 1590, six years before Saul Levi Morteira's birth in Venice. But while Morteira was born into a Jewish family and studied to become a rabbi, da Costa's early years were spent in a wealthy, respectable, New Christian family; his father held a public profile as a good Catholic. He was educated at home and as a young man, he writes, he had servants always at his command, and rode "a Spanish jennet to perfect myself in horsemanship, an art in which my father was so skilled, and in which I endeavoured to follow his steps." His family obviously was well versed in the manners of the Spanish nobility, as riding a horse was no laughing matter for a New Christian under the Inquisition. It was one of the areas of restriction that many Inquisitorial provinces had imposed, and members of da Costa's family had been accused of judaising. As such, their entitlement to horse-riding was a sure sign of endorsement from the Catholic elite.

In the absence of any other details about Uriel da Costa's Christian life in Porto, we can only rely on his own short, intense sketch of his past, written just before his death. From this glimpse offered by his memoir, it would seem that doubt gnawed at da Costa's Catholic faith at an early stage. Uriel da Costa studied law because, his autobiography states, social injustices stirred strong emotions in him. The young Uriel turned to religion—to Christianity—to quell his conflicted heart. But the eternal damnation of Roman Catholicism filled him with dread, so much so that he started reading more zealously the gospels and religious literature. Instead of finding solace there, he became more tortured than ever by renewed doubt, human misery and fatalism.

Da Costa soon realised that, for him, total absolution through the confession of sins was impossible to attain. This realisation struck him with despair. The first seed of doubt in Christian teaching was then sown in da Costa's mind, as he writes in his memoir.

> But as it was very difficult to shake off quickly a religion in which I had been educated from my infancy and which by a long unquestioning faith had taken deep root, I began when I was about twenty years old, to question the teachings concerning the afterlife. I asked myself whether or not they were forgeries and whether belief in them was consistent with reason.[2]

A much-perturbed da Costa decided that the Roman Catholicism in which he had been educated defied reason. However, he kept his doubt to himself for another five years, and became treasurer of his church. There, he turned to the Old Testament, and read the Pentateuch and the books of the Prophets. He found those less challenging and more appealing to his rational mind: "There seemed to be less difficulty in believing those things which were revealed by God Himself."

Secretly, he decided to return to his ancestral religion, at least intellectually at first. His inner argument for doing so, as he put forward in his slim autobiography, was that Moses only declared himself the deliverer of the Laws from God, who had revealed Himself to the man, almost catching him by surprise. Da Costa understood that man must not be under constraint by any mission to meet God. No obligation of true confession, and no fear of eternal damnation, had persuaded Moses to be where he was when God revealed himself. Da Costa started applying the tenets of the Old Testament to his life, privately. He spent all his time not taken up with a church official's duties on finding out how to become a Jew; how to take the oath and lead a life by the rules laid out in the Law of Moses. He knew he was committing the greatest heresy possible in Roman Catholic Portugal. If discovered, the consequences could be fatal. But he would not be discovered, as the spies of the Inquisition were not immediately drawn to a church official spending longer hours than usual at his Bible studies.

Soon after his father died, da Costa confided in his mother and brothers about his self-discovery, and he must have been deeply moved and surprised when his family supported his decision to return to Judaism. As one of a handful of influential New Christian families, they lived in an opulent part of Porto in a substantial house. He told his family that he had made necessary arrangements to board a ship bound for Amsterdam, where they would be able to live freely by their own convictions. It was highly risky for New Christians to travel without the king's permission. But they were lucky enough not to be caught, and at the end of a timorous voyage the da Costas—Uriel, his mother and two brothers—arrived in Amsterdam, "where we found the Jews professing their religion with great freedom, as the Law directs them. We immediately fulfilled the precept concerning circumcision."[3]

Uriel da Costa was twenty-eight when he arrived in Amsterdam in 1618, just after Menasseh ben Israel had taken over the rabbinical duties of Neve Shalom. The family, however, joined Saul Levi Morteira's Beth Jacob congregation. This was two years after the death of Samuel Palache, the more moderate founder-pioneer of the New Jewish community, whose idiosyncratic life as a seafarer, traveller, pirate and rabbi must have fascinated the newcomer, Uriel. The da Costas' arrival coincided with the second stage in the formation of the *Nação*, when the Mahamad was busy forging a religious, distinctly Portuguese Sephardi identity. It could not have been too difficult for the da Costa brothers to integrate, despite the peril of having to go through circumcision at a mature age. They were eager to prove their religious conviction; going under the *mohel*'s knife was the least of a New Jewish man's concerns.

Uriel da Costa was nearing thirty when the family joined Beth Jacob. At the time, this must have been considered very late to influence what was by then an established Jewish community. His knowledge of Judaism was purely bookish, and drawn only from the five books of Moses and the books of the Prophets. It would not be an exaggeration to deduce from his writing that, to his horror and dismay, da Costa was confronted by a discrepancy between his imagined Judaism and the version practised in Amsterdam. He saw that the rabbinical control and orthodoxy were no less rigid than what the zealous Catholic priests had exercised back home.

Within a few months of arriving in Amsterdam, he became estranged from the *Nação*, even from his mother and brothers. He was torn by his doubt as he began to despise the way Judaism was observed and the way that the rabbis, whom he describes as "an obstinate and stiff-necked race of men", were "vainly fond of the conspicuous seats in the synagogue and greetings in the market place". Da Costa became a recluse, living in self-imposed isolation away from the hubbub of the community. He also went travelling, to other cities in northern Europe where there had been a Jewish presence—Hamburg and Utrecht—to find support for his criticism of the Amsterdam rabbis' power. But his ideas were met with more vehement opposition in Hamburg, which was a prominent Jewish centre. It was there that the rabbis excommunicated him for the first time.

After much wandering, he returned home in a state of mind that belonged to a disillusioned émigré, who refused to be dictated to by the religious authority of his settlement. Da Costa still could not, even for the sake of community harmony or for his own family, who had left everything to follow him to Amsterdam, adhere to the religious regulations advocated by the rabbis. These, he found, were "quite different from those commanded by Moses. This provoked me to oppose them openly." He felt that Jewish rituals and customs were "invented" and that they contradicted what the primary source, the Torah, commanded. He told Morteira and other rabbis that their interpretations of Judaism had nothing to do with the original text. This landed him with a second excommunication, under Morteira's order. It was severe enough for his own brothers to sever all contact with him, fearing that the wrath of the rabbis and the *Nação* might befall the whole family. But Uriel da Costa was not to be dissuaded. Instead of asking for the rabbis' pardon, he started writing a tract in his defence, and to prove to Morteira's congregation that the customs and rituals they were practising were invalid under the Law of Moses.

The case of Uriel da Costa is regarded as the first recorded clash between the rabbinical tradition and what was now emerging in Amsterdam: the early modern Jewish voice. Traditionally, in Jewish ghettos, the rabbis served as the alternative judiciary. In free Amsterdam, the rabbis were entrusted with even more power than they had in Venice or Fez; here, they were the government, ruling over all aspects of Jewish civic life. Da Costa's knowledge of the precepts of Judaism was founded on the Old Testament, and the Christian interpretation of it with which he was well acquainted. Here, his first test was how to accept and be accepted by a community that was, rather, firmly rooted in rabbinical, normative Judaism.

Over the many millennia in the diaspora, the rules that regulated the lives of the Jewish community evolved to reflect an antipathy to assimilation into host societies. This often left the Jewish diaspora inward-looking. Hardly anyone challenged this attitude, because the all-powerful rabbis controlled not only marriages, births and funerals, but also the social welfare system. Uriel da Costa, who had lived a Christian and fairly affluent life in Portugal, would not have fully appreciated that it was an extraordinary achievement for the Jewish tradition to have survived since the Great Dispersion, despite repeated pogroms and discrimination against the community in all the countries where the diaspora had spread. The key to survival was total adherence to the strict rabbinical rules that kept at bay dilution of Judaism, including through assimilation into the surrounding society. Strictly speaking, the new Sephardi community in Amsterdam did not share the specifics of life in the ghetto, but Morteira and his ideological supporters were determined, as past rabbis had been, to import the spirit of ghetto Judaism, which "persisted tenaciously and eternally through persecution and expulsion, not in stray units such as the Inquisition ferreted out, but in ineradicable communities."[4]

As we know, Morteira dealt heavy-handedly with dissenting voices within the community, with the same determination to safeguard orthodox Judaism as he had been taught by his Sephardi masters in Venice and Paris before taking over rabbinical duties in Amsterdam. He was at once deeply troubled and irritated by the newcomer da Costa, who in his eyes was insolent, deranged even, repeatedly threatening to bring down the communal unity by challenging rabbinical authority. Morteira issued a severe *herem*, ban, against him, which remained in place for seven years.

THE DOUBLE LIFE OF URIEL DA COSTA

From his short memoir, it appears that da Costa was a deeply emotional young man, prone to tears. Life's injustices affected him terribly, and he spent agonising hours thinking over the judgment of his congregation in Amsterdam. Was this the religion of the Book of Prophets that he had chosen to embrace, to leave behind the rigid world of "paternosters and penances"?[5] Where in the Amsterdam *Nação* were the mercy, justice and righteousness of the prophets of the Old Testament? The rabbis appeared to him as the same closed-minded paternosters that he had encountered in Porto, and the multiple excommunication decrees evoked in him thoughts that his own people were now issuing an *auto-da-fé* against him. He had nowhere to hide.

Da Costa vividly describes the various stages of the *herem* or ostracism that he faced. The first chapters of his *tratus*, *Treaty on Examination of the Immortality of the Soul*, had been misplaced before the work was completed, and had fallen into the hands of the rabbis, who, in 1623, appointed a fierce critic of da Costa, Samuel da Silva, to publish an answer to the *tratus*. This rebuttal was called *Of the Immortality of the Soul*, and painted da Costa unequivocally as a heretic. Uriel da Costa now felt it necessary to publish the whole manuscript with a reply to da Silva's critique. This he promptly did the same year, thanks to Amsterdam's burgeoning printing press scene. He called da Silva a "ridiculous madman", without even, as he admits in his autobiography, having read his work. However, it was the views expressed in da Costa's tract on the immortality of the soul—his denial of this core belief of both the Jewish and Christian societies around him—that shocked the entire Sephardi establishment, from Amsterdam and Hamburg to Venice and Salonica.

"The next step they took was to set their children upon me in the streets. They insulted me en masse as I walked along, abusing and railing at me. They cried out, 'There goes a heretic, there goes an imposter,'" writes da Costa. Stones were thrown at his front door, windows vandalised. But his rebel soul was not to be dissuaded from his mission, which was to prove to the rabbis that their obsessive focus on rules and rites violated the Laws of Moses and the humanism of the humble Jewish Prophets. The rabbis were at a loss as to what else they could do about this New Jew's rebellion against the rabbinical establishment. They decided to take the matter of this "heretic" to the Dutch magistrate. This was probably one of the first cases from the Jewish community in Amsterdam to end up in the public court, a case that the *Nação*, even after consulting Sephardi rabbis in Venice, could not resolve by themselves. They complained that the Portuguese newcomer "had published a book to disprove the immortality of the soul in order to subvert, not only the Jewish, but also the Christian religion." The public prosecutor viewed this to be of grave concern.

It must be remembered here that the Amsterdam authorities' tolerance was a matter of showing leniency toward the faith of strangers among them, strangers who brought riches with them when they immigrated. The Calvinists would not tolerate defection from one's faith, since that would challenge their very existence—after all, it was the Reformation, the greatest defection in the history of Christianity, that had created the Protestants. In just the same way, the New Christians' desertion of Catholicism had forged the Jewish community in Amsterdam. The Calvinists and the Jews both believed that they held the bastion of truth, and for the sake of reining in more defection and more chaos, both sides were keen to ensure that everyone adhered strictly to his or her current faith. There was no room for apostasy.

The rigid ecclesiastical standards of the Calvinists meant that da Costa was soon arrested and sent to prison. He was bailed after ten days at a price of 300 florins—more than a rabbi's salary at the time—and his books were all confiscated. At this point da Costa's life was hit by a total sense of disconnect from the community for which he had left his ancestral land, and from the religion for which he had risked *auto-da-fé* of the most horrific kind. He no longer knew whether wearing a *sanbenito* and being publicly humiliated before the Portuguese king and his court would have been any worse than what he faced in the city that the Jews called their Dutch Jerusalem. His bitterness made him more and more reckless, and he started showing desperate tendencies toward thoughts that were treated outright as apostasy. He started doubting religion and God altogether.

We must take into consideration that this was 100 years before the Enlightenment would bring to European thought similar ideas and critiques of religious orthodoxy. Spinoza was yet to be born, and he would not publish his own debut "heretic" work for another twenty years. The thoughts that troubled Uriel da Costa were unsettling not just for the rabbis and the city authorities, but also disorientating for da Costa himself, the former church official from Porto. However deeply conflicted he was, Uriel da Costa was far from being mentally disturbed, as many rabbis and Jewish theologians have repeatedly tried to prove over the centuries. On the contrary, his responses to the autocracy of the rabbis, and the arguments he put forward in support of his own views, remained sharp until his death.

Da Costa penned his short autobiography after he had already decided to take his own life: "Let me here declare my mind freely. What should hinder a man from speaking the truth without reservation, who is just about to make his exit and to leave behind him a sad though true example of human misery?" Even at this point, the text is clear and his ideas have a sound structure; the progression of his philosophical resolution as he writes it down is almost "chronological". His vehement objection to the falsity of the rabbis is very well argued. The fearlessness with which da Costa expresses his points of views shocks his readers even today, but his reasoning is supported by his sound knowledge of the Old Testament—the only book on which he had based his religious convictions as a Jew. He holds up against the Law of Moses the customs and rituals of the congregation, and points out profound discrepancies between the two.

But then, things turn bleaker than he had ever expected they would—the law books themselves appear to have been "invented", by man.

> I began to ask myself whether the Law of Moses should be considered the law of God inasmuch as there were many arguments which seemed to persuade or rather determine the contrary. At length I came to the conclusion that it was nothing but a human invention, like many other religious legal systems in the world, and that Moses was not really its author.

This cannot be the language of a madman. This paragraph of da Costa's autobiography shows a modern man, and views that wouldn't enter mass consciousness for another century at least, if we consider Spinoza as da Costa's successor and the Age of Enlightenment as the vessel of his thoughts. If he was a conflicted man, that conflict was the piston of his rationalism. The contradiction that he saw in God's Law was something he describes as "contrary to the laws of nature". This is a precursor to the view Spinoza would offer the world, and which would spearhead Enlightenment philosophy: that God and Nature are interdependent. In this sense, Uriel da Costa was the first secular Jew in recorded history.

As he surmised that Moses was not the author of his Law, da Costa appears to have arrived at a somewhat calmer state of mind. Since his return to Amsterdam after being excommunicated by the Hamburg rabbis, da Costa had lived a miserable life, ostracised not only by the synagogue, but also by his own family members, his brothers in particular. However, he somehow ended up living with his nephew. When a certain cousin proposed to act as a mediator to bring him back into the congregation, da Costa jumped at the chance. It was the decision of a desperate man, not one suddenly repentant for his actions. His businesses had collapsed when one of his brothers, who controlled the family capital, refused to make any concession for him. Da Costa decided to be practical, pitied the rabbis whom he thought were intellectually inferior and not worth fighting against, and settled on a proverbial existence for himself: that if one lives in Rome, one should do what the Romans do.

> I began to reason with myself with the following manner: What can it profit me to spend all my days in this melancholy state, isolated from the society of this people and their elders, especially since I am a stranger in this country without any acquaintance among its inhabitants or even any knowledge of its language? How much better will it be for me to return to their community and conform to their ways...

These considerations persuaded him to return to the synagogue. Da Costa vowed before Neve Shalom that he would abide by its regulations, as the elders would expect of him.

However, no sooner had he negotiated this deal with his congregation than his nephew, who was living with him, brought a complaint to the synagogue that he had seen his uncle breaking the kosher rule. This unexpected news of fresh defiance made even the most lenient among the congregation turn against da Costa. The cousin who had negotiated his reacceptance by the community became his worst enemy, turning da Costa's brothers against him and doing everything to clear his own name—which meant doing everything to publicly humiliate da Costa. After this fresh fall from grace, da Costa's second marriage—after the death of his first wife—broke down, at the intervention of this cousin. While the latter launched a domestic war on da Costa, the rabbis carried on their public vilification of a man whose only disclosed offence at this point—since the previous *herem* had been lifted—was his alleged breach of the dietary law.

Da Costa does not say in his autobiography how long this situation continued, as he was more eager to describe the next, cataclysmic incident—the one that would break the last of his social standing and see him issued with another excommunication order. He met two Old Christian men, one from Spain and the other from England, who asked him what he thought of their desire to convert to Judaism. Da Costa told the men that it was an extremely bad idea, for they were better off with their old faiths. This might have been a trap, designed by da Costa's adversaries to catch him in the act of apostasy and place him under a proper, legal trial. When the men reported da Costa to the Mahamad, the governors' reaction was severe; they acted fast, and more brutally this time. The Mahamad resolved that the incendiary views of this repeated offender against Jewish unity in Amsterdam must be permanently stamped out.

Uriel da Costa was excommunicated, and the conditions of pardon involved not only public repentance, but also that the penitent must first be publicly disgraced before his case could even be brought to rabbinical attention. The particulars of this ordeal, da Costa wrote, conjured in his heart scenes of the Inquisition chambers and public squares where disgraced men and women were gathered and paraded, made to wear the humiliating *sanbenito*, and left for the general public to mock them, often for the rest of their lives. The shame would have far-reaching consequences: even the descendants of those accused at Inquisition trials would be stained with the humiliation for many generations, while the *sanbenito* worn by the convicted judaisers would hang on the church wall above their names. This ensured that the next generation of 'good' New Christians would never forget what had happened, and what would happen if they were to engage in acts of subterfuge or heresy.

Was it not the tiresome double life that he had led in Porto that had prompted da Costa's questioning heart to leave his native town? He had torn himself away from his ancestors' home because he could not live the false life of a Christian church official, devoid of intellectual stimulation—devoid of the truth, as he found through his reading of the Old Testament. He had jumped at the possibility of living in Amsterdam amid its intellectual liberty, and left his familiar, opulent life in Portugal, with its "woods and waters, the pleasant hills strewn with grazing cattle." Writing in his despair under Amsterdam's grey sky, in his lonely abode on a dark canalside road, da Costa reminisced about his worldly losses—the blue sky, the steep streets, the whitewashed houses gleaming in the sun in a warm and resplendent Porto. Had he not left all this behind in order to attend to the call of Reason?

Why, then, did the men of the Old Testament to whom he had submitted his spiritual life remind him of the Inquisitors whom he had managed to fool since his discovery of his ancestral Judaism? Why, after he had escaped the Catholic "hounds", did the religious police still hound him so, in presumably the safest place in Europe for Jews? He had been once fascinated by his people, who were believed to have been chosen by the Old Testament God Himself, a people that was interlinked despite its range of diasporic destinies for millennia. Da Costa's writing here shows that, after the betrayal of his nephew, his faith in his chosen destiny was irreparably shaken. He decided to resign himself to whatever was to come. The extent of his disillusionment could not be illustrated in words, his frustration knew no bounds. He had been repeatedly misunderstood by his own people, "a linked race" that he held in great awe, and that he believed to have

sprung from the mysterious East and the dawn of history, defying destruction and surviving persecution, agonising for its faith and its unfaith—a conception that touched the springs of romance and the source of tears—and his vision turned longingly toward Amsterdam, that city of the saints, the home of the true faith, of the brotherhood of man.[6]

The brotherhood of men, it appeared to da Costa, wanted the blood of their own "heretic" in Amsterdam, a city that he had embraced to escape from his double life back in Porto. Never in his worst fears, when he denounced his former Catholic faith, had da Costa imagined his life to turn to this— that his very existence would come under threat from fellow teachers of the Old Testament, just because he would not oblige with "ordinances far more galling" than those of the Catholic Church. What da Costa considered his simplest actions—how he ate, drank, slept and washed, when or how he worked, what he wrote and how he thought—the brotherhood had marked as heretical, as going against the intricate network of regulations ordained by the Oral Law. The 613 precepts of the Pentateuch became a noose around da Costa's neck, and their self-proclaimed upholders, the rabbis, wanted to rule "the most intimate recesses of life", exactly as had the elaborate, ceremonial Catholicism of his past. Da Costa felt he now faced a fearsome regime of Mosaic theocracy.

His autobiography at this point rushes to reach its end: his final submission to authority.

Da Costa's loneliness forced him to try another fresh attempt, to be humbled by the penance the rabbis had offered him, in return for his readmission into the Jewish congregation. Could he suppress his true faith once again and be—to use his memoir's famous phrase—"an ape among the apes"? After all, the Marranos were used to a double life. What difference would it make if he just went along with the rituals, as he had done in Catholic Iberia? If he just agreed to some public atonement to appease the mob, surely afterward he could just get on with his private life? Da Costa's new plea for reconciliation was accepted by the rabbis.

THE DOUBLE LIFE OF URIEL DA COSTA

On the day of his second readmission, to da Costa's great shame, his own people, his brothers and relatives, neighbours and acquaintances, reconvened to humiliate him in the synagogue. This was the situation he had feared all his life: "I dreaded nothing so much as to suffer disgrace." Da Costa's autobiography does not mention by name the rabbis who sanctioned this latest ordeal. But during a great part of his years of excommunication, Menasseh ben Israel was at the helm of Neve Shalom, the da Costa family's congregation. Da Costa did not blame the rabbi personally for his woes when he was excommunicated for the second time, soon after his readmission, but his *Treaty on Examination of the Immortality of the Soul* had tried to refute ben Israel's mysticism, spirituality and doctrine of the transgression of the soul, as laid out in the rabbi's own book, *De Resurrectione Mortuorum* (1636). No rabbis of the time publicised their views on da Costa's controversial pamphlet, which had been banned as soon as it was published. There are no records of what Menasseh ben Israel personally thought of the "heretic" among the *Nação*, but he could not have done anything to postpone or delay the merciless sentence handed down to da Costa as a precondition of his acceptance back into the fold. There are no records of the signatories to this latest bizarre ordeal before the congregation.

As he entered the synagogue, da Costa wrote, he was ushered again to the raised *teva* reserved for the penitent next to the *chacham*, the leader of the service. As da Costa mounted the *teva*, he was, as before, given a scroll from which he was asked to read—a lengthy recantation of all his transgressions, challenges and intellectual defiance against the rabbinate. This part of his account becomes both extremely dark and tragicomic. Da Costa described the executors of his punishment as vindictive men thriving on his misfortune and public disgrace:

> I entered the synagogue which was filled with curious spectators of both sexes. At the appointed time I walked up to the reading desk

which was in the centre and with a clear voice read aloud the form of confession which they had drawn up for me, namely, that I deserve to die a thousand deaths for the crimes I had committed ... To atone for these violations, I submitted to their sentence and was ready to undergo whatever they wished to lay upon me, promising not to be guilty of similar crimes in the future.

After he finished reading, "the chief elder" came up to him and asked him to go to a specific corner of the synagogue. He was asked to strip down to his waist, and his hands were tied over his head around a pillar. The verger in charge of delivering the punishment came forward, and with a leather whip gave him thirty-nine lashes. During the whipping, the congregation sang a psalm. Da Costa's description turned to mockery, joking that the elders stopped at this number because the Commandments stipulated that the number of stripes shall not exceed forty: "for these very scrupulous and pious gentlemen take due care not to offend by overstepping their bounds."

The *parnassim* lifted the excommunication order, but he was then asked to dress and prostrate himself across the doorway of the synagogue. The doorkeeper, da Costa vividly relates, then pressed his head down to the ground and held it there as the congregation walked over his body to leave the synagogue: "both young and old passed over me, stepping with one foot on the lower part of my legs and making ridiculous gestures, more like monkeys than human beings." The most difficult part for da Costa in this extraordinary public atonement was the fact that his own brothers and family members joined others and trampled over him. His disgrace was complete. A man without his honour is a dead man. His "detestable persecutors" had stolen away his cloak of self-esteem.

No Inquisitorial trial could match the humiliation of this dark ceremony at the synagogue, because in this, he was alone—at least being convicted of judaising and dying at the stake gave victims some kind of a sense of shared martyrdom. At this point in da Costa's *Exemplar*, the reader discovers his total loss of faith in humanity. He pauses briefly to describe the hatred and contempt of his own people, of being spat on by adults and children alike both before and during the ordeal. We imagine a broken man, full of painful reproaches, his head bowed by the terrible indignity he had just suffered, walking the grey streets back to his canalside home. Instead of a *sanbenito*, he wore a black cloak, and walked around the synagogue holding a black candle. Instead of the Inquisition inspectors and priests, there were rabbis in *tallits*, prayer shawls, who delivered the harshest penance in the history of the Jewish diasporic life. Far from the glory or comfort of martyrdom at the stake, he had been made to feel his life was worthless.

A final thought struck da Costa numb, because it took him right back to his Marrano life living among the Christians in Portugal. He shuddered as he reflected on his sudden conviction that, if Jesus were to come to preach in Amsterdam, the rabbis would crucify him, "like their forefathers decided to scourge him for opposing and condemning their tradition and hypocrisy". For da Costa, it was too much to live with. If he had come to share the Catholic belief that the Jews had killed their God—the view that had brought his people inimitable misery, Christian wrath and persecution for more than 1.5 millennia—then he certainly was no longer a Jew. He signed off the *Exemplar* with his original Christian name, Gabriel, which had been changed to "Uriel" when he joined the Jewish faith in Amsterdam. He wrote that he wished he had never done so.

But Uriel da Costa was not a Christian either. He had long ceased to be one, during those nightly candlelit studies of the Old Testament in his Porto church. The Jerusalem of the West that had once enticed him to leave the secrecy of Marrano life in his homeland had paradoxically brought about his end. Life under the constraints of the Inquisition at least had not cost him his faith in God. Da Costa felt powerless at the Amsterdam rabbis' limitless judicial power and authority to take away the liberty of individuals who did not agree with them. Why should he want to live the rest of his life fearing the oppression of the rabbis, "who under the mast of sanctity, like a thief in the night, come in by stealth and murder us in our sleep?" After the ordeal at the synagogue, a defeated and disgraced Uriel da Costa walked back to his dark home, wrote his short autobiography, and turned the pistol on himself. It was 1640.

Da Costa's philosophical works were mostly written in Portuguese. Why he chose to write his autobiography in Latin is an enigma. Perhaps he did not want it to be read by the synagogue informers who lurked about, or his cousin or nephew for that matter—legend says that, before he took his own life, da Costa tried first to shoot his brother and/or his nephew. *Exemplar Humanae Vitae* was first published in 1687, nearly half a century after its author's death. But it was an earlier work, *An Examination of Pharisaic Traditions*—an extensive critical attack on the rabbinical authority over the Oral Law in Judaism—that would immortalise da Costa the philosopher. His writings gave birth to the theological branch that would come to be known as "biblical criticism". These ideas were believed to have influenced Baruch Spinoza, a fellow Jew from the same synagogue, who would lay the groundwork for the eighteenth-century European Enlightenment.

Meticulous efforts were made by the rabbinical authorities to rid the community of all of da Costa's written work, for fear that they would threaten the foundation of the Jewish presence in western Europe. Despite this, the original manuscript of *Exemplar Humanae Vitae* survived, and was discovered in 1990 in the Royal Library of Copenhagen by three scholars, Herman Prins Salomon, Adri Offenberg and Harm den Boer. Uriel da

THE DOUBLE LIFE OF URIEL DA COSTA

Costa's life and work have since been re-evaluated. But even before this discovery, his views had already established him as one of the forefathers of European scepticism.

7

BARUCH SPINOZA

THE HERETIC WITHIN

Baruch Spinoza was a young boy, yet to have his bar mitzvah, when his congregation walked over the prostrated body of Uriel da Costa in the doorway of the synagogue in Amsterdam. There are no available documents that tell us who trod on da Costa that day. But we could very well assume that Spinoza might have taken part in the chastisement of this convicted heretic among them. Little did Spinoza know that, before long, he would pick up from where da Costa, a cousin on his mother's side, had left off; that he too would find himself in the forbidden area of questioning one's religion. What made this all the more unlikely is that Spinoza was one of Saul Levi Morteira's favourite students at the seminary of Ets Haim, of which his father, Michael or Miguel Espinoza, was a founding member. Miguel Espinoza was also an active leader of the Mahamad, his role important enough for him to be mentioned in the dedication to Menasseh ben Israel's long paper about the community's messianic aspirations, *The Hope of Israel*.

In fact, *The Hope of Israel* encapsulates what Spinoza would later fight to dispel: Jewish mysticism and the myth of a chosen people. Ben Israel's representation of the *Nação*'s and the general age's messianic hope, in both the Jewish and the Christian world, will be discussed in the next chapter. But for now, we shall take a look at the life and faith—or unfaith—of the Amsterdam *Nação*'s most famous member. It is a challenging prospect for any writer or historian to find a new angle on Spinoza. But, in the context of the mid-seventeenth-century upheavals of ideas, orthodoxy and apprehension amid which the Jews lived in Amsterdam, it is worth asking to what extent the philosopher and the *Nação* drew on each other.

The excommunicated philosopher did not live to see his position reinstated, nor his views glorified not just by the *Nação* of his birth but by the whole world, which would feed on the secular rationalism that he pioneered. The concept of a noble life beyond the parochial and based on reason, as he championed, was born not in a Dutch humanist educational institution, but in a yeshiva, the Jewish seminary of Ets Haim, where he studied under the tutelage of Morteira. Spinoza, father of the Enlightenment, elucidated, point by point, Uriel da Costa's first biblical criticism; it was given a solid platform in the voluminous work left behind by Spinoza, who lived only forty-four years.

Spinoza's family legacy was rooted in the same rich, sad and colourful Marrano past as we saw in da Costa's story. The family arrived in Amsterdam in 1604, but Spinoza's grandfather, Henrique Garcês, did not convert to Judaism for almost a decade, and was only circumcised after his death in 1619, so that he could be buried in the new Jewish cemetery in Ouderkerk. Even then, because the circumcision was not carried out until death, he was only qualified for a burial spot outside the fence—alongside the graves of Jews' servants and the children born of non-Jewish mothers. Judaism is passed through the mother and unless the mother has converted, a Jewish father cannot transfer his religion to his children.

Henrique's son, however, Spinoza's father Miguel Espinoza, would play a crucial role in the intellectual development of Amsterdam's Jewish community. He was one of the founders of Ets Haim, the seminary where young Jewish boys enrolled at the age of five to study the Torah and the Talmud. Miguel's son, Baruch or Bento—short for Benedict—was among its students. Both Miguel and Henrique must have had a powerful influence on Spinoza. When the da Costa family arrived in Amsterdam, Uriel and his brothers voluntarily went under the knife of the *mohel*, to comply with "the covenant with Abraham"—as circumcision is seen by the orthodox Jew. The Espinoza family, however, stayed away from formal acceptance into the Jewish settlement in Amsterdam for more than a decade. Had it not been for the Ouderkerk burial permit for Henrique, they probably would have remained apathetic to the Portuguese Jewish congregation for even longer.

Spinoza's maternal grandparents came to Amsterdam in 1604, so they were there almost right from the start of the community's formation, but Henrique and his wife spent a lot of time in Antwerp, running a dry fruit business with other New Christians there. While in Amsterdam, Henrique did not affiliate with any Sephardi congregations until his death in 1619, when he was given a Hebrew name, Baruch, and circumcised. Circumcision at death was common among the former New Christians, many of whom resisted the ritual cut even after officially converting to Judaism, fearing it would make it harder for them to return to Iberia. If they were captured by the Inquisition and their circumcision discovered, the consequences would be fatal. It could also be that Henrique Garcês still had a strong attachment to the Catholicism he was born with, and which he practised all his life. He was not the only one in the community who declined to take an oath in official Judaism; many had lived all their lives indecisive and were only "judaised" at death when a place for burial was needed—if one was not readily available at the Dutch Reformed cemetery, where many of the New Christians were buried. We should remember that many or most New Christians left their Iberian home for Amsterdam not, like Uriel da Costa, because they wished to return to Judaism, but because they were persecuted, or in search of better fortune, having heard about the amazing opportunities in a mercantile empire.

Many of the undecided New Christians, though they kept good terms with their Sephardi brethren, resisted joining the Portuguese Nation in Amsterdam. Many among them had become accustomed to Catholic thinking, literature and ways of life, and, despite being given the chance to become part of a self-governed Jewish nation, some waited in hope that one day they would be able to return to Iberia. Perhaps Spinoza's grandfather chose not to go through circumcision while alive because he wanted to return and be buried in Portugal, under a blue sky in the shadow of an olive grove. Perhaps he could never call the cold grey northern European port city his home, and the ancestral religion to which his people had returned remained alien to him. Perhaps he saw in graven images the highest sophistication of artistic expression of man's link to God.

Other members of Henrique's family were openly Jewish and involved in the building of the *Nação*. However, historians believe that his ordeal at death, which Spinoza heard about growing up in Amsterdam's sheltered Jewish community, must have left a strong impression on his young mind. He must have grown up hearing his grandfather's story, and also his rabbi Morteira's regular sermons outlining the importance of circumcision. Morteira would frequently quote from the scriptures and say those who were able to undergo but resisted circumcision would risk *karet*, excision from the Jewish People, and would have no part in the world to come. They could not be saved. This "salvation" refers to the messianic redemption that more or less all Jews believed in: that, when the Messiah came, all Jews would be raised from the dead and gathered together before the march to Jerusalem. Morteira, therefore, chillingly doomed for eternity those who died uncircumcsised.

Baruch Spinoza's young life was blighted by a series of deaths of close family members. He lost his mother at the age of six. Subsequently he visited the cemetery in Ouderkerk to bury his elder brother, his sister, his grandmother—Henrique or Baruch Senior's wife—his stepmother and then his father, Miguel, in 1654. He was twenty-two. The Jewish historian Yosef Kaplan suggests:

> Quite probably during his visits to the cemetery he lingered near the grave of his namesake, 'Grandpa Baruch', from time to time. He must have inquired into the reasons why he was buried outside the fence, far from the other members of his family. At some stage he must have heard the story of his grandfather's posthumous circumcision and this certainly made an impression on him. The insult to 'Grandpa Baruch' whose grave was placed beyond the fence probably disturbed the grandson Baruch, perhaps arousing sorrow and bitterness. When he cut himself off from the Jewish community after his excommunication in 1656, and articulated his criticism of Judaism, he also found a way of expressing his contempt for the ceremony of circumcision, which the elders of his community imposed on his dead grandfather.[1]

In his *Tractatus Theologico-Politicus* (Theological-Political Treatise), Spinoza is vociferous about his antipathy to what he believed to be Jewish self-righteousness and observance of ancient rituals with no modern, logical basis. In fact, his polemics against the Jewish practice of circumcision at times seem obsessive; he even links this custom to the loss of vigour of the Jewish People, suggesting it was why they did not have a state, when other, more virile nations, such as the Chinese, had established empires. Kaplan has a hypothesis on this sarcastic tone in Spinoza's writing:

it would not be preposterous to assume that the insult to his grand-father, who was buried outside the fence of the cemetery, because he had not been circumcised during his lifetime (and thus retained his full virility until his death!) also played some role in the attitude of the philosopher who chose to live beyond the fence of Judaism.[2]

This vehement opposition could not simply have been a product of Spinoza's later education outside Judaism and of his veneration of Cartesian rationalism. It was steeped, it seems, in private grief from his early childhood. Kaplan argues that Baruch was traumatised by what had happened to his namesake. And how terrible it must have been when the *parnassim* did not even fulfil the dying wishes of his grandmother, Maria Nunes, also known by her Hebrew name Miriam, who wanted to be buried beside her husband at Ouderkerk. Baruch Junior was sixteen when Miriam was buried inside the main cemetery, as the *parnassim* certified her Jewish credentials as impeccable. In fact, all other members of Spinoza's family were buried inside the fence. Baruch Senior's resistance to the ritual cut must have seemed so insolent to an unforgiving *parnassim* that he was cast out, as if he had already suffered a manmade *karet*. We could perhaps speculate that Baruch Spinoza decided he, too, would have no part in that small world, the "little sanctuary" of the Jewish nation on the banks of the Amstel.

At Ets Haim, Spinoza was a top student under Saul Levi Morteira—who would serve him the famous ban, the *herem*. But before any of this could be thought of, he was one of Morteira's favourite students, becoming a Talmudic scholar by the time he was thirteen. The community patriarch was immensely fond and protective of his star pupils. He wrote the following in 1652, in the introduction to his student Moses Israel Mercado's commentaries on *Ecclesiastes* and *Psalms*:

> Now, God be praised, about forty "armed soldiers" in the war of Torah regularly eat at my table, some of them masters in Mishnah

and Talmud, some in the legendary and rhetorical texts, some of them eloquent preachers, some focus on the simple meaning of Bible, some are poets, some experts in books of metaphysics. For all of them, reverence for God is their treasure. All of the scholars who have visited us observed this with astonishment; they examined these students and said, "God's blessing is upon you, and we bless you in God's name."[3]

Morteira was impressed by the diverse talent of his students and proud of their various pursuits of knowledge. It is extremely likely that the young Baruch Spinoza was among the students praised here. He probably still had not "come out", so to speak, with his questioning of Judaism; at least publicly, he was still a "warrior" of the Torah and of the *Nação*, armed with knowledge of the Old Testament and the Law of Moses. It is hard to imagine in reading these words that Morteira, Spinoza's teacher and mentor, would have become one of his fiercest critics only a few years later.

There have been various speculations on the master's initial thoughts about his pupil's deviation, which began not long after the above passage was written, and all of these suppose that Morteira at first understood Spinoza's views as a temporary anomaly, a frivolous rebellion of youth. Morteira probably did not have the slightest idea in 1652 that, just four years on, he would be issuing the harshest *herem* on one of his favourite "armed soldiers" of the Scriptures. Baruch was known to the community as Benedict, or Bento, which means "blessed". But he turned out to be one of its most conflicted souls—even more so than his intellectual predecessor Uriel da Costa, whose views and mental condition had been denounced by both his contemporaries and later historians as a product of derangement, paranoia. Some described da Costa as a martyr to the split personality syndrome born of the Jews' transition to modernity. Morteira undoubtedly thought Baruch Spinoza was similarly a product of what the Jews had resisted historically: assimilation into the contemporary world.

Spinoza engaged in a violent mental struggle to break free of the age-old constraints that he believed kept the Jews' so-called ancient heritage alive. The philosopher argued candidly in his work that the Jews had survived not despite anti-Semitism, but because of it. Doubting the Jews' ability ever to have a nation or kingdom of their own, he argued that their religion had become their "nation"; as such, this religion, with its unforgiving orthodoxy, would hinder the possibility of creating a sovereign Jewish state. Spinoza wrote in *Tractatus Theologico-Politicus*, after his excommunication, that *"imo nisi fundamenta suae religionis eorum animos effoeminarent"*; Yosef Kaplan explains that this declaration states "explicitly that under the influence of their customs, [the Jews'] spirits had become effeminate. For this reason they lacked the vitality necessary to re-establish their state."[4] With this reference to lost masculinity, we see again Spinoza's implicit reference and visceral aversion to circumcision, among other intricate rituals and ceremonies of the ancient tribe to which he had once belonged.

As da Costa had been two and a half decades before him, Spinoza was an internal threat to the *Nação*. But while da Costa's rebellion was blamed on his Marrano past and the inner struggle that he had suffered ever since arriving in Amsterdam, Spinoza's views could not be treated lightly or dismissed as a result of assimilation into a host culture. He was a Talmud and Torah scholar to begin with—not a Marrano immigrant like da Costa, he had been born into the community, brought up and taught by the rabbis in Amsterdam, to which the whole Sephardi world looked for direction. The *Nação* was alarmed that a heretic like Spinoza could destabilise the high, holy status of Dutch Jerusalem. His views had to be restrained and his presence restricted as quickly as possible. There was no time for negotiations involving Venice and other Sephardi centres, as had been the case during Uriel da Costa's multiple excommunications. A homebred heretic like Spinoza did not deserve a second chance.

Saul Levi Morteira left behind volumes of handwritten manuscripts that contain his polemical work on the vices of Christianity, yet nothing is available on what he thought of his prize pupil who challenged everything he had ever taught him. It could be that he did not want to leave a record for posterity of his most insubordinate student somehow getting away from the *herem* and pursuing a life where he further developed his heretical thoughts. Did the rabbi ever try to talk him out of them? Did he try to persuade the young philosopher not to tarnish the image of their community, which was enjoying the status of a free people in Europe, just short of full sovereignty? But how could Morteira have convinced a sceptic like Spinoza of the need for the Jews to remain connected to orthodoxy, because their future kingdom would be the final one when all others had perished in the coming of the Messiah?

We do not know how or whether the master tackled his unruly pupil, but several imagined stories have developed about the relationship between Spinoza and Morteira, and the latter's early reaction to his student's anarchic ideas in a deeply orthodox community. These talk about Morteira's initial bafflement at Spinoza's irreverence towards observing Shabbat and dietary rules—two of the most important pillars of Judaism. In this imagining, Morteira tried to coax Spinoza into proclaiming that he still believed in a Jewish God. He implored him to repent for expressing such apostasy. As his direct teacher and mentor, and as the personal rabbi of the Espinoza family, Morteira had known Spinoza since he was a child. He had taken the little boy whose mother had just died under his tutorship at Ets Haim, the seminary co-founded by Spinoza's father, Miguel.

Another of these stories reflects on the inner conflicts of both men and the difficulties they had in understanding each other, leading to a total breakdown in communication. Jean-Maximilien Lucas wrote the earliest biography of Spinoza, in 1719.[5] He presented a picture of what might have happened in the days leading up to the philosopher's conflict with the *Nação* and his excommunication by Morteira. Apparently the initial charge against Spinoza, for his contemptuous views of the Law books and the rituals of Judaism, was brought to the leadership of Kahal Kadosh by two young men of the community. Morteira, according to Lucas' story, was sceptical at first of the accusations against his pupil. He tried for some time to convince him of the truth of Judaism. At first he threatened to issue a *herem*, only if his pupil chose not to keep his thoughts to himself. But Spinoza was not to be dissuaded from his position.

This must have come not just as a blow from a disobedient young student, but a major setback in Morteira's teaching, in his twilight years as a rabbi. Many later historians writing about Morteira criticised him for his ban on the *Nação*'s most famous son. But the rabbi must have thought that he was acting as he did for the unity of the Jews in Amsterdam and the Sephardi diaspora, which by then was vast, with a strong presence in the Americas. Excommunicating Spinoza was necessary to preserve the orthodox character of the *Nação*, which, in the half-century since the Yom Kippur service of 1603, had managed to establish itself as a successful entity of New Jews amidst a Calvinist society.

Morteira had been leading the former New Christians to normative Judaism almost from the beginning of the community's life in Amsterdam, and now he was faced with one of his brightest students threatening to bring down that very structure. From his polemical work, today in Amsterdam's Ets Haim library, it is evident how he loathed Christian thought, including the humanistic evolution of the religion. The Christians, he believed, had been and always would be the Jews' worst persecutors. Throughout his life, Morteira tried to pinpoint the vices of

BARUCH SPINOZA

Christianity and keep his community on alert against embracing assimilation with open arms—even in the unprecedented golden age of "Dutch Jerusalem". Assimilation was death to the Jewish hope of Israel.

But it seems that his wrath against his stubborn student was driven as much by personal disappointment as by orthodox duty. Unlike certain other prominent rabbis of the *Nação* such as Menasseh ben Israel, Isaac Aboab da Fonseca and Samuel Palache, who had been distracted by outside pursuits and inter-faith interests, Morteira never really left his community. Since he had taken over Beth Jacob's rabbinical duties in 1618, he had devoted his life to protecting his congregation from being led astray by the remnant of the Iberian culture that kept encroach-ing on the community, and from the revolution in the Christian thought in the host country. He, like other traditionalists, thought that Spinoza was influenced by the culture and philoso-phy born of the new humanism and deconstruction of Christianity in western Europe. Spinoza could not be dismissed outright—as da Costa had—because of the personal depth of spirituality that was evident in Spinoza from very early on. In an imaginary vignette of his early years by the leading cultural Zionist Israel Zangwill (1864–1926), the young Baruch is por-trayed with empathy. The nobility of his character and profun-dity of his vision are clear in these opening lines of "The Maker of Lenses":

As the lean, dark, somewhat stooping passenger, noticeable among the blonde Hollanders by his noble Spanish face with its black eye-brows and long curly locks, stepped off the trekschuyt on to the canal-bank at s'Gravenhage, his abstracted gaze did not at first take in the scowling visages of the idlers, sunning themselves as the tow-boat came in. He was not a close observer of externals, and though he had greatly enjoyed the journey from Utrecht along the quaint water-way between green walls of trees and hedges, with occasional

157

glimpses of flat landscapes and windmills through rifts, his sense of the peace of Nature was wafted from the mass, from a pervasive background of greenness and flowing water; he was not keenly aware of specific trees, of linden, or elm, or willow, still less of the aquatic plants and flowers that carpeted richly the surface of the canal.[6]

The reader visualises a lonely soul, with an almost ascetic self-reflection that singles him out from his environment and "the general bellicose excitement of the populace", as Zangwill goes on to describe the canal-side. Morteira, who despised mysticism and was therefore a strong opponent of both the esoteric Kabbalah movement and ascetic aspirations, must have felt awed by the inner nobility of this young man he taught.

In the above excerpt, Spinoza is coming home to Amsterdam from Utrecht, where his job is to grind and make lenses. The physical stooping must have resulted from his day's work. He is returning after the official publication of *Tractatus Theologico-Politicus*; he has already been excommunicated, but is returning to see a Christian teacher whom he venerated. It seems from the general excitement and hate speech of onlookers, of whom the daydreaming young man soon becomes aware, that the authorship of this pamphlet—on which Spinoza's name did not appear—has been leaked. Its denial of God and refutation of Judeo-Christian theory has won him the wrath not only of his own community, but also of the States General, to which Spinoza has been presented by the *parnassim* as "the traitor to State and Church."

Zangwill imagines profanities such as "Traitor!" and "Godless gallows-bird!" screamed at Spinoza by passers-by. He is accused of forsaking the established creed by advocating freedom of thought and "fearlessly" contradicting "every system of the century." Even Dutch tolerance cannot cope with Spinoza's scientific treatment of the Bible, and his own synagogue has pleaded with the States General and the city regents to banish this renegade from "New Jerusalem", having already issued its own public ban against him. Before a rabbinical tribunal personally presided over by Morteira, Zangwill quotes the *herem* against Spinoza:

> we excommunicate, expel, curse, and execrate Baruch de Espinoza before the holy books ... Cursed be he by day, and cursed be he by night; cursed be he when he lieth down, and cursed be he when he riseth up; cursed be he when he goeth out, and cursed be he when he cometh in. May God never forgive him! His anger and His passion shall be kindled against this man. On whom rest all the curses and execrations which are written in the Holy Scriptures...[7]

As Zangwill points out, for this community of refugees from Spain and Portugal, who had regained their Jewish faith in the free and fair Dutch Republic after years of persecution and hidden Marrano practices, it was hard "to have that faith doubted for which they or their fathers had given up wealth and country." But Bento de Spinoza, blessed with an uncompromising inner truth, would not break under an excommunication order, nor would he be stifled by the rabbinical threats to his family against speaking to him. The light that burned within the young man— lens-maker by day and philosopher by night—would not let him waver under the visceral hate of his own people.

Spinoza was expelled from Amsterdam a few months before the death of Morteira in 1660, when the city authorities acquiesced to the rabbis' and Calvinist clergy's demand that he be banned. The choice was between an intellectual exile from his new philosophical theory, or a physical exile from his family and friends with whom he had grown up and studied in the Jodenbuurt. He chose the latter, and the world would later be inspired by this father of the Enlightenment—although his major work, *Ethics, Demonstrated in Geometrical Order*, would not be published until 1677, the year of his death and two years after the building of the majestic Portuguese Synagogue, the Esnoga. Perhaps, by then, the third generation of Portuguese Jews in the Dutch Republic was finally freed from its fear of displacement, and even internal heretics could no longer threaten the tenacity of the Amsterdam *Nação*, with its conspicuous house of worship.

Had he been alive, it would have eased Morteira's wrath a little to learn that his talented student was not a godless apostate after all—he just believed that God and Nature were indistinguishable. He saw God in everything, everywhere. Morteira, like other veteran rabbis in Calvinist Amsterdam who believed rigorous ritual constraints were necessary for the infant Jewish community's survival, failed to understand or accommodate a rationalist—the bringer of an original philosophy based on mathematical calculations of how mind and body, reason, and the path to freedom are intertwined. A skilled optician, Spinoza ground and shaped lenses to enhance vision. His philosophy was driven by the same rationale: that its application to life would illuminate the path to spirituality, currently cluttered by rituals and rabbis. A man manacled by rites and liturgy was a short-sighted man. Who better to guide a people to spiritual clarity than their own lens-maker?

Yet, in his lifetime, Spinoza's community could not appreciate its golden hero. His philosophy heralded a cultural revolution, born of the previous century's religious strife, which had split nations and creeds all over Europe. As he made his lenses on the upper floor of a Utrecht warehouse, his solitary, spiritual life brings to mind a Buddha-like figure. Here, through a series of "propositions", Spinoza formulated his thoughts on God, or Nature—*Deus, sive Natura*. With geometric precision, his *Ethics* refuted the Judeo-Christian conception of a transcendental God, instead arguing that God and Nature are causally and necessarily, connected: one cannot exist without the other. It was mathematically implausible, Spinoza concluded, that a god in the Judeo-Christian tradition could not have created this universe. He did not marry; perhaps that would have taken away the isolation he needed to write hundreds of thousands of pages of ethical trea-tises in his short life.

Was Spinoza influenced by the radical theologians of the Protestant Reformation? This is a question to which many his-torians and philosophers have sought answers. Although Lucas' *La Vie de Spinoza* was not published until 1719, there had been an earlier sketch on the philosopher's work from 1699, *Der Spinozismus im Jüdenthumb*, by Johann Georg Wachter. Wachter claimed that Spinoza might in fact have been a product of Jewish mysticism, which the Europeans would be learning frenziedly throughout the eighteenth and nineteenth centuries. Important works on this subject by an Italian ex-Marrano, Abraham Cohen de Herrera, were circulating in Amsterdam around the time that Spinoza was questioning the orthodoxy of his community. It seems he got hold of Herrera's books in Spanish translation while still a student at Talmud Torah, including *Gate of Heaven*, because certain passages of his *Ethics* can be traced back to Herrera's work.

Spinoza left Amsterdam in 1660. He would never return to the Jodenbuurt. Morteira died the same year, leaving behind a community that would continue to be deeply orthodox. In the 1660s, the *Nação* prospered in all areas of trade, diplomacy, edu-cation and social welfare. It had defied Spinoza's prediction that, since the Jews lacked vigour, they would not become a state. Not only were they prospering, they were thriving as a well organised, specifically Jewish community. They had evaded assimilation altogether, except in business, for their high society dealings. Even Spinoza, after all his intermingling with the Dutch intel-lectuals, did not speak the language very well, and had a thick accent. He wrote his philosophical treatises in Latin.

The lay members of the *Nação* were bound in every respect by their essential Jewish identity. There were almost no intermar-riages with the Dutch Christians—but that was also due to the

Dutch law we met earlier banning such liaisons, which was welcomed by the rabbis. The community would maintain the status quo of growth, intellectually and economically. Breaking social boundaries was not an option—not without being branded heretics—and that was true for both societies. And had the rabbis and regents not proven that the demarcation line between the two communities was working in the Dutch Republic? Amsterdam presented an ideal situation, where the Jewish community could grow rich and influential, even hobnob with the Dutch bourgeoisie, but never have to give up being Jews. This was an imagined national–religious–cultural border, not a ghetto wall. It preserved the social order on both sides.

The community grew so confident that it became restless—the question was, what would be the next step? Will any nation ever remain content with its rate of progress, however stable, and say that it has grown enough? In the third quarter of the seventeenth century, the *Nação*'s leading members approached their rabbis and asked them to devise the next step for this Jewish Nation in exile.

8

HOPE OF ISRAEL

IN "THE LAND OF MILK AND CHEESE"

The next step was the most pressing question in Vlooienburg 400 years ago. The manmade island on the east bank of the Amstel River was the safest home for the Jews of Europe, their Jerusalem of the West. Could they truly now stop wandering? Was Amsterdam the last stop on the long road of exile? The *Nação*'s answer to its restless population was that the Jews' last stop was, and would always be, the Jerusalem of the East, from which they had been exiled and to which they would return in a messianic age.

So they settled for Amsterdam as their penultimate home, awaiting signs that would usher in the final phase of their wandering. They felt very comfortable, secure. The persecution, pogroms and Inquisition were dark chapters in the past that would never be repeated. What more could the Jews want? They prospered beyond belief without compromising their re-discovered Judaism—in fact, they succeeded because of it, as their specialised expertise and contacts in trade and diplomacy had made their presence indispensable to the Dutch economic boom.

Here, they could wait for the coming of the Messiah. It did not matter when the final call to march to Jerusalem would be made by the Saviour, whose arrival was predicted by a widespread Judeo-Christian messianic anticipation in the mid-1600s.

Standing on the edge of today's Centraal Station, built in the nineteenth century, one can easily visualise the seventeenth-century artists' Amsterdam. There was water everywhere; it was all harbour. Amsterdam was a unique city with an inland sea. If one looked west from the Jewish quarter, the Jodenbuurt, one would only see riverboats and ships, masts and flags, along what is today the Damrak, a partially filled-in arm of the Amstel that was then a landing wharf. This busy stretch of the Zuyderzee, the south sea, came right into the heart of Amsterdam, and the city thrived on this unusual natural feature. The harbour was an integral part of city life, where sailors could land safely, protected by the city's boundaries. The inland sea port also meant that Amsterdamers thronged from morning till night along the inner arm, coming into daily contact with the sailors. The stories they brought in were greedily devoured by the population, hungry for seaborne riches: new discoveries, spices, exotic tales. The harbour was the international news channel of its day. According to a rather unfavourable late-seventeenth-century report by the French ambassador at The Hague, the Jews were apparently constantly on the lookout for "news". He wrote, "They pay as much attention to the news as they do to business."[1]

This "news" that the Jews were crowding around the Dutch harbour to hear was of signs, tales, legends and rumours that would inform their hope of Israel. Wealthy merchants, street peddlers, the Sephardi elite or the Ashkenazi poor—the Jews of Amsterdam would keep their ears open around the harbour and listen to returning sailors' stories, searching for clues that would confirm this hope of ending the diaspora, even if the Jews' material success and stability in their Dutch Jerusalem might complicate their relocation to Jerusalem of the East. The search of the Jews for signs of the messianic age had never ceased during the millennia in exile, not even in the special time and place of the *Nação*. Amsterdam's Portuguese Jews were the makers of their own incredible good luck, bestowed, they felt, by a clearly pleased God—just as the Dutch had reclaimed the land from the sea and thought it was they who were God's chosen people: "It had become a commonplace for the protestant Dutch to see themselves as the New Chosen People, saved by miracles from the idolatrous image-besotted Catholics."[2]

Certainly, the mid-seventeenth-century Dutch were living through a miracle, as Amsterdam ruled the oceans and the land. To use the oft-quoted Dutch term *overvloed*, the Republic overflowed with riches. Its borders were open to whoever was able to add to that flow of progress, or simply wanted to bask in its success. This was truly a promised land, as much for its native citizens as for the outside world: "as it was said in olden times, a land flowing with milk and honey, truly that is Holland and here in Amsterdam where there is a land and a city that overflows with milk and cheese."[3] So the Dutch adopted a self-perception as "Israel–Holland".[4] The Dutch national poet, Joost van den Vondel, wrote his epic *Passcha* (Passover) in 1612, three years after the Twelve Years' Truce, comparing the redemption of the children of Israel with the liberation of the Seven United Provinces. William I of Orange, who had led his people to freedom, was often likened to Moses of the Hebrews. Moses had a stammer, and William was known as William the Silent. This was in line with the Calvinists' preoccupation with drawing on the Old Testament for parallels to the Dutch miracle. Across the River Scheldt—the Red Sea of the Low Countries—lay the northern provinces, "Israel–Holland", protected by God's providence.

In this Dutch Reformed milieu, bells were also tolling the imminent arrival of the Saviour. The liberation of the United

Provinces was seen as a precursor to the Second Coming. Just as the centuries of persecution had been but a divine test of the Jews' endurance and steadfastness, so had *overvloed* been for the Dutch: the flooding of the polders, the bursting of the dykes, the constant battle against nature to hold onto the reclaimed land and build a good life on it. These two peoples, brought together by a celestial plan on Europe's northern shore, complemented each other's messianic expectations. Both considering that they were favoured by God among the races, they awaited the final miracle—the Coming or Second Coming of a redeemer. Where else would news of that arrival be announced, its imminence felt, but in the world's richest and most stable city, Dutch Jerusalem?

Amsterdam was bursting at the seams with frenzied expectations among the Calvinists, many Protestant dissenters, and the Jews. The latter had arrived in the north following calamities, as predicted in the books of the prophets, which foretold that such calamities would precede the arrival of the Messiah. The Spanish Inquisition was a tragedy, but also part of this prophecy, and the 1648 Treaty of Westphalia, which ended Spanish supremacy in Europe, was hailed as the final demise of the enemy of the Jewish people. What could still hold back the Redeemer? Hope flooded Jewish writing, art and popular thinking. This was expressed in Rabbi Jacob Judah Leon's obsessive architectural drawings of the Temple of Solomon, which were published in the 1640s. The *Nação* executed these model etchings and built a temple in their image.

Other important works published in Jewish Amsterdam in 1647 were commentaries on the messianic promises from the Bible, first compiled in Venice in the early sixteenth century by Don Isaac Abravanel, a Portuguese Jewish statesman expelled by the Spanish Edict. These treatises were hugely important for the Jews, who were looking for direct signals of the end of exile. The most important precondition had already been met, the Jews' terrible suffering at the hands of their enemies—for what could be worse than the near-eradication of the faith by the Spanish Inquisition? And what could better prove that the Jews were on the path to redemption than the miraculous and total return to Judaism after 200 years of Catholic life in the Iberian lands of idolatry? The Dutch miracle also informed the Jewish dream of "Israel", a metaphor for a people, as well as a nation—their *Nação*.

In 1645, there was news of a terrible incident in Dutch Brazil, which would eventually lead to a crucial legal decree aimed at protecting Dutch Jews outside the Republic. During a Portuguese rebellion against the Dutch in a Brazilian island just off Recife, the Portuguese captured a Dutch militia, which had a squadron of thirteen Jews. The Portuguese commander separated the Jews from the Christian Dutch and burned the captives alive. It was revenge raw and political, dating back to the New Christians' defection from the Portuguese Crown and accession to the *Nação* in Amsterdam. This brutal act was condemned by the Dutch States General, and the *parnassim* petitioned The Hague for soldiers of the Hebrew Nation to be treated like other Dutch nationals.

Appealing to the Calvinists' devout faith in the Old Testament, the petitioners quoted Queen Esther's plea to King Ahasuerus: "If it pleases the king, give me my life—that is my petition! Grant me my people—that is my request."[5] The impassioned plea of the *parnassim* included a reminder that the God of the Old Testament rewarded gentiles who showed kindness to the Jewish Nation.

In response, on 7 December 1645 the States General issued a historic charter that declared Holland's Jews to be Dutch subjects, and that they should be considered citizens like any other inhabitants of the Dutch Republic. This declaration, known as the *Patenta Onrossa* or Honourable Charter, is regarded as "the first charter of equality a sovereign state conceded to the Jewish nation in the Western Hemisphere." As we know, full citizen-ship—or what would be known as emancipation—would not come about until 1796, but in the colonies the *Patenta Onrossa* was as good as full rights. The States General decreed that the Hebrew Nation in Brazil must be protected from any damage to person or property, in the same manner as all citizens of the Seven United Provinces.

Though at first glance it seems that these equal citizens' rights were to be exercised only in the context of the colonies, where Jewish commanders were fighting to uphold the Dutch cause and exhibiting unequivocal loyalty, the next part of the *Patenta* leaves no confusion. According to historian Arnold Wiznitzer's *Jews in Colonial Brazil*, it instructed that the Jewish Nation must be protected, and there must not be any distinction or division between the rights of its members and "those of our other nationals." In this way, the Jews would be encouraged to "further the service in this state and that of the puissant West India Company."[6] In other words, the States General's decree was to be extended to wherever there were Dutch interests. Wiznitzer argues that such an official statement of protection for Jews by a Christian nation was unique in the seventeenth century.

Let us look at another landmark that defined the 1640s as an extraordinary decade. While the old Sephardi Jewish synagogue was reconstructed into a more grandiose building in order to house the united congregation—the one described in contempo-rary art as the "Temple of the Jews" and later visited by the Stadtholder and the Queen of England—the foundation stone was being laid of a very important building on the wharf. Designed by the Haarlem painter Jacob van Campen, the new town hall erected over the next decade would dominate the cityscape with its magnificent beauty and strategic importance in the lives of the Amsterdamers. What was more, it was built in the heart of Amsterdam, "an imperial monument in a city state".

On the floor of the citizens' hall at the centre of the building, an enormous map of the world was engraved in marble, with all the world's oceans represented. When citizens took a stroll, the world was literally at their feet, and it was proclaimed to all visitors that Amsterdam and its trading network ruled the waves. The city itself was positioned right in the middle of the floor, just as Jerusalem had been depicted in medieval maps. Holland was now truly Israel–Holland, the geographical and commercial centre of the world.[7]

It was not only the Jews who liked to refer to Amsterdam as their Jerusalem; the seventeenth-century Calvinists called the 1648 town hall "the temple of freedom".[8] In the same year as the construction of the town hall began, the Peace of Munster was signed, marking the Spanish Empire's recognition of the Dutch Republic and so the end of the Eighty Years' War. Stability and peace, and the restoration of the Jews with civic power, were all primary requirements for the Second Coming. A messianic frenzy now took over the imagination of the Jews living in freedom and stability in Amsterdam. They strolled along the harbour listening out for travellers' tales from the New World that might ignite the hope of Israel. "Israel" here is an amalgamation of the Jewish diaspora and its hopes of a nation, a homeland, and return to Jerusalem. All this would be fulfilled by the Messiah.

Once Amsterdam's Jewish Nation became convinced that the incredible pace of its success could culminate in the manifestation of the Redeemer, there was one thing left to do: locate the Ten Lost Tribes, who must be found and united with the tribes of Benjamin and Judah, the rest of the Jewish diaspora, before the Messiah's appearance. One particular story from this time, out of many possible sightings of the Lost Tribes, led to unprecedented exhilaration amongst those who were predisposed to messianic expectations, in both the Jewish and Christian worlds. The news was brought to Amsterdam from the Americas in August or September of 1644 by a former Portuguese Marrano, Antonio de

Montezinos, who after his formal conversion had taken the Jewish name of Aharon Levi. We shall refer to him as Montezinos, the name that was recorded in most historical documents relating to his story. Montezinos' sensational tales made way, for the first time, for a direct Judeo-Christian dialogue that spread beyond the Dutch Republic. They facilitated Assistant Rabbi Menasseh ben Israel's mission to settle Jews in England and other parts of northern Europe that had previously banned them.

Montezinos was born in Portugal, in the city of Villaflor, to Marrano parents. At the age of forty, he travelled to the Indies, having secretly embraced Judaism. In the city of Cartagena in Spanish New Granada (modern-day Colombia), he was caught and imprisoned, accused of judaising. As the Inquisition was not yet established in Cartagena, and there was no tribunal, the case against him was soon dismissed. After he was freed, Montezinos went to the river port of Honda, where he had previously met an Indian called Francisco, who had told the Marrano before his incarceration that he knew an isolated place of "a hidden people", on the other side of the mountain range. They set off on an arduous journey across the Cordilleras. The two men trekked through the dense jungle for more than a week before arriving one morning at the bank of a great river, which Montezinos likened to the Talmudical river of Sambatiyon.

It was the Cauca. Francisco told Montezinos that beyond the dangerous, fast-flowing river lived some strange Indians. As they camped on the riverbank, a delegation of these "strange Indians" came to meet Montezinos. Upon their meeting, the men recited in Hebrew the *Shema Israel* prayer:

Shema Israel, Adonai elohenu, Adonai echad.
Here O Israel, the Lord is our God, and he is One.

The *Shema* is the Jewish profession of faith. Hearing this, Montezinos was about to jump into the river to swim to the other bank and locate the "hiding place" of the rest. But they stopped him, and did not allow him to cross during the days he lingered on the riverbank hoping to learn more about the men who, by now, he was convinced were descendants of the Lost Tribes. Montezinos did not go to the other side to see their settlement, but around 300 of them apparently came to see him, Aharon Levi, a representative of the two tribes from whom these men's ancestors had been separated. They gave him "a curious message consisting of nine propositions" to take back with him.[9]

Montezinos was now sure he was seeing before him people who were Hebrews, or had descended from the ancient Hebrews. He recounted their markedly different physical features in such vivid detail that, to his Jewish audiences in Amsterdam and Pernambuco, Brazil, the men were none other than descendants of the Lost Tribes: "Those men are somewhat scorched by the sun, some of them wear hair long down to their knee ... They were comely of body, well accoutred ... They were tall, handsome, they cut a fine figure."[10] The men's complexion does set them apart from the Native American Indians, as would the beards Montezinos described them as having.

After some days waiting in vain on the riverbank for the men to return, he left with Francisco to go to the Jewish communities in Brazil and Holland, and deliver them the cryptic message that the "strange Indians" had given him, the code of which the former Marrano could not break. Montezinos came to Amsterdam and recounted his journey and his discovery to Menasseh ben Israel, among other leaders of the community. Across the Cordilleras, in an area crisscrossed by a fast river, he had come to a people who might be the Ten Tribes dispersed following the Assyrian captivity. The story spread fast, and reached both the Jewish and Christian worlds long before ben Israel began documenting it in *The Hope of Israel*. It caused a huge sensation, given the enormity of the subject in the post-Reformation world. Whether or not Montezinos' story was true mattered little in the context of a messiah-obsessed generation in northern Europe and in the Jewish diaspora in general.

After he arrived in Amsterdam, Montezinos took an oath in the presence of Menasseh ben Israel and other "honest men" of the Mahamad, that his meeting with the strange Indians was true. Ben Israel lent Montezinos' story his personal approval in *The Hope of Israel*:

> I myself was well acquainted with him for six months together that he lived here (Amsterdam); and sometimes I made him take an oath in the presence of honest men, that what he had told me was true. Then he went to Pernambuco (in Brazil), where two years after, he died, taking the same oath at his death. Which if it be so, why should I not believe a man that was virtuous and having all that which men call gain.[11]

It would be particularly implausible to think that Montezinos was lying, ben Israel said, because he could not have taken his oath lightly. As it concerned eternal life, Montezinos, a Marrano saved from the curse of idolatry, would not have jeopardised his chances of salvation by committing such a grave perjury.

Montezinos came to Amsterdam as the two iconic buildings, the Jewish Temple on Houtgracht and the Town Hall on Damrak, heralded stability, success and heroic achievements of the Portuguese Jews and the Dutch Reformed Christians. Both had put behind them past traumas of foreign bondage and forced dominion, and with the Peace of Munster their common enemy, Iberia. Exhilaration was in the air, conjoined by a sense of wonder: was this the end of the old ways? Was the next era, the realm of salvation, beckoning from the New World? Montezinos' account fuelled the already burning curiosity of northern Europeans in search of final redemption. As Henry Méchoulan and Gérard Nahon explained in their introduction to *The Hope of Israel*, "It had an extremely strong impact on the 'Nation' of Amsterdam, on well-read Jews and Christians, and indeed on

Menasseh ben Israel, who was to write, from the starting point of this amazing adventure, its Messianic sequel, *Esperança de Israel*."

Menasseh ben Israel used Montezinos' tales as a peg to launch his own messianic arguments in *The Hope of Israel*. Its English version was presented by the rabbi as a petition to a certain English theologian, John Dury, to make his case for the advent of the Jewish Messiah as a prerequisite for universal salvation. The work was actually commissioned; until its publication in 1650, the zeal of messianism—one of the essential pillars of Jewish faith—had been kept private by the Jews, fearing their host nation might regard it as an indirect denial of Christ the Messiah. Now, amid the cross-faith messianic excitement of the age, ben Israel was asked as a Jewish rabbi, by an interested, foreign, Protestant audience, to comment on the veracity of Montezinos's story.

This was groundbreaking. The Jews' hope of Israel had been unrequited in the Christian world, where they had settled and suffered. It was often mocked in plays and other literature in the Catholic south. The Jewish *esperanza*, hope, was lampooned in Spanish theatre as a "degrading Jewish mentality", a "hope of the fools". Here now was ben Israel, trying to prove that this was not, after all, the hope of the losers, but had been substantiated. Ben Israel weighed up the explosive issue very carefully. He was not going to stir up that old mistrust among his Christian friends: the suspicion that the book might undermine Christian faith in the Second Coming. Jewish messianism, he emphasised, has nothing to do with the denial of Christ's Second Coming. He foregrounded the Jews' belief that a "coming" was imminent, and was worth paying attention to.

Among Protestant theologians, frantic calculations were underway for the date of the Second Coming and the conversion of the Jews. Most put forward 1656 as an auspicious date. This might have been the reason why Oliver Cromwell—a staunch believer in the Old Testament and the messianic prophecy—allowed Jews to re-enter England in that year. The mid-1600s saw the peak of millenarian speculations concerning the onset of the messianic era, when, among other things, the Jews would be given sovereignty and returned to Israel. Millenarianism was widespread among English Protestants, and ben Israel was well aware of it. It was precisely this that had emboldened the rabbi to write his famous letter to Cromwell, arguing that the Jews and Christians shared a common interest and belief in restoring the Jewish nation, to create the necessary conditions for the return to Jerusalem and, for the Christians, the Second Coming.

The story of Montezinos produced rapturous responses from Christian theologians and statesmen, who became desperate to find out whether there was any truth in what the former Marrano had seen in the Indies. As Méchoulan and Nahon explain,

> The second coming, so long awaited by the Christians, cannot take place as long as the Jews do not have their political rights restored to them in the Holy Land, where finally they will all be united; hence the fundamental importance of the problem of the Ten Lost Tribes, which must at least be located geographically in anticipation of the great day of reunion.[12]

Montezinos' tales inspired hope that the Lost Tribes had finally been geographically located, in the Indies. To those predisposed to messianic symbolism, he offered proof that the prophesy in Deuteronomy was beginning to come true: "And the Lord shall scatter thee among all people, from the one end of the earth even unto the other; and there thou shalt serve other gods, which neither thou nor thy fathers have known, even wood and stone" (Deuteronomy 28:64). What, ben Israel asked, was England waiting for? Would it help in completing this process of "scattering" that must precede the (Second) Coming? Would Cromwell accept the return of the Jews to live amongst the English Nation?

This was the theme of *The Hope of Israel*, a short and important petition to an English establishment still ambivalent as to whether or not Jews should be allowed back. It is an excellent pre-modern work of advocacy by a determined activist campaigning for immigration rights of a long-deported minority. England was hesitant, its borders well guarded against a possible influx of olive-skinned people whose strange habits and customs they knew only from the generally derogatory portrayals of Elizabethan theatre.

John Dury and his fellow Protestants had not expected such an elaborate reply to their request that ben Israel confirm the veracity of Montezinos' story, but the rabbi could not miss a chance such as this to present the Jewish cause to an important Christian country that still barred Jews, having expelled them in the thirteenth century, and to speak directly on interfaith matters to co-leaders of Christianity. The last time he had had an opportunity to address a representative of England was during Henrietta Maria's visit to the synagogue in 1642. But on that occasion, as we saw in Chapter 5, ben Israel confined his address to formalities and a diplomat's tribute to royal dignitaries. He was also probably conscious of Henrietta Maria's background—that was not the right time, standing before a Catholic queen, to broach the subject of readmitting Jews to England.

Almost ten years on, things had changed drastically in northern Europe. England had moved from absolutist monarchy to a parliamentary system after the defeat of the royalists and the beheading of Charles I in 1649. Cromwell was renowned to be as good a statesman as he was a Protestant. His interest in the Second Coming was well known, and the diplomat in ben Israel wanted to gain from it. Though he was careful not to topple the balance in the Judeo-Christian dialogue emerging after centuries of anti-Jewish prejudice, ben Israel turned what was meant to be a short reply of a passage or two into a lengthy "review".

As well as being a superb work of advocacy for the resettlement of the Jews, *The Hope of Israel* was a manifesto for Judeo-Christian co-existence, outlining how the two strands of messianism could merge into one universal theme of wellbeing. The Jewish messianic hope did not have to challenge the foundation of Christianity—that the Messiah had already come, as Jesus Christ, and would come again. If the two faiths hadn't agreed the first time around, they could now make it up, after 1,600 years of bloodshed and a great deal of suffering. Ben Israel's book marked a watershed in the history of hostility and mistrust between the Jews and the Christians. It was a powerful call for a lasting entente to overcome medieval xenophobia and pre-modern prejudices. All the while, the rabbi pursued his mission to fast-forward his and the Jewish Nation's messianic vision.

Within a few years after the English publication of *The Hope of Israel*, one of the last hurdles was overcome. Ben Israel had had to reassure the English authorities amid their fear that all of Amsterdam's Jews would now flood into London. At least for now, he told Cromwell's ministers, the resettlement was only for those Spanish–Portuguese Marranos who wanted to break free of their Catholic cover and publicly become Jews. The re-entry of the Jews into England was made legal in 1656, when Cromwell granted them limited access to settle. Soon, many of the Iberian New Christians who were already in England on business contracts came in from the Marrano cold and declared their true, Jewish identity.

However, having accomplished this major victory, and having convinced his Christian readership that the discovery of the Lost Tribes was imminent, ben Israel turned to publishing further theological treatises, rather than insisting on an investigation into the "strange Indians" of New Granada. In spite of Montezinos' account, and the enthusiasm it generated in the Sephardi, Ashkenazi and Christian worlds, no expeditions left for the Americas to follow the Marrano traveller's trail and verify his story. For a decade, the messianic craze within the Jewish community remained somewhat contained. Ben Israel started spending more time in London, under Cromwell's direct protection. He even received a handsome allowance for living expenses. We know that he did not get on particularly well with his chief rabbi, Morteira; it is probable that ben Israel felt more appreciated in England, and was pleased with the attention he was getting—both favourable and unfavourable—following the tremendous success of *The Hope of Israel*'s English translation.

Meanwhile the Jews of Amsterdam were growing richer and more established in the community. The Sephardi merchants, living in palatial canalside houses, had the means easily to conduct more than one expedition into New Granada. Montezinos died in Recife in 1648, but before his death he was able to pass on to the *Nação* the last of the nine requests by the "strange Indians": to "send twelve men ... who were skilful in writing."[13]

The message could only mean that the self-proclaimed descendants of the ancient Hebrews were inviting a delegation of scholars from the enlightened Jewish community of Europe. Perhaps they wanted their stories to be recorded by bona fide members of the community. Why did ben Israel, who had the backing of both a powerful Christian nation and his own Amsterdam community, not elaborate on this important point in his 1650 work? He wrote a whole book in defence of Montezinos' story, yet did not take further steps to verify it. Why did no one else among the rich and influential Dutch Jewry follow it up with an expedition? Were they afraid that the tales might prove to be untrue? Could it be that, while feeling enthused by the idea of redemption and return to the Holy Land—"an article of faith", in the words of Maimonides—the well-established Sephardi merchants of Amsterdam were not ready to relocate to Jerusalem? Was that why they would pay for their "Temple" to be built in Amsterdam?

The Jewish Temple was an emblem of architectural perfection; it symbolised the realisation of the exiled New Christians' dream of liberation, establishing the most autonomous home the Jews had known since their expulsion from the land of their forefathers. They created a sovereign community, one strong enough to take on the world on near-equal terms. This miraculous achievement could only have happened in the Dutch Republic, which was "two centuries ahead of the rest of Europe in respect of freedom and tolerance".[14] From the late sixteenth century, Amsterdam had been seen as the culmination of Jewish aspirations, the end of a long journey. The mid-seventeenth century was the peak of the great messianic age, and yet the Jewish hopefuls did not pursue their quest for information on the Lost Tribes, in the Indies or elsewhere. It could not be that they were waiting for the tribes to come to them—several times in Jewish history self-proclaimed messiahs had come forward, but they were all proved to be false. The leaders of the Jewish Nation did not pursue Montezinos' lead because they did not want to risk being disappointed.

It would be fair to say that the merchants of Amsterdam's Jewish Nation, living a prosperous life that would have been beyond their wildest imagination only two decades earlier, were not ready to uproot themselves from their Dutch Jerusalem. One can even detect a hint of complacency in the community's attitude and lifestyle during this extraordinary period, almost as if there was no need to go after the Messiah. The talk could be there, and aspirations could be freshened as and when the community needed them for spiritual inspiration. For was it not the messianic hope that had bound together the Jewish nation in exile for millennia? But there was no rush; they did not have to abandon their lovely, gabled double-fronted houses for the land of their ancestors.

By the 1650s, an extensive network of charitable organisations like the Dotar had been established, run by the Jews and for the

Jews. Interestingly, there was even a stipend for those who wanted to go and live in the Holy Land.[15] The real Jerusalem was not an obvious choice of residence; it was a destination for those who were not solvent enough to make a life in Amsterdam. Jerusalem of the East was not, or so it seemed to the seventeenth-century Amsterdam Jews, an alternative home. Rather, it was a resettlement scheme and rehabilitation project, set up by the wealthy Portuguese Jews, for impoverished or "unwanted" Jews—those who could not afford to help maintain the Jewish Nation's privileged status in Amsterdam.

Furthermore, following the death of his second son while on business in England, Rabbi Menasseh ben Israel seemed to have lost interest in life. He had already lost one son in Brazil. He broke down both emotionally and physically; after Cromwell helped him to ship the body back to Amsterdam, where his son had wished to be buried in the Jewish cemetery at Ouderkerk, he lasted just six more months. Perhaps the messianic fervour would have continued to produce more volumes of inter-faith literature, had ben Israel been around longer. The iconic rabbi of the *Nação*, the age's most prolific advocate of interfaith dialogue in the Judeo-Christian milieu, the spokesperson of the Jewish messianic aspiration and its relevance in a Christian world, died in 1657, a year after his most historic achievement for the community: formal approval for the readmission of the Jews into England.

Spinoza left his religion and community before finding acceptance, respect and praise for his philosophy in the Christian world. Menasseh ben Israel had remained a deeply religious Jew and a rabbi of his community, while still reaching out to the Christians. He was attentive to both their reverence for and rejection of the people of the Old Testament, and managed to make them listen to his presentation of the Jewish cause. One man was the pioneer of European liberalism; the other the promoter of an interreligious discourse across a spectrum of nations.

Ben Israel's personal petition to Oliver Cromwell for the readmission of the Jews was one of the most important pamphlets challenging historic European prejudices against the Jews, and celebrating the benefits of a multicultural society with equal rights for all. In that sense, he was one of the first Jewish theologians to campaign for a binational state—a turn of phrase that would become an oft-used expression in the context of the Israeli-Palestinian conflict three centuries later. Nahum Sokolow, considered to be the first historian of modern Zionism, analysed ben Israel's character at great length in his *History of Zionism*, calling him "the bard of the Jewish National idea."[16] *The Hope of Israel* was probably the most successful booklet ever published on the Jewish hope for salvation. It became extremely popular during the last seven years of ben Israel's life. Amongst the Jewish diaspora in Europe, it contributed to the development of a whole new conviction, one that would become a political concept. Two centuries on, it would be called Zionism.

9

THE MESSIAH WHO ALMOST CAME

Messianism did not dissipate with the death of the author of *The Hope of Israel*. It was kept alive by his zealous congregation in Amsterdam, the diaspora and the sprouting Sephardi Jewish communities in the New World. Its breadth and veracity were constantly being tested throughout the mid-seventeenth century. The merchants of Amsterdam, strolling along the landing wharf facing the newly completed town hall, would instinctively stop by the harbour and linger, watching the sea and the ships—a typical Dutch waterscape that has been painted and etched thousands of times. News of the existence of Jews in Cochin, southern India added to the thrill, bringing closer the coming together of the Jewish diaspora.[1] Menasseh ben Israel had mentioned this Jewish colony in his petition to Cromwell, in an anxious attempt to impress the Lord Protector "with the worldwide usefulness of his people."[2] Menasseh stressed the wealthy and influential position of the Jews in India, which would soon occupy a central place in English/British colonial ambition.

The existence of the Cochin Jews also excited European Christians, preoccupied throughout the seventeenth century with messianic auguries. Jan Huygen van Linschoten, an early Dutch traveller who had been in Cochin in the previous century, wrote in 1587:

> The Jewes have built very fair stone houses, and are rich merchants, and of the king of Cochin nearest Counsellers; there they have their Synagogue with their Hebrue bible, and Moses Law, which I have had in my hand; they are mostly white in colour, like men of Europa and have many faire women. There are many of them that came out of the country of Palestina and Jerusalem thether, and speak over the Exchange good Spanish; they observe the Saboth and other judicall ceremonie and hope for the Mesias to come...[3]

From van Linschoten's description it seems that these Jews were Iberian refugees of the first Sephardi diaspora of 1492. The Jewish presence in southern India had previously been documented by the Portuguese, soon after Vasco da Gama's arrival at the Malabar Coast in 1498. *The Hope of Israel* also said that one part of the Jewish population in Cochin was white, and the other of a "tawny colour". It was with Amsterdam's Jewish printing press, launched into the mainstream trade by ben Israel, that the first prayer books of the Cochin synagogue were published. The community sent a delegation to the southern Indian town with the books and messages of solidarity.

The Hope of Israel was published in Dutch in 1666, nine years after the death of its author. Over the decade that had passed, it seemed that the quest for a messianic manifestation continued at a steady pace, though the "frenzy" was over amid the success and complacency of the Republic's Jewish Nation, at the height of its progress. As we saw earlier, the paintings of Jewish merchants by Dutch masters such as Rembrandt, Bol and Govert Flinck started to resemble Dutch burghers, in their physical traits and the clothes they wore. Their women and children displayed the finest silk and imported lace. The men wore wigs with long curled hair according to the fashion of the time, and women showed off the

French and Italian *haute couture* in their dresses and bonnets. Paintings of the interiors of seventeenth-century Jewish homes also show black African servant boys and girls, linking the Sephardi merchants to the thriving slave trade in which they were involved, alongside their Dutch compatriots and other Europeans. Among some of the richest Jews in the Ouderkerk cemetery is the small, modest gravestone of a servant or slave boy, Eliezer, who was brought, by some accounts, to Amsterdam by the merchant Belmonte, presumably from the Americas. There are no other graves of servants, slaves or non-Jews in this main, oldest part of the cemetery. Most probably he was converted by his master to Judaism, and given the name of the biblical servant Eliezer. He died on 27 March 1627.

One could say that this was the "milk and honey" moment in the history of the great Jewish exile. Who would want to go to Jerusalem of the East, leaving all this—the silk and lace; the printing press and the imposing public synagogue; the trip to the *mikveh* with servants brought over from the New World; the lavish entertainment in their grand houses on Herengracht, the city's most prestigious street; their official recognition as the Hebrew Nation by the Dutch Republic? Amsterdam was experiencing a golden age for Jewish self-determination. By the 1660s, the Ashkenazi Jews—who had arrived some decades earlier—were also becoming prosperous. The communities came into daily contact, and although intermarriage between the two denominations was not permitted, the Sephardim were on the whole accepting, even welcoming, of the Ashkenazim's bolstering of the Jewish population in a Protestant city. After the infamous Polish Chmielnicki or Cossack massacres of 1648–57, when Amsterdam was flooded by Jewish refugees from Poland and middle Europe, the *parnassim* set up a fund to rehabilitate the destitute Ashkenazi arrivals.

The world was in awe of the Sephardi Jews' breaking of the old boundaries and stereotypes. The Christian world and the Jewish diaspora alike could hardly believe the official re-entry of the Jews into England. In another groundbreaking move, shortly before his death, Menasseh ben Israel had struck up a dialogue with the Queen of Sweden about settling Jews in the prosperous Hanseatic belt. The Christians were watching with curiosity the rise of the Jews, whom they used to see as hook-nosed, turbaned and "horned" gross caricatures, as brokers in the World Trade Mart, and as an intellectual powerhouse that lent to the dawning of European scepticism in the ideas of a neighbourhood rebel called Baruch Spinoza. By the 1660s, the Dutch-born Portuguese Jewish intelligentsia was hobnobbing daily with Christian compatriots in the realms of art, theatre, music, and pioneering philosophy.

Why, then, would the Mahamad in Amsterdam and the new Jewish congregation in Brazil—in effect an offshoot of the Dutch Republic's Hebrew Nation—follow up on the lead of some sun-scorched "strange Indians", when they had tobacco farms to attend to, sugar mills to supervise, a slave trade to approach, thought-provoking and challenging Judeo-Christian literature to publish? The guild rules were becoming farcical, so relaxed that many Jews had already joined the medical profession, some had invested in joint ventures, and a printing press was a common sight in Amsterdam's Jodenbuurt.

Since the 1620 invention of the "Dutch Press", a specialised weighted typeset, the Republic had become even more prolific in publishing a significant amount of religious literature, as well as atlases, books on cartography, copies of etchings, and so on. More books were published in the Dutch Republic in the seventeenth century than in most European countries put together. The highest proportion of publications, about 33 per cent—a staggering 22,000 books—were printed in Amsterdam alone. The Dutch Press dominated until the mid-eighteenth century, when England and Germany took over. Since printing was a new trade, Catholics, Jews and other immigrants could join. The

Jewish Nation became a leading light in Dutch publishing. The printing trade also thrived in the Republic because of the absence of a state religion and lack of effective censorship. There was a Europe-wide demand for all kinds of literature, from all the predominant faiths. By 1650, around half the urban Dutch population, both male and female, could read and write—a phenomenal achievement for an early modern society. The higher the literacy rate rose, the more the demand grew for books, almanacs, periodicals, prayer and song books, and newspapers.

Jewish printing presses around this time were publishing volumes of Hebrew textbooks for non-Jewish "Hebraists": Protestants who believed in the Second Coming, for which the restoration of the Jews to a social and political institution was an essential prerequisite. There was also great demand from artists for basic Hebrew-language books, as the style of depicting Hebrew letters in Old Testament-themed paintings was popularised by Rembrandt, among others. It was amid this demand from the Christian Hebraists in the Republic that Menasseh ben Israel's iconic book finally saw its publication in Dutch, in 1666. *De Hoop van Israel* also came out the same year as twenty-four high-profile members of the *Nação* wrote to Shabbatai Zvi of Izmir in modern Turkey, hailing him as the Messiah.

Shabbatai had indeed proclaimed in 1665 that he was the Saviour the world had been waiting for. The jubilation at this news spread far and wide and took the Sephardi, Ashkenazi and Protestant worlds by storm. The tales of Montezinos were thought to have prepared the Amsterdam community to readily accept Shabbatai Zvi as the Messiah, and the *parnassim* was quick to act. The Jewish Nation's governors could not wait for the Messiah to come to them and lead them to Jerusalem— they collected signatures of prominent leaders of the community on a special paper with an Amsterdam hologram, and put together a delegation to take the document to Zvi in Turkey.

The signatories asked the self-proclaimed Messiah if the time had come to join him in the march to Jerusalem, the homeland of their forefathers.

The men set off with this message and had reached Venice when the devastating news hit that Shabbatai Zvi was not, after all, the one. He was in fact a false messiah, a traitor to the Hebrews. The delegation in Venice was waiting at the sea crossing when they heard that Shabbatai had converted to Islam and was now working for the Ottoman sultan. This was a disgrace, the greatest setback since the New Christians' return to Judaism. The rabbis and the *parnassim* had been so cautious until now that they had not carried out an expedition into the Americas following Montezinos' story. But in this instance they were tragically fooled, shamed by the claim and brief appearance of a fake messiah. It was a scandal in the eyes of their Christian neighbours.

The Hebrew Nation was devastated at how quickly the much-awaited "news" turned to bad news; the flicker of hope of the great "coming" had been abruptly put out. It seemed that the integrity of the community was shaken. Before its morale could be punctured irreparably, the rabbis took drastic steps to distance themselves from the pseudo messiah and from those who still believed in him—there were strong followers of the messianic movement who believed that the Turkish messiah had been forcibly converted, and who hoped he would soon break free of his quasi-Islamic identity, imposed by the Ottomans, and lead his people to Jerusalem. Even today there are remnants of what came to be known as the Sabbatean movement. In the Ottoman Empire, those who converted to Islam with Shabbatai Zvi secretly followed Jewish rituals. These crypto-Jews were known as the Dönmeh; some are still thought to be active in Turkey.

Despite the shocking disclosure of Shabbatai's demise and the biggest trauma since their flight to the Dutch Republic, the Jewish congregations in Amsterdam, Brazil and the diaspora were determined to move on. They clung to their successes in their adoptive homelands and waited, patiently, for another beacon to light the path to eternal salvation. The second half of the seventeenth century would be different. The setback of Shabbatai Zvi meant that the messianic movement went somewhat underground, clearing the way for exemplary stability and steady economic growth both in Amsterdam and in the satellite communities in the Americas.

Meanwhile, the messianic anticipations in the Sephardi world had dispersed across to the pockets of Ashkenazim in central Europe. They devoured the tales of the Marrano adventurer, Montezinos, and this strengthened their communal unity with the Sephardim. Montezinos' story would continue to travel throughout the eighteenth and nineteenth centuries, to the scattered Jewish settlements in Russia, Poland and Germany. What impact, if any, did they have on those small communities of Ashkenazi Jews who were not lucky enough to bask in the *Nação*'s extraordinary success?

The messianic literature was primarily a product of the Sephardi Jews. Historians have tried to trace the "dawning of Zionism" through the mass distribution throughout Europe of messianic pamphlets, books and songs. Such circulation of literature was possible because of the ubiquitous Dutch printing press, which, according to the Republic's official bibliography, produced some 67,000 titles in 1601–1700. In the printing houses dotted around Amsterdam's Jodenbreestraat, extensive Jewish literature was published in all the European languages, including Yiddish, and of course in Hebrew, the *lingua franca* of the Jews across the Sephardi–Ashkenazi divide. From *De Hoop van Israel* came a large number of Hebrew translations, which reached the Sephardi and Ashkenazi diasporas around the globe. They were priced affordably, as they were printed on non-expensive paper for mass distribution. The result was unimaginable, taking the

Jewish people into previously unchartered waters in consolidating the Jewish hope of return from exile to Jerusalem, as a unified people. This literature succeeded in bridging the old denominational divide.

The following excerpt, from Méchoulan and Nahon's introduction to *The Hope of Israel*, tells us of the reverberating impact these mass publications would have on the history of the Jewish exile for centuries to come.

> It was the booklets in Hebrew, peddled in Russia and Poland and read in Jewish families in the evenings, which without doubt worked underground, conveying the miraculous and the real, Holy Scripture and secular knowledge, the scent of distant lands and the imminence of the Return. The Sephardic Messianic manifesto beat a royal way through the steppes, forests, and villages of the Ashkenazi Jews.[4]

The Portuguese Jews, then, are credited with the creation of a vast body of pamphlets on messianism, which preoccupied both Jewish and non-Jewish readers of the seventeenth and eighteenth centuries. History was being made, the future of the Jewish people was being shaped by this literature—but all the while the writers or architects of that future remained unaware of their role: they were ushering in an altogether different stage in the quest for a Jewish homeland. There was now a pan-Judaic movement, no longer limited to the aspirations of educated and well-established Sephardi citizens in the Christian world. From England to the Russian hinterland, a new chapter was fast emerging.

Meanwhile, in Amsterdam, a large section among the Jewish hopefuls refused to give up. They were not disheartened by the embarrassment that the Shabbatai Zvi story had caused. Shabbatai was the highest-profile Jewish convert to Islam. In the aftermath of the event and its vast publicity, many in the Sephardi diaspora felt they were being treated as a laughingstock by some sections of the Christian and Islamic worlds. The Protestant position was reinforced by Shabbatai's demise. The

Christian Second Coming was the ultimate truth, the Jews were told. Jesus was the true Messiah, on whose return the Jews would all convert to Christianity. But some started looking for ways to prove the sceptics wrong, reiterating that Shabbatai Zvi had been a victim of forced conversion—just like the New Christians. As they found their true path, so would Shabbatai, and he would lead them to Zion. This put the *parnassim* on alert. They prohibited talk of Shabbatai Zvi both within the community and in public. Anyone caught with proclaiming allegiance to him risked being excommunicated. The embarrassment of the false messiah episode was further exacerbated by an old memory passed down from the Iberian ancestors. At no other time did Spanish mockery of the Jewish *esperanza* haunt them as tellingly as it did after 1666.

Since there was no immediate hope of return behind a messiah figure, the best the Jewish Nation could do was to make their time in exile worthwhile. Like their Dutch Reformed compatriots, they too called their home "Holland–Israel". The "Temple" must be built in Amsterdam, their Jerusalem on the Amstel, since the alternative endeavour under the banner of Shabbatai Zvi had so tragically failed. The Sephardi community in Amsterdam and its satellite establishments in the Americas concentrated on further improving their current status in a glorious exile. The Jews in Amsterdam worked even harder to obtain greater professional advantages in Dutch institutions. They were not allowed into the architectural guild, but they could employ Dutch architects to execute Jewish designs and Jewish motifs. Since the return to the Holy Land could not be made, at least not yet, the temple must be erected here in Amsterdam, home to the Western hemisphere's most successful Jewish Nation.

One of Menasseh ben Israel's old rivals, Rabbi Isaac Aboab da Fonseca, had gone to Recife to serve as rabbi of the Jewish congregation there, Zur Israel. He had returned to town after Dutch

Brazil was lost to Portugal in 1661. Aboab, who took over as chief rabbi after Morteira's death and would lead the Amsterdam Sephardim throughout the second half of the century, was very much caught up in the Sabbatean excitement, which broke out soon after his return. Some, such as the Hamburg rabbi Jacob Sasportas, believed that Aboab remained secretly loyal to the Sabbatean movement even after Shabbatai Zvi's collective denouncement by Jewish communities in the Dutch Republic and around the world.[5] This would not be revealed until much later, when Aboab moved to Salonica to join the crypto-Sabbateans there. Aboab, however, was fully supportive of the *parnassim*'s instruction to the community to prosper in Amsterdam as best they could, as if this were their Jerusalem. In public, he fully distanced himself from the Sabbateans.

More and more Sephardim were drawn to Amsterdam, from the crypto-Jewish world and from North African and other European ghettos. Amsterdam became the jewel in the Sephardi crown. The old synagogue on the Houtgracht could not cope with the increased volume of newcomers into the faith. It was under Chief Rabbi Aboab's direction that the Sephardi community bought a piece of land for a new synagogue in 1670, at the top end of Jodenbreestraat, which today is on the corner of Meijerplein and Mr. Visserplein. A year later, in 1671, an Ashkenazi synagogue was inaugurated not far away. The work began to replace the existing Portuguese synagogue with a much bigger, several times enlarged replica of Solomon's temple. It was much easier for Aboab to preside over the community and supervise the building of the new synagogue, since his old rival, ben Israel, was no longer alive. He appointed Elias Bouman, one of the seventeenth century's most renowned Dutch architects, to incorporate the existing designs of Jacob Judah Leon Templo.

Bouman's building contractors used 3,000 woodpiles for the foundations on the Jodenbuurt's waterlogged ground. The pace of work was fast—the community had to be protected from a sense of despondency befalling them after the catastrophic end of the so-called messiah. The new house of worship would decisively proclaim the strength of the Jewish faith among the former New Christian community, a faith that had survived despite centuries of Inquisitorial oppression and intimidation. Not only had this conviction, dormant in their Catholic lives, leapt out and blossomed in Amsterdam's liberal air, the Jewish tradition that was reinstated in Amsterdam became the Jewish Enlightenment, *haskalah*, setting a world example for Sephardi Jewry. For the proud Jewish Amsterdamers, their faith must remain invincible, regardless of how many pseudo messiahs came and went before the true salvation was reached. And until that happened, they must continue to prosper materially and spiritually. This was the best they could do, until a divine intervention would set in motion their last journey: the return to the *terra santa*.

The high-arched, towering brick-and-wood Portuguese Synagogue, the Esnoga, was completed in 1675. The *Nação's* hope of Israel was made material, on Amsterdam's soil.

The golden city in the golden age of the Dutch Republic was no longer a temporary refuge, as it had been seen during the first half-century of messianic expectations. It was beginning to look like the final stop in the Jews' wandering through exile. The comfort and security that had arisen from the *Nação's* collective sense of stability had been envisioned in Jessurun's play, *Diálogo dos Montes*, performed in 1624, in the early days of the community's life in Amsterdam. Mount Sinai, upon which the Law was given to Moses, offers this verdict:

> Soon may your offspring blest,
> O sovereign judge, for whom we daily pine,
> As recompense for all your labours here,
> In royal apparel dressed
> Restore the ancient line;[6]

The labours of the Jewish Nation had been rewarded by its survival, blessed enough in Amsterdam for the Saviour to be predicted to appear in "royal apparel" to restore the ancient people.

The message of this verse was internalised by the community. There was no doubt that their good fortune, after having been "tossed at sea", was a sure sign of their chosen status. Their privilege emboldened them to build, in the most successful Christian country of its day, a permanent Sephardi synagogue, a magnificent Jewish house of worship. Its wood was of the finest Brazilian variety from Recife; its glass and interior fineries were imported from Venice and other European cities. Shaking off the momentary humiliation of the fall of Shabbatai Zvi, the Jews of Amsterdam went back to business as usual—not only that, the Portuguese Jews pooled all their resources to prove to their own community, the Christian world and the Sephardi diaspora around the globe that they had truly settled in their Holland–Israel. The Esnoga cost 186,000 florins to build, and became the largest synagogue in the world. The inauguration, which coincided with Hanukkah in 1675, lasted an entire week.

These grandiose ceremonies were intended to offer much-needed reassurance to a congregation disheartened by the debacle of the messiah, and to direct them towards a new approach to redemption: to make the most of what they had already been blessed with. We can almost hear the undertones of contemporary Protestant ethics in this approach—it would not be a wild exaggeration to assume that Jewish thought was exposed to or influenced by it. This solution was convenient, too: since the waiting time for the Messiah in royal apparel, could be of any length now, the messianic goal of the Jews had become less tangible and more symbolic. They would no longer have to chase after signs of the Lost Tribes, to calculate dates for the grand arrival. The coming of the Messiah had been spiritualised, becoming part of the popular imagination and a greater hope in redemption not just for the Jews, but for everyone. In a way, the

THE MESSIAH WHO ALMOST CAME

demise of Shabbatai Zvi and the building of the splendid Esnoga universalised the Jewish hope of Israel.

In numerous times past, the Jews' great aspiration had turned to devastating hopelessness, such as when King João II (1481–1495) of Portugal joined Spain in persecuting the Jews who were expelled from there and who took refuge in Portugal. The Jews dealt with their lows in the Dutch Republic through constant evocation of similar examples from their history, from which they drew strength. The past was poetry, a source of trauma and glorious pride for a people whose turbulent history had been documented as much in popular literature as in historical manuscripts. Don Isaac Abravanel, the distinguished fifteenth-century finance official of the Portuguese court, turned to writing heartrending prose after João II became king:

> Then came an evil day for all people and especially Israel—a day of darkness, lamentation and oppression. Death quickly mounted his windows and terror gripped his palace. She filled the halls, grasped the knife to slay his son, and slew him as the divine sentence decreed. Thus a spirit passed and went unto his God even as the chaff blows from the threshing floor. And the daughter of Zion was left as a booth in the vineyard without a support.[7]

But the Jewish Nation had not been defeated. Just as "a spirit passed and went unto his God even as the chaff blows from the threshing floor", the Marranos had passed on the burning spirit to their people, who had dispersed, but kept it burning. Every time an unprecedented calamity struck, it was in this spirit that they found direction for continuity. The last line of Abravanel's memoir—"It was a time to remember our glories and our misfortunes"—became the motto of a people for whom misfortune lurked never too far behind incredible success.

This spirit or *esperança*, hope, made the long exile bearable, glorious even, and was burning bright once again. This innate light was exactly what ben Israel—who wrote enthusiastically about his connection to Abravanel, his wife's ancestor—had put forward in his long discourse with European leadership seeking to dispel the Christian world's old prejudice about the Jews. Tuning into the Christian millenarian curiosity then abroad, the rabbi-diplomat had calmly stressed the blessed status enjoyed by the Jews. The light belonged to his people—this was the secret of their survival. Méchoulan and Nahon elucidate poignantly what ben Israel had tried to achieve for his people:

> Menasseh Ben Israel has interpreted a melody whose theme was known by all his own people. It was in that context that his composition, with all its newness, its strangeness, and its exoticism, took up the song of hope which the former Marranos of the "Jerusalem" of the North had never quite lost and were now finding again.[8]

The week-long opening ceremony of the Esnoga in 1675 was attended by both Jewish and Christian dignitaries—another testament to the Jewish Nation of Amsterdam's new, modern approach to reaching out. If Uriel da Costa were alive at this time, he probably would not have been excommunicated; Spinoza would not have been banished from his community. One could say that the process of breaking free from the cloistered mentality of Jewish life in Amsterdam had been set in motion by the internationally bestselling *Hope of Israel*, and now by the building of the Portuguese Synagogue. Foreign travellers passed by and marvelled at the splendour of the "Jewish church", and at the prosperity of a people who had been subjected to centuries of misconception, prejudice and daily mockery in Europe and elsewhere. The community felt immensely proud of their new house of worship, which dwarfed the nearby churches. It had broken free of the terror of the Inquisition and the strictures imposed by conservative rabbis such as Morteira against trusting the Christians. The open-to-all Hanukkah ceremony during the Esnoga's grand inauguration had now established that real dialogue could be established with the Christians. Though "assimilation" was still much discouraged in the community, integration was now welcomed.

It was also something the Calvinist rulers favoured: to live and let live. At this point it seemed that Dutch society was showing early signs of "pillarisation"—of segments of its citizenry living along religious lines. The mutual tolerance of cultures was a novel creation of early modern Dutch society; the Jewish and Christian religious bodies both adapted to it willingly. As it helped the Hebrew Nation to prosper while remaining a Jewish entity, it also served the more orthodox Calvinists, who believed in preserving the purity of the Christian faith. But the difference between late medievalism and early modern culture in Europe was that the former believed in annihilation of the "other", while the latter accommodated and "tolerated" the other, even though this was motivated by self-interest on both sides. In this approach, the anomalous Dutch Republic exceeded all others. The goodwill of its Calvinist rulers was transmitted to the Dutch general population and the intelligentsia, who were fascinated by the Iberian strangers who, just half a century after their arrival, matched the Dutch bourgeoisie in wealth and scholarship.

The Jodenbuurt had now become a permanent, imposing feature of the cityscape, boasting in the Esnoga the finest example of Dutch new classicism. Artists wanted to record the Republic's most celebrated landmark. From its ostentatious erection, the "Temple" was painted and engraved in many famous pieces. The inaugural event was immortalised by the Dutch printmaker Romeyn de Hooghe, who created a copperplate of the ceremony. Numerous prints were made from it and sold or distributed around the world. De Hooghe engraved on both sides the names of the influential members of the *parnassim*, as well as the names of the architects and the building committee. He also engraved— and therefore preserved for posterity—the names of the community's wealthiest merchants, whose generous funding had helped build the magnificent monument, probably the most important that had been constructed in the Sephardi world.

The Esnoga was also written about in contemporary travelogues and other literature. Visitors came from all over the world to bask in its splendour and scale. Never in the history of Judaism since the destruction of the Second Temple had the Jews had the privilege to worship in a building as majestic, public, and talked about as the Portuguese Synagogue of 1675. The Esnoga's foreground, on the Amstel tributary that flowed into the great open sea, became a popular promenade destination. Men, women and children came and enjoyed the views, and the awe-inspiring building of the Jews that towered over the Christian churches.

10

REMBRANDT'S NEIGHBOURS

One wonders how Rembrandt (1606–69) would have painted or etched the Esnoga had he been alive then. He had lived a stone's throw away from Mr. Visserplein, where the Portuguese Jews built their temple-synagogue, at the top end of Jodenbreestraat. Its geometric precision showed the most sophisticated realisation yet of the pride of an enlightened immigrant nation, and the sparse classical design expressed that Nation's humility despite being tremendously successful. The one-storey structure that surrounded the main Esnoga also housed a smaller daily house of worship, mainly for the use of schoolchildren and students of the yeshiva Ets Haim. Today it is used as a winter synagogue, which can be heated.

During his lifetime Rembrandt relentlessly drew, etched and painted his exotic neighbours—in the flamboyant outfits of the merchants, if he fancied a splash of colour on his easel, or else the simple Ashkenazi vagabonds and peddlers who poured into Jodenbreestraat from middle Europe, as well as new Marrano immigrants from the Iberian Peninsula who fell on hard times after losing all to the Inquisition. As we know, it was during the seventeenth century that Moses started appearing in Dutch paintings without horns, and the Dutch masters stopped displaying a "demonological exaggeration" of the figure of the Jew—the prominent hooked nose, the long beard and turban. By the mid-century, the appearance of the Portuguese Jewish merchants and other professionals bore almost no distinguishing features to mark them out from the gentiles of Amsterdam. The remaining visibly Jewish Amsterdamers were mostly the Ashkenazim, and perhaps the rabbis.

The Old Testament was the most popular theme during this period, with the old Jewish stereotypes retouched by Dutch masters such as Rembrandt and Lievens into essential characteristics of the figures of the Bible. Their style enhanced "the narrative immediacy of scripture painting so that Rembrandt gives us not only a David, but a St Matthew and a Jesus with the features of his Jewish neighbours on the Breestraat."[1] Well-off Jews had been having their portraits painted for some time by renowned artists. One of the more famous etchings is of Dr Ephraim Bueno descending a staircase; we meet a man with a mischievous grace and a perfectly trimmed Van Dyke beard, starched white cuffs turned back over a black coat, and a stiff white collar. To the naked eye, this figure from 1647 could be a member of the Calvinist regent class, a rich burgher.

The portraits and paintings of the seventeenth-century Jews show how they lived, or how they wanted to be seen by future generations of Jews. Those who posed in these pictures were not mere models for the artists; they commissioned these works and sat for them in their finest clothing and jewellery, smiling their happiest smiles. These men, women and children were no different from any other rich members of society in the pre-photographic age, who wanted to have their portraits etched in black and white, or painted in rich colours by artists they could afford. The rich Sephardi merchants also commissioned engravings of their sumptuous houses by artists like de Hooghe, such as the double fronted canalside Belmonte residence at the most sought after address on Herengracht.

From this point of view, the fact that Rembrandt painted the Jews is not remarkable. So did de Hooghe, Bol and others. Why, then, has Rembrandt been described by historians as the particular friend of the Jews? Why was the same term not used for others like de Hooghe? The latter painted and etched more Jews, Jewish buildings and Jewish ceremonies than Rembrandt did. It is through de Hooghe's marvellous illustrations of Jewish rituals and prayers, of the synagogue interiors and of the majestic canalside Jewish houses that we learn much about Jewish life in Amsterdam in this period.

But there is a marked difference between the works of de Hooghe and Rembrandt. While de Hooghe was a real-life illustrator, Rembrandt added emotion to his characters, expressions that were beyond what a human camera—the illustrator of the pre-photographic age—could capture. Rembrandt's careful drypoint and brushstroke took ample artistic license, so that his sitters transcended the parochial. The Dutch master looked at his Jewish subjects not as Jews, but as fascinating human specimens who could be visualised in many shades of colour and expression. The etching of Ephraim Bueno was not remarked by its maker as being of a "Jew". Like many of Rembrandt's works, it was untitled. It was only much later—when the face in Rembrandt's etching was found to bear a strong resemblance to another on a different painting by Jan Lievens, titled *Ephraim Bueno*—that art historians connected the painter and his subject. One wonders whether, without this second painting of Dr Bueno, we would have known the man on the staircase was a Jew at all. He looks like a typical Dutch burgher.

This is where Rembrandt's greatness lies. Steven Nadler, a professor of Jewish Studies, says in *Rembrandt's Jews* that the master was a true artist, not a mere illustrator: "De Hooghe documented the world while Rembrandt created his own. De Hooghe pictures the Jews of Amsterdam; Rembrandt, although using his Sephardic and Ashkenazic neighbours as models, transcends their particularities to achieve the representation of ideal human types within biblical proportions."[2] Rembrandt's humanistic approach to even evil or complex characters from the Old Testament meant that they appeared to seventeenth-century viewers in a totally new light. For example, the figure of Bathsheba is depicted by most painters exactly as she is described in the Bible: as a wily seductress of King David. But Rembrandt's Bathsheba appears to us first of all not as an idealised beauty, as a nude seductress is meant to be—instead, the wounded look on her face suggests a great human dilemma. While she is forced to betray her husband, she is only the victim of an abuse of power, and her contemplative, tormented expression exudes the quandary she is in, thinking of the fatal consequences her actions will entail.

Rembrandt's Jews never fitted the run-of-the-mill caricature of the Jew in European painting and literature. One of his most recognisable etchings is of his friend and neighbour, Menasseh ben Israel. Rembrandt lived on his street, next to the Pinto House, which belonged to one of the wealthiest Sephardi merchants, Daniel Pinto, with whom Rembrandt had a recurrent boundary battle. Walking today along Sint Antoniesbreestraat, which follows on from Jodenbreestraat toward the Centraal Station and the harbour, one imagines how the two men's paths must have crossed daily. From the tall windows of his studio in the attic of Rembrandthuis, where Rembrandt taught his students, one could see the house of ben Israel, one of the most scholarly Jews of his time, along with the homes of other prominent Sephardi figures. There are various accounts of the so-called friendship between Rembrandt and ben Israel. There was undoubtedly considerable interaction between the two men, for some of ben Israel's books were illustrated by his famous neighbour. But were they really "friends"? Or was it a relationship between a commissioning client and a painter?

Ben Israel was not the only Jew whom Rembrandt had been asked to paint. And the Dutch master was not the only artist hired by the Jews to depict their portraits and ceremonies. But Rembrandt was probably the most prolific of all the seventeenth-century Dutch artists who dealt with Jewish sitters and Jewish themes. One fifth of Rembrandt's portraits of men are of Jews. One of the earliest Dutch municipal records tells an amusing story about a commission for a painting that went wrong for the client, a moderately rich Jewish merchant, Diego D'Andrada. He had asked Rembrandt for a simple portrait of his daughter to hang in his house, and had paid most of his fee up front. But the extremely disappointed D'Andrada filed a complaint against the artist in 1654 at the public notary's office, saying the portrait looked nothing like his daughter. He wanted the artist to retouch it or change the style of the painting, which Rembrandt refused to do. We do not know what happened with this dispute, but it illustrates the kind of regular, even petty interaction Rembrandt had with his neighbours in the Jewish quarter. Did it amount to real friendship? There remain no specific details of Rembrandt's dealings with the Jews apart from the fact that he painted them and illustrated their books, in return for cash. Records show that Diego D'Andrada paid him an advance of 75 guilders, with the remainder to be settled when the painting was finished.

Many historians are sceptical specifically about the depth of Rembrandt's "friendship" with Menasseh ben Israel. Mirjam Knotter, a Rembrandt scholar who works at the Jewish Historical Museum in Amsterdam, has this view:

> Most of the "stories" about Rembrandt being a friend of the Jews started in the nineteenth century. The people of Amsterdam

thought, others have Rubens, we must have Rembrandt. Let's talk about Rembrandt, starting with, "He was such an amazing friend of the Jews." But there's no proof—in fact he fought with the Jews! It's a myth. The story was invented in the nineteenth century.[3]

Fight with the Jews he surely did. The most visceral of these disputes was his protracted legal battle with Daniel de Pinto over who should pay for construction material to shore up the foundations of their sinking houses on Sint Antoniesbreestraat, hastily built on a landfill on the manmade island of Vlooienburg fifty years previously. De Pinto took Rembrandt to the Public Notary Office, complaining that the artist was not paying enough for his share for the building work. He then withheld rent for Rembrandt's basement, which he was using to store tobacco. That left the Dutch master, already steeped in debt, enraged. Rembrandt had been leasing his basement to de Pinto and other Jewish merchants of the Jodenbuurt for storage since the damp subterranean cellar was no good for a painter and his work. The bickering between de Pinto and Rembrandt ceased only when the artist was declared bankrupt and his possessions confiscated. There are no records showing that he ever paid de Pinto.

What these stories prove is that Rembrandt's relationship with the Jews was conditioned by typical neighbourly behaviour— rows over the garden fence, disagreements on the party wall, nothing extraordinary to say that he went out of his way to befriend Jews. But what it does tell us is that he did not see the Jews as outsiders. Our records of Rembrandt's bickering with his Jewish neighbours do not bear the hallmarks of the anti-Semitic demonisation of Jews that had obsessed Christianity. The fact that these ordinary details of his contact with the Jews have survived also demonstrates the high frequency of everyday interactions in the Jodenbuurt between the Dutch and the fairly recent Iberian immigrants. Rembrandt's Jews were his creative inspiration and the source of his knowledge in Hebrew, which

1. Title page of Rehuel Jessurun's *Diálogo dos Montes*. This one-act play was performed in Amsterdam's first Jewish synagogue to the Beth Jacob congregation in 1624.

2. *Hof van den Baron Belmonte*, a typical canalside house on the Herengracht. Manuel de Belmonte is distributing alms to the poor. Engraving, Romeyn de Hooghe, c. 1700–05.

3. *Jewish funeral near Amsterdam*, featuring the tombstones of Isaac Uziel and Eliahu Montalto. The plot for the Jewish cemetery at Ouderkerk, Beth Haim, was bought in 1614. Etching, Romeyn de Hooghe, 1680.

4. Pages from Saul Levi Morteira's polemical work *Providencia de Dios con Israel* (undated). The chief rabbi, who led the Beth Jacob congregation from 1618 and the united congregation from 1639 to 1660, tirelessly preached Jewish orthodoxy in his sermons and writings.

5. and 6. Title pages showing the stamps of Menasseh ben Israel's printing press, which he founded in 1616 amid Amsterdam's booming publishing scene.

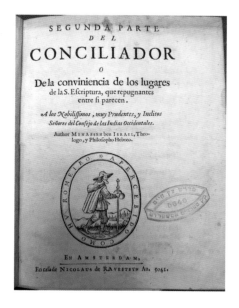

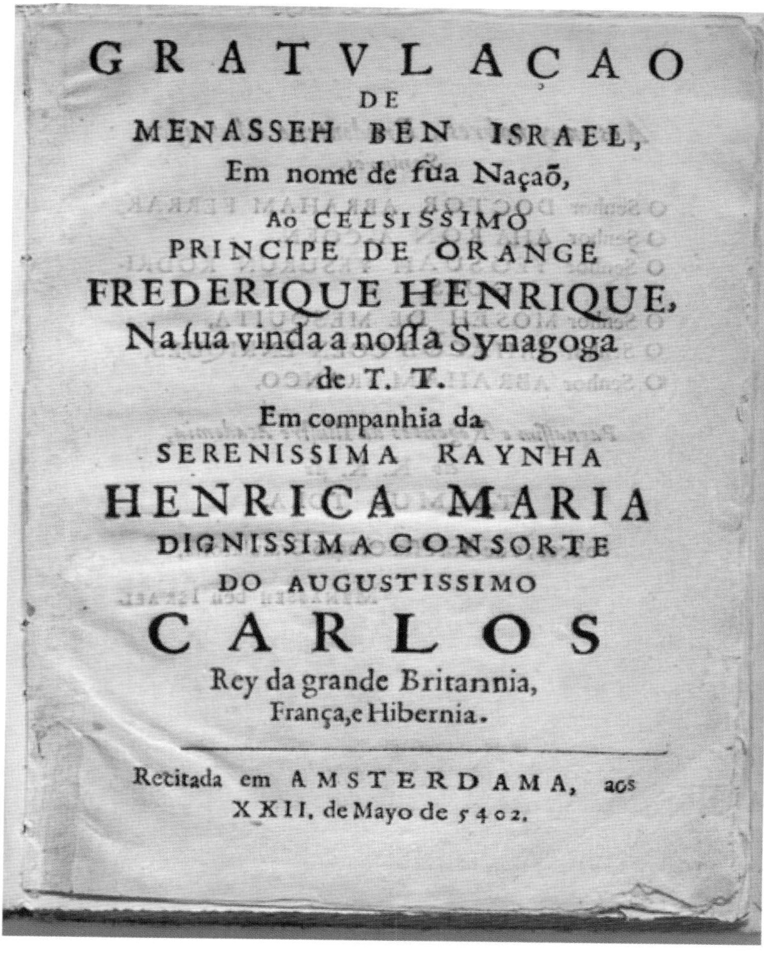

G R A T V L A Ç A O

DE

MENASSEH BEN ISRAEL,

Em nome de fua Naçaõ,

Ao CELSISSIMO
PRINCIPE DE ORANGE

FREDERIQUE HENRIQUE,

Na fua vinda a noffa Synagoga
de T. T.

Em companhia da
SERENISSIMA RAYNHA

HENRICA MARIA

DIGNISSIMA CONSORTE

DO AUGUSTISSIMO

C A R L O S

Rey da grande Britannia,
França,e Hibernia.

Recitada em AMSTERDAMA, aos
XXII, de Mayo de 5402.

---

7. Title page of ben Israel's ceremonial pamphlet celebrating the 1642 visit
of the Prince of Orange and Henrietta Maria, Queen of England, to the
Portuguese Synagogue.

8. Dedicatory poem for Amsterdam's new Town Hall (completed 1655) by Constantijn Huygens, who addressed the councillors as "Founders of the Eighth Wonder of the World". Later engraved by Elias Noski with the Hebrew tetragrammaton, YHVH, at the top.

9. *Letter by 24 members of Yeshuot Meshiho to hail Shabtai Tzvi as Messiah,* 1666.

10. *View of the Great and Portuguese Synagogues in Amsterdam.* The Ashkenazi Great Synagogue (left) was completed in 1671, the Portuguese Esnoga (right) in 1675. Gerrit Adriaensz Berckheyde, oil on canvas, c. 1675–80.

11. "The Glory of the Amstel and its Senate", as de Hooghe referred to his depictions of the new Esnoga. This gives a reverse view of the two synagogues facing each other, and shows the busy canal life in between. Etching, 1675.

12. *The Portuguese Synagogue in Amsterdam during the inauguration.* Romeyn de Hooghe, etching, 1675.

13. Cohanim golden washbasin showing the Judgment of Paris, commissioned by the Portuguese Jewish community. Abraham Warnberger II, 1670.

14. Phoenix seal of the United Congregation of Talmud Torah, on the Mahamad office carpet. The phoenix emblem, first used in Neve Shalom prayer books, reflects the survival and rebirth of the Portuguese Jewish community in Amsterdam.

15. *Ephraim Bueno, Jewish Physician.* Bueno was one of Rembrandt's neighbours in the Jodenbuurt (Jewish quarter). Etching, 1647.

16. *Moses Breaking the Tablets of the Law*, showing two tablets in the Jewish tradition, competent Hebrew lettering and a humanised Moses. Rembrandt, oil on canvas, 1659.

17. Illustrations to Menasseh ben Israel's *Piedra gloriosa*, showing Nebuchadnezzar's dream, Jacob's Ladder, David and Goliath, and Daniel's vision of four beasts. Rembrandt, etching, 1655.

Fig. 18: Hendrik Jacob Curiel, with his half-Indonesian wife, Apalonia Curiel-Jiskoot (far left), and two village women (c. 1930).

19. Newspaper article (last paragraph) reporting Hendrik Jacob's NSB record and arrest of his family members, before they were sent to an internment camp. *Vrije Stemmen*, 21 August 1945.

20. Death, on a tombstone in Beth Haim cemetery, Ouderkerk aan de Amstel.

21. Jacob's Dream, on a tombstone in Beth Haim cemetery, Ouderkerk.

22. The hand of God cutting down the Tree of Life, on a tombstone in Beth Haim cemetery, Ouderkerk.

he displayed so skilfully in his Old Testament paintings. As Steven Nadler says, "much of what we think about Rembrandt and his art stems, ultimately, from his decision to live there."[4]

The Jews were also his difficult, noisy neighbours, who disrupted his work with construction and lawsuits—apparently, during the year 1653, when de Pinto was overseeing the fortifications, Rembrandt produced just one piece of work: *Aristotle with a Bust of Homer*.[5] But some Jews might indeed have been his friends. He almost certainly got to know ben Israel and other scholarly Jews on a different, more congenial level. It is difficult to prove when the myth of "Rembrandt's Jews" came into popular imagination. The Jodenbuurt was called such simply because the Jews outnumbered the Dutch on this triangle on the Amstel River. Vlooienburg would later be connected to the mainland by filling in the canals, and Sint Antoniesbreestraat would be joined with Jodenbreestraat.

It was at 4 Sint Antoniesbreestraat, in a tall, narrow, gabled redbrick house with a network of subterranean cellars, that Rembrandt lived, taught his students, and produced his famous etchings and paintings. He was surrounded by both his wealthy Jewish neighbours and the Ashkenazi vagabonds who passed through his street peddling trinkets, begging or loitering on corners. From his top-floor windows, he could see the *Nação's* earlier synagogue, built in 1639, following Jacob Judah Leon Templo's drawings. Though a smaller structure, the old synagogue on the Houtgracht had an interior of similar design to that of the later, grander Esnoga. The Houtgracht synagogue of Rembrandt's day was immortalised in a 1662 engraving by Jan Veenhuysen, *Der Jooden Tempel of Sinagoge*.

From what survives of Rembrandt's dealings with the Jews, again what strikes us most is the ordinariness of these encounters between equal citizens. Mirjam Knotter agrees that Rembrandt had an amazing eye for the exotic. However, she reiterates that she is not convinced by the artist's "special relationship" with the Jews, a notion romanticised over the following two centuries— first by Dutch intellectuals who wanted their own Rubens, and later by the Jews themselves, who paid homage to the great Christian artist who had painted them without distorted physical features or insignia to set them apart, as had been the norm in Christian art for many centuries. Not only the Jews but also other subclasses of European society were typically depicted in a derogatory or special manner that accentuated their lower social status. The heretic appeared in yellow *sanbenito* with devil's horns, the prostitute in red, the Moors with the crescent moon—and the Jews as we know, with various physiognomic deformations and caricatured expressions.

Compare Hieronymus Bosch's Jew in *Christ Mocked (The Crowning With the Thorns)* from c. 1510 to Rembrandt's Jews, whether scruffy Ashkenazim or Sephardi nobility. Bosch's characterisation of Jesus' tormentors is grotesque, reflecting the virulent anti-Semitism of Catholics at the time. The man on the left has both a crescent moon of Islam and a yellow star of the Jews on his red headdress. His long, hooked nose is another identifying mark that inundated early modern Christian art. The Jew, if not beaky-nosed, was thick-lipped and his features bulbous. He had upturned eyes that exuded lust and greed. By contrast, Rembrandt's Jews portray the artist's unparalleled skills in conveying characters in mid-expression. He generously brushes them with humanism. The meticulous observation of mundane, joyful and pensive faces, in both his paintings and etchings, established his place as the most celebrated portraitist of his age. The richness of expression in his characters, the intrigue and penetrating, erudite eyes are all typical of Rembrandt's Jews.

Ephraim Bueno's illustrious pose on the stairs epitomises the security and comfort of the makers of the Dutch Golden Age, not the personified evil of the Boschian tormentor of Christ.

REMBRANDT'S NEIGHBOURS

Rembrandt's famous *Jewish Bride* emanates the softness of expression in a loving couple; the richness of the red and the brocade embellishments in their clothing denote their high social status. Many of Rembrandt's works identified with the Jews—in particular his work on the Old Testament theme—happened to be of sitters who were also Jewish. Another interesting feature of his "Jewish" work is the theme of suspended emotion: characters caught mid-expression. Look at the hesitantly positioned hands of the characters in *The Jewish Bride*—it is hard to know their relationship, the emotions conveyed by their hands and sideways glances. The painting freezes a certain equivocation in the interaction of the characters, the universal mystery that is beautiful when left unexplored. This marked a sea-change from traditional Western art using Jewish models. Other Dutch masters such as Jan Steen also painted Jews without specific derogatory iconography, but Rembrandt was the most celebrated artist of his time who broke free of the style that had mocked the Jews for centuries. His sympathetic portrayal made him popular among the Jews not only during his lifetime, but also many centuries afterward—gratitude to an eccentric artist whose humanism defeated Christian prejudice and made great art.

This seems to have led the Jewish imagination to run wild in later centuries, resulting in stories of a special relationship. But the ties between Rembrandt and the Jews of Amsterdam might well have been built only on the fact that the Jews often paid heftily for the portraits, paintings and etchings that show their daily life in Amsterdam. Or perhaps these artworks have simply recorded the way the Sephardim wanted to be portrayed, in grand houses with servants, dressed in their finest silk and jewellery. This was the first time that Jewish subjects, like their Christian Dutch contemporaries, could pay de Hooghe, Lievens, Rembrandt and others to document their rich lives and worldly possessions—and so instead of the deformed physiognomy of the past, we find opulent drapery, marble or chessboard floors, pearls and gold lace on women and girls; richly coloured gabardine and crisp, white cartwheel collars around men's contented faces; curiosities on the mantlepiece, to exhibit their seafaring ventures around the world.

Rembrandt received 500 guilders for a piece. Owning a self-portrait in the pre-photographic age was not a big deal, certainly not in the seventeenth century's mercantile milieu. Both the ordinary portraiture of Jews and the illustrations of special events, such as de Hooghe's *Circumcision Ceremony in a Sephardic Family*, were typical of the time. Those who could afford it would hire an illustrator as one would today hire a photographer or videographer for weddings, anniversaries and bar mitzvahs. One estimate proves how commonplace such work was: a recorded 5 million paintings were commissioned in the seventeenth-century Dutch Republic, for a population of 800,000. But amid the mass demand for realistic and popular art, Rembrandt managed to inject unique emotion and depth into his characters. Instead of prosaic portrayals of contemporary and Old Testament scenes, Rembrandt's renderings exuded panache and spirituality that transcended the mundane.

His Ephraim Bueno's mischievous eyes linger in the memory of the viewer, his relaxed posture on the stairs riddles one with questions of where he is about to go, what he is about to do. Is he going to a business meeting? Is he about to visit a patient, or receive visitors in his sumptuous living room? Will his Ashkenazi or African servant serve the guests refreshments? Did Rembrandt just catch him by chance on his way out? Compare this to the older Bueno by Jan Lievens: his eyes have become distant, and have lost Rembrandt's playful spark. The old man is sitting in a similar relaxed pose, but there is no impending tension. Lievens has not pained the moment of suspended action in a game of musical chairs—the sitter has posed for him. Like a photographer, Rembrandt waited for his subject to appear, followed them around and caught them in mid-action. It was this, as well as the deep humanism in his work, that established him as the most influential portraitist of the age.

A friend of the Jew? Probably, yes. But did he go out of his way to befriend them so that they could be sitters for his artistic creations? Probably not. He would hardly have been able to avoid bumping into them in the Jodenbuurt. On Saturday mornings, working in his attic studio, he could probably even hear the faint chant of the service coming from the synagogue on the Houtgracht. And across the street he would call out to Saul Levi Morteira and Menasseh ben Israel, the rabbis whose advice he might have sought for his Old Testament paintings. On his way out for a stroll along Damrak, if he saw his next-door neighbour Daniel de Pinto, he would probably quicken his pace to get away from the nagging tobacco merchant and his property dispute. These were Rembrandt's daily acquaintances, but, Mirjam Knotter says emphatically, "Rembrandt was not a friend of the Jews". "In fact some of his bad characteristics were blamed on the Jews. It was often said that he was affected by the Kabbalah!"

What about his love of the Hebrew language? Did he not learn from the rabbis, in particular from his friend and neighbour, Menasseh ben Israel? "He didn't really know Hebrew," explains Knotter. "In fact he made mistakes and in his painting of Moses with the tablets, the Ten Commandments are wrongly written." In any case, in those days Protestants often learnt Hebrew; Rembrandt's attempt at painting Hebrew letters was not out of the ordinary.

Having said that, in *Moses Breaking the Tablets of the Law* (1659), what we see first is the artist's attempt at depicting the delivery of the Ten Commandments to Moses, according to the Torah: in two tablets rather than one, as in Christian art, which had featured in churches all over. Rembrandt's Moses holds aloft the tables broken in two, the first five Commandments hidden by the second. Rembrandt either made a deliberate break from the Christian tradition, or he did so because it was easier to draw a two-part tablet on one canvas. But the most likely explanation is that he was truly influenced by the Jewish tradition, according to which Moses smashed the first set of tablets in his frustration to see his people worship a golden calf when he appeared from Mount Sinai. The first set of commandments was to do with man's obligation to God directly, the second, which remained intact, with man's duties to the world and its people. This is a strong Jewish message: by fulfilling ethical obligations towards one's fellow human beings, one can regain the Covenant with God. We know, we can see, that Rembrandt painted his Jewish neighbours with this same humanist message in mind.

"Affected by the Kabbalah" is probably not an exaggeration. Who wasn't, in the great age of messianism? Was that not what made Menasseh ben Israel the most famous Jew in Europe, bold enough to submit a petition to Christian theologians about Montezinos' rambling story of the mysterious Lost Tribes? Was the Protestant world not deeply enthused by the Judaica, Jewish studies, in order to find a direct link to the Bible? As well as Menasseh ben Israel, Aboab da Fonseca, among other influential rabbis, was a renowned Cabbalist. He had also been well known amongst the Dutch artists and Christian theologians, and was etched by Aernout Nagtegaal, when Christian interest in the Jewish mystical movement was at an all-time high, and the studies of Jewish tradition, Aramaic and Hebrew were introduced in departments of higher studies at the Dutch universities.

In order to appeal to this specialist interest of the Dutch elite, many artists attempted to use Hebrew letters in their Old Testament-themed work. The result was a new way of looking at the Jews and their language as had not been explored previously by any other European society. The Protestant world was fascinated by the fact that the Jews continued to conduct their religious services and their reading of the Bible in the original Hebrew. The Law of Moses could not be deciphered in all its nuances without first knowing the language in which it was written. Rembrandt tried to reflect this general Protestant view in his painting of Moses with the tablets, going back to the original sources and showing Moses bearing two tablets, as mentioned in the Old Testament, and, most importantly, normalising the Jews. Moving on from Michelangelo's Moses with horns, Rembrandt paints the prophet as an ordinary man with a scruffy beard and tufts of hair on his pate, his face showing the exertion one would naturally feel while bearing two stone tablets down a mountain in the desert. Moses' ordinary face exudes the most extraordinary pain as he carries the Law to mankind, led astray during his absence and worshipping a golden calf.

In the Protestant imagination, the golden calf embodied the intermediary priests and saints and rituals of the Catholics. The light around Moses' face is the light of the Protestant Reformation. Rembrandt's Moses interacted with God in person—the Calvinists wanted no artificial or human intermediary in order to reach God. The letters and words of the Bible were good enough for the true believers. In a way, then, Rembrandt's Moses is the Christian Reformation personified. His tormented expression reflects the angst of Reformed theologians battling the various Protestant sects within the Church as well as the clandestine Catholics. The glow in which his face is bathed is the glow of the supreme truth held by the Reformed Church: salvation through returning to origins, the bestowal of the Tablets of the Law.

The portrayal of the Jews and their biblical significance in this light established Rembrandt as the most important painter of Judaism. Jewish historians enthusiastically analysed him as the one who knew the Jews and their language best. Other artists had tried to draw Hebrew in their work before, but the script had been reduced to caricature, whereas Rembrandt's Hebrew was exquisite, near perfect. Mirjam Knotter's claim that "He even got it wrong!" is countered by historian Steven Nadler: "no other non-Jewish painter in history equalled his ability to make the Hebrew—real Hebrew—an integral element of the work." At least eight of Rembrandt's paintings display the script. It is true that, in his earlier work, the characters sometimes appeared to be a mock Hebrew, bearing only a loose resemblance to the true script. But by the time he painted *Belshazzar's Feast* in the 1630s, Rembrandt had become confident, and tried as best he could to prove his prowess, to show that he had learnt the language from the bona fide Jews on his street. The way he painted letters such as "aleph", "mem" and "pe" could be out of a print; their precision is extraordinary. Although his rendering of the letter "nun-sofit" appears to be a "zayin", this minor slip is understandable, as he was copying from a handwritten script. Here he copied the Aramaic–Hebrew words from Daniel 5, 25–31: *"mene, mene, tekel, upharsin"* ("numbered, numbered, weighed, divided")—meaning that God has numbered the days of King Belshazzar's rule, and his kingdom will be divided.

Since the eighteenth century, historians have been intrigued by the mystery behind Rembrandt's repeated attempts at perfecting the Hebrew script in his paintings. Who was the person who scribbled writings down for the artist to copy, the cryptic writing on the wall by God's hand in Belshazzar's banqueting hall? They almost certainly came from the city's Jewish community, and must have been a scholar, a teacher of Ets Haim, a rabbi even. The individual most often identified as Rembrandt's Hebrew teacher was Menasseh ben Israel, the etching of whose face is one of Rembrandt's most important pieces, setting in stone his position among the greatest portraitists the world had ever produced.

Much has been written about ben Israel's influence on *Belshazzar's Feast*, which is a prime example of Rembrandt's unique skills in capturing suspended motion. The banqueters' expressions appear as if they have just encountered the Medusa's head. The luminance on their petrified, shell-shocked faces encapsulate the force of the ominous, cryptic Hebrew warning on the wall of their imminent doom, written by a divine hand. The glowing letters illuminate the banqueters' fear, their disbelief at the prophecy that their days are numbered, as they knock over some sacred golden utensils stolen from the Temple in Jerusalem, the act that has brought about their downfall. It is widely believed that ben Israel, who was friendly if not friends with Rembrandt, helped the master with the Hebrew in this piece.

Even if he was not a friend, ben Israel must have been an important acquaintance of Rembrandt—otherwise, why would he have agreed to illustrate the rabbi's important messianic work, *Piedra gloriosa* (The Glorious Stone)? It is unlikely Rembrandt did it for money, because ben Israel was going through financial problems at the time of its writing. He was commissioned to draw four etchings for the book, at a moment when the artist himself was facing bankruptcy. His life was in disarray and so was ben Israel's, steeped in a leadership battle with the most powerful rabbi in Amsterdam, Saul Levi Morteira. Ben Israel published the work in 1655, as a response to the messianic quest of his own people and his Christian friends, who were curious to read a Jewish rabbi's explanation of the matter.

Rembrandt was thought to have been a believer, like most of his compatriots. His was an immensely religious period in world history, which had just witnessed the splintering of the old Christian faith and the emergence of the new. The religion of the convert can be laced with exaggerated piousness, in an effort to prove loyalty to the new faith. The more emphasis was put on the return to the original biblical text in order to reach God, the greater the demand grew for elucidation of the Bible on the painter's canvass. It became an all-powerful artistic theme. Apart from pandering to his rich Dutch Reformed commissioners, Rembrandt might also have considered his own salvation. Otherwise, why did he bother to perfect the Hebrew script? Demonstration of civil and neighbourly attitudes towards the Jews was also integral to the behaviour expected of a good Protestant. So when a neighbour, a scholarly Jew, asked him to illustrate a book that put forward arguments for the coming of the messianic era, in which Holland–Israel would play a crucial role, Rembrandt could not have turned him down.

The four frames illustrate the dream of Nebuchadnezzar, Belshazzar's predecessor, of the "great statue" and its interpretation by the Prophet Daniel. Another obvious reason why Rembrandt took on this job might have been the connection between these pieces and *Belshazzar's Feast*, which had been received with great acclaim in the Christian world. It would not be a wild assumption that Rembrandt did not want to miss the opportunity to create a prequel to his earlier painting. Besides, he might even have felt honoured to have been asked to make the etchings, when "Europe's most famous Jew", ben Israel, could have gone to others. Amsterdam was inundated with artists in the mid-seventeenth century. Every person of reasonable means owned one or more paintings.

The desire to acquire biblical images to hang on the walls of one's home was made all the greater by the fact that very few paintings from before 1566 had survived; this was when vicious iconoclastic attacks, known as *beeldenstorm*, purged the Dutch Republic of images, enacting literally the Second Commandment. This was one of the foremost manifestations of the views of the Protestant Reformation. Over the subsequent decades, it had led to a phenomenal rise in personal collections of art that embraced biblical stories. This work also helped the laity to understand the

Bible, since no saints or religious icons were now present as points of reference. A pious population would often commission religious art from northern Europe's numerous masters.

In the four etchings for *Piedra gloriosa*, first we see the feet of the great statue in Nebuchadnezzar's dream. A mighty stone severs its arms, belly and legs, which symbolise the past kingdoms where humanity was enslaved by evil tyrants. Then we see David killing Goliath, and Jacob has a dream of a celestial ladder with angels playing on it as his head rests on a smooth stone. These point to one and only one message: that the age of eternal, universal justice was well within view. Messianic salvation was not just a hypothesis, but a possible reality. In his book ben Israel codified this message: that the launch of a significant epoch had been deeply felt by the religious people of Dutch Jerusalem. For Rembrandt, *Belshazzar's Feast* was the fulfilment of the Prophet Daniel's promise, depicted in the etchings: that the days of the evil kingdoms were numbered. And to ben Israel's readers, the message could not have been timelier. The Catholic kingdoms, whose monarchs were the many Belshazzars, would be destroyed at the dawn of an imminent, messianic age.

Ben Israel had been dead for two years when Rembrandt painted *Moses Breaking the Tablets of the Law* in 1659, and had left for England two years before that. Who helped Rembrandt with his Hebrew this time, for the Ten Commandments? It seems he had almost perfected the language by this painting; the style exudes confidence, the Hebrew letter-end after each Commandment dropping with a long, confident brushstroke. The hesitant artist's cautious display of a rudimentary knowledge in *Belshazzar's Feast* had evolved into a deeper grasp of both the script and the Scripture. But the rabbi could still have been Rembrandt's teacher—the concept of the painting might already have been born before ben Israel left Amsterdam. Rembrandt might also have asked some of his other Jewish "sitters", such as

Ephraim Bueno, for help with the Hebrew. Whichever path he followed to learn to write correct Hebrew, he had almost mastered the art.

Ben Israel was gone, but the presence of the Hebrew language and the Hebrew Nation remained a constant feature in the artist's life. Rembrandt scholars have suggested the theme of the painting, and the idea of the particular posture in which Moses raises the tablets above his head, came from Rembrandt's visit to the synagogue on the Houtgracht. He must have seen the festival of Shavuot there, and the ceremony of Hagbahah, in which a selected team from the congregation opens and raises high the Torah scrolls, during the week-long celebrations of the giving of the Pentateuch to the Jews. Even if it was a deep interest in greater salvation according to the Calvinist doctrine that made Rembrandt one of the greatest painters of Old Testament-themed art, he also remains one of the most sympathetic depictors of the Jews.

None of his paintings or etchings tells us of the problems and arguments he had with Daniel de Pinto or other Jewish neighbours. His characters instead exemplify superior human traits: the graceful poise of the old man in an armchair, rabbis disputing the Law, the triumph of Mordechai, Moses bringing down the Law, Dr Bueno descending a grand staircase, a scholar in his study. Even the vagabonds in some of Rembrandt's tronies, thought to be Ashkenazi refugees, represent benign human emotions. The trauma of their recent exodus from central and eastern Europe was anaesthetised by Amsterdam's tolerance and religious freedom. And the memory of persecution of the older Jewish immigrants, the former New Christians, was transformed in Rembrandt's work into one of the greatest stories of human regeneration and rebirth.

These are the themes that Rembrandt's Jews convey to viewers. No other Christian artist before him had painted the Jews and Judaism in such a balanced, positive light. It is as though he wanted to use the stories of biblical tenacity among Old Testament characters to convey the Dutch miracle, the success story of facing a strong, hostile Catholic empire to the south. *The Triumph of Mordecai* (c. 1641), illustrating a simple Jew's victory over the powerful, evil idolator Haman, is a poignant metaphor for William of Orange's victory against Catholic Spain, which liberated the northern provinces that would emerge as the Dutch Republic. As we mentioned earlier, William of Orange, who led his people to freedom but did not live to witness their final triumph, was often likened to Moses. Having led his people across the Red Sea from Pharaonic bondage into freedom, he too did not live to reap the fruits of his achievement.

The use of the historic plight of the Jews to describe the struggle of the Dutch Reformed movement against Catholic Spain was popular among Calvinist regents and theologians, and this was reflected profoundly in the art of the seventeenth century. As we saw earlier, the Dutch liked to think of themselves, too, as the children of Israel, who were persecuted but always found God's providence. While the Jews were gearing up for the messianic revelation, their "first coming", the Protestants were excitedly predicting the possible year for the Second Coming of Jesus.

At a point when paintings and contemporary literature were giving unprecedentedly favourable publicity to the Jews living among the western nations, it seemed that the Dutch regents were lining up behind the Jews for guidance as to the exact nature of the final redemption. And since the scriptures demanded for this both good treatment and reinstatement of the Jews in the Christian nations where they lived, Rembrandt's art created a real sensation in his lifetime. Many in the Dutch Reformed Church saw Amsterdam as a place where the Jews would congregate before converting to Christianity and marching to Jerusalem. The future voluntary conversion of the Jews was very important for the Protestants, and Rembrandt's work clearly reflected their self-interested benevolence. For why on earth would they convert if they were treated badly? This was one of the reasons why the Calvinists despised the Inquisition. The Jews must be enticed, not forced or intimidated, into the fold of universal salvation under the Christian gospel.

The shared Judeo-Christian naming of Amsterdam as a "New Jerusalem" was probably the first battle for intellectual and religious ownership of a notion called Jerusalem. Not only was the city's central place in Dutch thought literally set in stone on the marble floor of the town hall, Amsterdam was also positioned as the centre of the world in seventeenth-century maps printed on Amsterdam's presses. Amsterdam was Dutch Zion to the Jews, while the Dutch also believed in their city's momentous biblical significance. Particularly after the arrival of Ashkenazi refugees in long beards and scruffy clothes during Europe's religious Thirty Years' War (1618–48), Amsterdam indeed looked like a sort of biblical theme park. The Dutch looked forward to an economic miracle, and the Jews, basking in that miracle, felt comfortable enough to hope for Israel. Amsterdam was the only city in seventeenth-century Europe where Judeo-Christian expectations merged: to reap greater material success and spiritual dividend.

The synagogue on the Houtgracht was routinely filled not just with members of the Jewish congregation, but also with gentile visitors curious about the people of the Old Testament and their intricate customs and rites. They would come to see the beautiful handwritten scrolls of the Hebrew Bible, wrapped in brocade and silk and held aloft during the service. Many Christians came to Amsterdam to learn about the Jews, and handbooks that were printed in the city taught them about Judaism. This overwhelming curiosity and desire for knowledge of the Jews was also embedded in the joint great expectation: that universal peace and rule of law would be established imminently, to last 1,000 years. No artist portrayed this millenarian hope as skilfully as Rembrandt.

Even the most vehement sceptics of his real intentions in obsessively portraying the Jews and the Old Testament would agree, as the art historian Shalom Sabar has noted, that the Dutch master was strongly influenced by the Sephardi community of his neighbourhood, a "carnival of nations" inhabited by figures considered to be straight out of the Bible. An artist, particularly a portraitist, seeks out unusual, strong, interesting faces. Rembrandt would not have become the master he was without the Jews around him.

Rembrandt died in 1669, two years before the Ashkenazi poor of his street would see their first Great Synagogue erected, and six years before the building of the magnificent Portuguese Esnoga, just a few hundred meters apart. Romeyn de Hooghe's famous etchings immortalised the great setting of the synagogues, which announced the presence of the Jodenbuurt's residents, old and new, as permanent. Rembrandt drew his neighbours looking like Dutch burghers, and now they belonged not just to the Republic, but also to their Temples in this great city. Art historians have often wondered how Rembrandt would have etched or painted the inauguration ceremony at the Esnoga, how his dry point would have rendered the chiaroscuro of the rabbis, the congregation, the guests and dignitaries under the light of the 1,000 candles that hung from the high ceiling, lighting the interior as they do today.

Even if he was not a friend of the Jews in his lifetime, the Jews of later centuries befriended Rembrandt. Jewish historians in their numerous tributes elevated the position of the Leiden-born artist who has left behind the world's finest collection of Jewish-themed art, embodying the fabulous century of the Jewish Golden Age on the banks of the Amstel. The historian of Jewish art Franz Landsberger, in *Rembrandt, the Jews and the Bible* (1946), wrote passionately about this Jewish gratitude toward the Dutch master: "in this era of European Jewish tragedy ... here was a man of Germanic ancestry who did not regard the Jews of Holland of his day as a 'misfortune', but approached them with friendly sentiments, dwelt in their midst, and portrayed their personalities and ways of life."[6]

Other Jewish historians of the twentieth century also chose not to see that more documentation was available of Rembrandt's petty fights with his Jewish neighbours than of his mythical "friendship" with and compassion for a select few Jews who may have given him Hebrew lessons. Mirjam Knotter holds the view that any extraordinary friendship between Rembrandt and the Jews would not have escaped the obsessive record-keeping of the Dutch. Yet the municipal archives from this period only have details of minor, trivial incidents, such as a burglary by a Christian thief in Rembrandt's cellar leased to Jewish tobacco merchants.

Whatever the nature of interaction was between Rembrandt and his Jewish neighbours, the artist's legacy and the stories of his "friendship" with the Jews, in particular with Menasseh ben Israel, lived on—not only during the great Jewish tragedy of the twentieth century, but also in the art and thought of the Amsterdam Jews in the immediate aftermath of Rembrandt's death in the late 1660s.

The crowns of the ark of the Torah scrolls in the Esnoga, built after Rembrandt's death, are decorated with the commandments in two tablets, as Rembrandt divided them in *Moses Breaking the Tablets of the Law*. As Rembrandt had painted the letters, gold on black stone, so did the synagogue artist, who hewed them in copper on black wood, in exactly the same five and five division. The Israeli art historian Shalom Sabar noted this interesting influence, remarking that the Hebrew letters, in their "colouring and appearance", are "reminiscent of [Rembrandt's] painting." It would not be at all outrageous to suggest that the person behind the inlaid copper letters on the black wood of the synagogue ark had used Rembrandt's piece as inspiration, even copied it.

This would not have been the first time a Jewish artist imitated Rembrandt's "Jewish art". When ben Israel published a second edition of *Piedra gloriosa*, he gave the job to a local artist from the Jewish community, Salom Italia. In his rendering—of much poorer quality—we see Rembrandt's four plates copied almost detail for detail, except for the fourth frame with its bodily representation of God, which is forbidden in Judaism. This depiction of God in the first edition might have been the reason why ben Israel commissioned a Jewish artist to copy Rembrandt. Asking one of Europe's most famous artists to tweak his own work would have been an audacious and undiplomatic act, the sort of thing that Menasseh ben Israel, the great negotiator-diplomat, stayed clear all his life.

11

THE *MAKOM*

"THE GLORY OF THE AMSTEL AND ITS SENATE"

"The Glory of the Amstel and its Senate" is how Romeyn de Hooghe described his famous etchings of the Esnoga's inauguration in August 1675. He was proud to have been asked to serve as the chief artist capturing this event in the awe-inspiring "builder's masterpiece", the most impressive architecture yet built on the Amstel, marking almost a century of upward mobility, unprecedented privilege and rare elevation of the Jews' status as the Hebrew Nation in a Christian country. By the start of the eighteenth century, Amsterdam had become the biggest and most important Jewish city in the world.[1] Jewish scholars came to Amsterdam to have their work published, as the city became the unrivalled centre of Hebrew and Yiddish book printing.

While this had been a tremendous success story, we must not forget that the former New Christians from Iberia, who had grown into the *Nação* and been recognised with their Ashkenazi co-religionists as the Jewish Nation, were thriving in Amsterdam within a self-governed Jewish community, rather than in a liberal Christian Dutch culture. As we know, while most rabbis including

221

ben Israel advocated better integration into Dutch society, they kept assimilation or acculturation at bay for as long as possible, fearing that the new faith of these former Catholics, who had been Jews for only two generations, would not otherwise hold.

In *Diálogo dos Montes*, Rehuel Jessurun presents the mountains' arguments before the judge, the biblical King Jehosaphat, that they are all equally qualified to be judged the best of all. The structure of Dutch society at the height of Amsterdam's prosperity was like the Mounts of Zion, Sinai, Olives, Hohar, Carmel, Gerizim and Nebo: with multiple parallel communities of settlers that held together the social seam. The city's magistrates, like Jehosaphat, heard the arguments and woes of the different communities before peacefully resolving their differences. The losing parties accepted the judgment and bowed their heads to the winner.

In a way, seventeenth-century Dutch society was a precursor to *verzuiling*, or pillarisation—the segregation of different religious beliefs and denominations, co-existing peacefully but not interacting at a social level. The pillars are social institutions, not individuals. The individual only matters so long as they stick with their particular institution of origin. Such a society could be built of different *zuilen*, with the inhabitants of various faiths not necessarily merging or learning about each other's cultures. Integration under *verzuiling* is only economic, not social. The Jew could do business with the Calvinist, without taking part in or being invited or obliged to attend Christmas and Easter festivities. Likewise, their Calvinist business partner would not need to learn about the Jewish holidays.

The Jews were under strict instruction from the Dutch Reformed regents to maintain their separate religious orthodoxy within the Jodenbuurt's autonomous structure. They were told, and the rabbis agreed, that this was essential for overall stability and people management. Each community, and not the central government, was in charge of maintaining law and order within it. This was a model also adopted by the Ottoman Empire, which kept different communities behind specific demarcation lines in order to exercise effective control over each of them.

Amsterdam became the *makom*, simply the "place", for the Jews to dwell in and be free. The Ashkenazim popularised the Hebrew word *makom* as the Yiddish *mokum*. As we know, this bedraggled people, fleeing persecution, pogroms and massacres in a middle Europe savaged by the Thirty Years War, were at first given shelter and charity by the city's well-established Sephardim, before they too grew into an independent and successful community in their own right. The Protestant authority also left them to be who they were: another deeply orthodox people. The two communities formed two important pillars of Dutch socio-economic stability.

All over Europe, Catholics and Protestants, Jews and crypto-Jews, Huguenots and gypsies, were being murdered or chased out of their homes, their properties and possessions confiscated wherever a community found itself a religious minority. Amsterdam offered everyone a safe haven—not only a refuge, but freedom to practise their religion. When the New Christians arrived from the Iberian Peninsula, they were allowed not only to live as Jews, but also to openly reconvert to Judaism, a religion historically treated with great suspicion, akin to apostasy. Its followers had been seen as those who murdered Jesus Christ. And yet, the New Christians of Amsterdam were given residency permits and full freedom to be Jews as early as 1616. The rest was history.

"Live and let live" requires a mindset practised by various societies in history, including the Ottoman Empire. It worked in the divided early modern societies, whose various strands did not meet at a grassroots level. In Spinoza's time, and even before, there was interaction only at an intellectual level, where artists met merchants and painted their portraits, philosophers met fellow thinkers and exchanged ideas, Christian theologians discussed the works of Jewish rabbis. But how many stories are there of Ashkenazi refugees and Dutch humanists mingling socially? We know of no interaction between Menasseh ben Israel and a Dutch fisherman, or any ethnic Dutch of lower status. The "friends" of Rembrandt were not the poor Ashkenazi refugees dependant on Sephardi charity, nor even the ordinary members of the synagogue; it was exclusively rich Jews with whom he mingled, quarrelled and made up, or didn't. Even in hierarchical feudal societies a certain amount of interaction took place between masters and servants. But in Amsterdam's pillarised structure, the Jews usually did not, and were definitely not encouraged to, have Christian domestic workers or nurses for their children. Sexual liaisons between the various ethnic groups were forbidden, in order to maintain "purity of blood" of the different segments.

I have heard from descendants of the *Nação* in Amsterdam that this system was necessary in the seventeenth century for the survival of a formerly persecuted minority. In a deeply religious world, one's faith identity was interlinked with one's ethnicity and nation. This categorisation of society along ethno-religious lines, and the concurrent live-and-let-live policy, meant that the former New Christians were able to rekindle their ancestral Jewish faith and Sephardi tradition—not just save it, but create a golden age for Sephardi Judaism in Amsterdam. Without the unifying force of religious orthodoxy among the Portuguese Nation, Sephardi Jewry would have remained scattered around the world, confined to isolated pockets of the Ottoman Empire, Italy and North Africa. The Jewish settlements in Brazil, Suriname, the Dutch East Indies and England would have remained an unattainable dream. A strict religious separation in a free land, rather than absorption of the lesser faiths into the dominant Christian religion, saved the New Jews from dissolution.

In other words, without it, had the Iberian immigrants all become Dutch, the *Nação* would not have been established in Amsterdam. Menasseh ben Israel would not have written *Esperança de Israel*. His book's message of hope for return to an ideological Zion would not have been translated into Hebrew by his printing press in Amsterdam, and would not have had its far-reaching ramifications for subsequent Jewish thought in Europe. From the banks of the Amstel River, it was transmitted via travellers' routes throughout the eighteenth and nineteenth centuries to what was left after many pogroms of the Russian and central European Ashkenazi communities. There, according to the "first historian of Zionism", Nahum Sokolow, the Sephardi ben Israel would be posthumously memorialised as "the bard" of modern Jewish nationalism. And among the Ashkenazim of middle Europe, the *Nação's* hope of Israel would metamorphose into a quest for Zion.

PART II

FROM RICHES TO RAGS

12

ABRAHAM PALACHE

STILL A WANDERING JEW

"I almost walk out of all those books about my ancestor. I'm still wandering, in modern times!"

Sipping coffee in the outdoor cafe at Entrepotdok, a canalside walkway along the old eastern docks, Abraham Palache reminds me again that he is the twentieth-generation descendent of Samuel Palache, the famous diplomat-rabbi from Fez, a typical wandering Jew of the seventeenth century. That first Palache of Amsterdam came to the promising, open and tolerant city to teach the New Christians Judaism, "to cure them from the Catholic epidemic!"[1]

His descendant Abraham is a Dutch Portuguese Jew and a world-renowned vaccinologist, working on influenza. His travels take him to most parts of the world, providing local solutions to a global disease. This wandering Palache of the twenty-first century says that it was not so straightforward, the story of tolerance and acceptance in the Dutch Republic. He looks at the glassy surface of the canal. Intermittently bypassing tourist boats slice through its calm water, decorated with a vintage flare and a theme in mind: to revive and continue the Old Amsterdam. The carnival of nations is still here, traversing the city's waterway, admiring its unique, manmade cityscape. The canals and their water flow are regulated centrally by a medieval system of dykes—so the level is never too high, never too low. Just as the city's authorities have ruled a richly mixed population coming from all over the world, allocating each group just the right amount of tolerance, just the right amount of freedom—not too much, not too little.

"They were autonomous as long as they stayed within the law. I think that's one of the characteristics of a successful community. They knew how to respect the municipal law—probably that has to do with their historical background. You had to always adjust, always make sure your neighbours don't get suspicious of your alien lifestyle. So on the one hand you depend on your neighbours for their favours not to point their fingers at you, and you're kind of tolerated, but on the other hand that brings responsibility."

Abraham says the Portuguese Jews very quickly mastered the art of showing respect for the extant law of the Dutch Republic, and that gave them refuge. The secret of the Amsterdam Jewish Nation's success lies in its ability to adapt. Its method of survival was to get a full grasp of the dynamics of Dutch society, and they were accustomed to this act: "They did it before, in all the societies they passed through on the long road of exile before coming here." The Jews knew they could not do anything that would cut short their stay, because there was nowhere else to go. On the long road of exile, they had lived in the Middle East, North Africa, Spain, Portugal, France, Italy, the islands off the Atlantic coast of Morocco. Their relative success in the Muslim world and the stability for several centuries in Muslim Spain taught them how to be flexible, how to comply with rules—even if that meant living under curfew at nightfall, in segregated quarters within walls, often with trade and other restrictions. Before the Seven United Provinces opened their doors in the late sixteenth to early seventeenth centuries, there were very few countries that would welcome Jews.

So, unsurprisingly, after they came to Amsterdam they quickly became an extremely flexible community, ever so obliging—because they were unsure how the Dutch Protestants were going to see these outwardly Catholic Iberians with Jewish hearts. Abraham says although the New Jews of the *Nação* then formed a strict orthodox community, they were very different from other Orthodox Jews in the Sephardi diaspora and the Ashkenazi pockets around Europe. The Amsterdam Sephardim stood apart, with unique characteristics distinct from those of the "oriental" Sephardim in the Middle East and the Muslim world. They enjoyed more flexibility and freedom in their outlook on life, one of the main reasons being the need for leniency from their leaders, to take into account the habits of these former Catholics. Religious rules were very important, but they were not set in stone. The Portuguese Jews tried to adapt to their history, and to the culture of their host society. Nowhere had Jews achieved greater success in their resettlement and starting over than in Amsterdam, their Dutch Jerusalem.

* * *

How, then, did the same city, after three centuries of extraordinary mutual growth and co-existence, transfer 140,000 of the Netherlands' Jews into the Hollandsche Schouwburg theatre on the eastbound tramline, before bundling them off to Nazi death camps?

Seventy-five per cent of the Dutch Jews perished there—the second highest percentage loss of a national population in Europe, after Poland, where the figure was 90 per cent. What happened, what was happening, during the century prior to

World War II? Until the end of the eighteenth century, although Amsterdam's supreme place in the world trade was waning, the Jews still had high status and enjoyed incredible privileges and good fortune both at home and in the Sephardi diaspora. It is puzzling to think that this "sanctuary", the Dutch Jerusalem, the finishing line at the end of a long, tempestuous odyssey, should have simply vaporised. Was the brief Jewish miracle in Amsterdam no more than a big historical accident?

After my conversations with Abraham and other descendants of the *Nação* in today's Amsterdam, I came away with the feeling that perhaps the migration of the New Christians to the Seven United Provinces was a chance arrival of a group of enlightened economic and political refugees, drawn by a virgin project of mercantilism in a brand new, anomalous entity called the Dutch Republic. There, they made unimaginable progress in a very short amount of time. Many of the descendants I spoke to said that the so-called tolerance of three centuries had been self-interested; that the Dutch Christians had only temporarily set aside the historic suspicion of and rivalry with the ancient Hebrews; and that, when the profit of the Golden Age was no longer there, and the much-impoverished Jews of the twentieth century did not bring in the wealth and resources their ancestors had, those old hostilities jumped right back in and found their familiar breeding ground in a Christian nation.[2]

Since the northern provinces had separated from the traditional monarchy, the Dutch Republic had never really established a true identity. It had no precedent upon which it could model itself. The regents were ruling a divided state, improvising rules as they went along. The States General's office was in The Hague, and from there they would issue a general decree on a particular matter, but the seven provinces that made up the Republic each exercised their own rules. Amsterdam was not the Dutch Republic, but this city that was in effect a city-state liked to think so. When the Jews were given freedom to live in Amsterdam and practise their religion, build houses of worship and a cemetery, other Dutch cities barred them not only from settling there, but even from staying overnight in public inns or visiting some of the cities for business. When Amsterdam was disrobed of the Dutch miracle that had kept it soaring above all other world cities, it came down to earth with a jolt. The interdependent trade connections of the merchant classes that had held in place the city's rich status quo began to crumble, and in less than half a century—by the middle of the nineteenth century—Amsterdam had already been far superseded by London.

The tolerance of the city was challenged by the intolerance of the provinces from which domestic economic refugees began arriving in the late eighteenth century. The Jews had by then been well integrated into Amsterdam's social and intellectual fabric, and in 1796 received their Emancipation, equal citizens' rights, which meant that no guilds or restrictions could stop the Jews from working in any area, including government offices. There are various theories, some of which we have discussed, but still—what took the Dutch so long to assign this fundamental right to the Jews? If the French Revolution of 1789 had not unleashed in western Europe the magic words of liberty, equality and fraternity, the Dutch perhaps would have waited even longer.

The answer is deeply rooted in a historical reality: that, until the eighteenth century, there was no such thing as individual citizenship for everyone, as society had a corporate structure. It was only after the French Revolution that the category of individual citizenship was introduced into European thought. After France in 1791, the Netherlands was the second country to give Jews equal citizenship. It took many more decades for others, including Great Britain, to arrive at that point. But the question lingers: why was it France, and not the Dutch Republic, with its pioneering ideology of tolerance and liberty of conscience, that was first?

The reasons are manifold. We could safely say, without going into detail beyond what this book sets out to explore, that both sides in the Dutch Republic were in agreement with the status quo: to keep the parallel institutions, pillars, or corporate structures, running side by side, as had been the case since the late sixteenth century when the Seven United Provinces became a republic. The separation of society into autonomous religious segments had originally been devised by the Dutch regents to keep order between Catholic renegades and Dutch Protestants. It was institutionalised later for effective and economical governance—an early model of decentralisation. And for the Jews, the system worked very well. It was hugely encouraged by the *parnassim*—the leaders of the Mahamad board of wardens—to protect both the integrity of the *Nação* and the power that the rabbis exercised over the community to maintain its orthodoxy.

When assimilation happened, you got heretics like Spinoza, who threatened to wipe out the Jewishness of the community with the virus of scepticism. The rabbis did not want the Jewish Nation to join the wave of this early modern European vice. The New Christians had not suffered for centuries before re-establishing their true Jewish identity and community in Amsterdam for it to be wiped out again by a new fad in the Christian West. Full citizenship was feared, as it would have meant an end to the rule of the *parnassim*, and so the rule of the *halacha*. The rabbis resisted it right up until 1796.

With the breakdown of the old system and the dissolution of the Mahamad, chaos unfolded. Though it was not at first visible as such, it was there. Freed from the communal religious and cultural grip, the Jews were now equal by law to the Dutch, and could join any profession they liked. But generations of constraints and the resultant lack of experience or precedents stunted the Jews' initiation into the numerous professions that now became available to them. This also created professional alienation. Before, there had been separation, which was different from mistrust and envy. Now there was suddenly increased competition, and with this came jealousy. The Dutch had been suspicious of the Jewish merchants' wealthy status before, but in a way understood or even accepted, coming from their long familiarity with social stereotypes that linked the Jews with financial dealings. Now, mainstream society was no longer exclusively Dutch Reformed—anyone could become anything. There were Jewish doctors, lawyers, professors, retailers.

As the economy declined steadily, and then steeply following the bad performance of the Dutch East India Company in the last decades of the eighteenth century and its final loss in 1800, the 1796 Emancipation led to further transformation in the fate of the Dutch Republic and its Jews. Liberty, equality and fraternity served a big blow to the much-cherished orthodoxy of the Amsterdam Jews when compulsory secular education was introduced for poor Jewish children. In 1806, it was ruled that the Jewish schools were to teach the general curriculum alongside the Jewish one; they could continue to operate and even received state funding. This lasted until 1857, when the Netherlands decided no longer to fund separate religious schools. The Jewish Nation dissolved them and sent the children to state schools. Did this sudden, and to some extent forced, assimilation by the Dutch authorities have an adverse effect on communal relations? Did resentment continue secretly, for a century, before Nazism brought it all out in the open? Did the general Dutch population resent their Protestant children having to share classes with the new Jewish intake and come face to face with their esoteric traditions—circumcision, fasting, the Passover week of unleavened bread, the kosher diet, the Saturday Sabbath?

Parallel to these questions, more recent scholarship into the Dutch Shoah or Holocaust has also revealed a "Dutch Paradox":

the number of victims, much higher than in any other western European country. This new scholarship asks how the Netherlands managed to keep its tolerant reputation for so long, when the statistics of the Shoah indicate the contrary. One of the ways to understand the historical dynamics behind the high number of casualties among the Jewish population is that the Jews were so well assimilated into the Dutch society at the time of the Nazi occupation that both they and the general Dutch Christian population were in disbelief: the tragedy that was to happen so fast over the next five years was beyond everyone's imagination.

The historian Anna Hájková talks about a Second Dutch Paradox, which examines the considerably low number among the deported Dutch Jews who survived, compared with, for example, Jews from Czechoslovakia or Salonica who were sent to the camps. "The percentage of Dutch survivors was 1.48 percent, in contrast to 10.3 percent for the Czech Jews. The Dutch Jews had a strikingly low survival rate. Even the Jews of Salonika, who spoke no German and were unaccustomed to the Central European climate, had higher survival rates: 2.52 percent."[3]

Hájková's research argues that this second Dutch exception can be understood through the Dutch Jews' specific adaptation to the camps, their withdrawal and sense of passivity. This "regressive mode" goes back to an earlier time, she argues, because Jewish assimilation in the Dutch Republic was very different from that in France or central European countries. Traditionally what the Dutch tolerance created was a fairly isolated, albeit independent, community, with little or limited contact with the wider "gentile" society. As a result, the Jewish Nation had "only little external experience, war and anti-Semitism."[4] Perhaps the Dutch Jews, even after being deported to Westerbork transit camp and from there on to the killing centres all over Europe, were still in disbelief that this was actually happening.

We could project these possible scenarios onto the events leading up to World War II in order to understand the inexplicably cold-blooded collaboration of certain sections of Dutch society that gave away the Jews to the Nazis. The commendable Dutch Resistance could not fight an invisible force that had been eating away at society from its very core. The early setting of the pillarisation of the society created a situation ensuring that social divisions were camouflaged by the many cloaks of toleration. The *verzuiling* was a significant factor behind the isolation in the camps of the Dutch Jews, who, historically had grown alongside, rather than with, the mainstream society surrounding them.

The breakdown of the old social structure with the collapse of the economic miracle also seemingly took the last layer of decency from a generation whose ancestors had grown up set apart from their neighbours by a tough set of restrictions founded on the law of segregation. The exposure was so inglorious that it embarrassed and shamed the remainder of Dutch society, as it watched with powerlessness the dalliance of the depraved *zuil*, segment, with xenophobia.

At the apogee of the Jewish Nation's fulfilment in the Dutch Republic, the Portuguese Jews built their magnificent 1675 temple-synagogue. It was a testament to their total and perhaps, following the disappointment of Shabbatai Zvi, even ultimate attachment to their Dutch Jerusalem, to Israel–Holland. This was not only the heyday of the Sephardim in the Christian state; it was also where the Ashkenazi Jews settled comfortably and built their own Great Synagogue. Not as ostentatious as the Esnoga, it was still flashy enough to show the good fortune that these formerly destitute war and pogrom refugees had made in Amsterdam, their *makom*—the "place" that they called home.

During the ignominious 1940s in Dutch history, when the occupying German soldiers destroyed, looted and vandalised the Great Ashkenazi Synagogue, the Portuguese Synagogue was spared. The Nazis, in an evil twist of their dark tale, marked it for a grisly purpose: this was where the Nazi commander, Ferdinand aus der Fünten, had first wanted the Dutch Jews to be assembled before their deportation. But the plan was later cancelled—the tall windows, designed after Solomon's Temple, made the building a target for the nightly Allied bombardments, as it was impossible to hide the flame of even a single candle lit inside. The windows were too numerous and huge to be blacked out, the interior too cavernous to be used as a garrison. It was cold, without power or a heating source, and could not be used as a detention centre or for any other purpose. There are also other disturbing theories, which will be discussed later, as to why the Portuguese Synagogue was spared from Nazi vandalism. They left the building alone, and did not ransack it as they had the Ashkenazi house of worship.

The Jewish detainees were held instead further east, near the docks and right by the tramline, at the Hollandsche Schouwburg theatre, nicknamed the Jewish Theatre. This is where some 3,000 men, women and children would be gathered every week, before their final journeys to various camps. The theatre had a capacity of 300—it is hard to imagine the conditions in which the Dutch Jews spent their last days before being bundled into the weekly trains. From the Hollandsche Schouwburg, trams would take them to a train station; from there, most of the Jewish captives would be brought to the transit camp of Westerbork, some to Vught. Carrying selected inmates from the transit camp, further trains would depart for Amersfoort, Herzogenbusch, Bergen-Belsen, and Auschwitz-Birkenau.

This was the dismal coda to the incredible story of the most commercially and intellectually self-made Jews in modern history—in the city that they had believed was their Dutch Jerusalem, in the theatre about which they had been so passionate since they began their new life in Amsterdam. How ghoulishly discordant the allegorical *Diálogo dos Montes*, performed in their first synagogue in 1624, would sound in the 1940s Jewish Theatre of Nazi-occupied Amsterdam. Jessurun's Mount Gerizim accepts Mount Sinai as the victorious mountain chosen by the judge, Jehosaphat, because that was where the Law was given to Moses:

> Gerizim: *Sovereign thrones from which the word descends,*
> *Bestowing wisdom and authority,*
> *To be observed to all eternity,*
> *The highest, purest truth man apprehends...*

And here is how Jehosaphat replies:

> *In memory of that miraculous story*
> *Enacted there, to your illustrious height*
> *Laurels, diadems, crowns are ever due.*[5]

There were no laurels, diadems or crowns for the inmates of the Hollandsche Schouwburg. After an illustrious performance of over three centuries, the leading actors in the Dutch miracle were murdered in just three years: 1942–5.

As the Netherlands and the world were left soul-searching, wondering whatever had gone wrong with the famous Dutch tolerance, 5,500 Jews crept back into the ghost city, to the macabre, empty Jodenbreestraat, to find traces of their old lives there. If Spinoza had been alive then, would he have been wagging a finger at the pathetic last numbers of his people who had excommunicated him, saying, "I told you so," and that mutually exclusive societies are ultimately self-destructive? Maybe not. He was a recluse, and the exclusivism of his own community had so pained him that the dispirited young philosopher had never looked back after being ejected from it.

Those Spinoza felt closer to, the Christian humanists—what would they have done? Would they have identified and neutralised the third force that had not only shaken the foundation of the Dutch tolerance, but shamed it, obliterated it? They would not have been able to isolate it. What pillarisation of society also does is to give perfect alibis to those who, after all misdemeanours, wish to retreat back into their ethno-religious cloister, their hideout. To punish the individual perpetrators of wrongdoing, one would have to punish the entire *zuil*.

* * *

I have invited Abraham Palache to breakfast. We meet on a summer morning in Entrepotdok, eastern Amsterdam, close to the old Jodenbuurt and a stone's throw from the Resistance Museum. The museum, which has a massive Star of David on its façade, deliberately displays the value of Dutch humanism on which the Netherlands prides itself. The Resistance was strong, says Palache, "but do you know why they're making such a big deal over a little girl, who became an icon of Dutch Resistance?"

He is of course talking about the most famous Jew of Holland, Anne Frank. "They're trying to hide the shame of World War II," says Palache. "Otherwise, why should the Dutch tolerance focus so hard on the tragedy of a little Jewish girl who didn't even survive?" The ineptitude that was there, says Palache, the failure to locate the third force that had been in action for some time and which had succeeded in obliterating the city's almost four centuries of Jewish presence, was too much to be reckoned with by the Dutch liberals. What, then, is the moral of this tragic story? I ask Abraham, whose ancestors first set foot in Amsterdam in the 1600s. Is there a lesson to be learnt? Is Dutch society still functioning on a dark legacy of segmentation? Live and let live?

Abraham says that Amsterdam's Sephardi community today continues to adapt, to merge host cultures and cultures of origin. The Jews who originated from the Portuguese Nation in the seventeenth century and who live in today's Amsterdam have preserved that legacy of versatility and a liberal attitude to life. "At least that's what I'd like to believe. But it's hard to prove—because we're so few left. We're 650 members at the Esnoga, 200 families, and only a handful, sixty maybe, are active in the community life." Abraham Palache has been a member of the *parnassim*—or what remains today of that old board of synagogue wardens—for thirty years. What motivated him to get involved was the desire to rebuild the community, to reconstruct its broken morale, to try to bridge the postwar period and modern times.

One of the difficulties in keeping the community in Amsterdam has been the *aliya*, literally the 'going up'—the phenomenon of young people leaving for Israel. For the survival of the community, this is a problem, says Abraham. But, at the same time, it is a natural evolution. It would have been something else, if not Israel. "The most important thing is, they are happy, they are in a place where they feel more comfortable." At the same time, Abraham agrees, the modern State of Israel has put an end to the old diasporic way of life. Intermarriage with non-Jews, the rampant secularism of the West, lack of community life especially in urban centres—all have contributed to the dwindling number of Portuguese Jews in Amsterdam. "Whether we like it or not, the community is dying out."

At the same time, there have been some interesting intercontinental movements of Sephardi Jews. Most of the young Portuguese Jews in the Netherlands move to Israel when they finish college, but many Eastern Sephardim—from Israel, Morocco, Iraq—have in recent years relocated to the Netherlands, to become part of the old Sephardi congregation. They have agreed, voluntarily, to accept the rites and rituals of the Western Sephardim. "The Amsterdam community is still surviving, but not totally with its original descendants. That is extremely interesting." Abraham says that he is happy for the community to grow in this way, accepting other Sephardi Jews without a Portuguese background, into the congregation. "We have to do this, for the sake of survival!" It is not very different from when the burgeoning Amsterdam *Nação* of the 1600s needed the old Sephardim from the eastern diaspora, and even the Ashkenazi refugees from middle Europe, to grow as a strong religious group. Then as now, it was important to enhance the Jews' demographic ratio to protect them from dissolution.

As part of the postwar generation growing up in Amsterdam, Abraham knows first hand the pain and frustration of being a tiny, diminishing community. The decline started with his parents, during the war. His father's battle to protect the community from disintegration continued during and after the conflict, when he returned from Buchenwald. Abraham tells me that he himself joined the *parnassim* to pick up from where his parents had left off; he is committed to reviving the community. The *Nação* must live on, in spite of the memory of the recent genocide, assimilation and *aliya*. His parents' generation suffered the pain of losing all, when the ground beneath their feet just caved in overnight; when it seemed that Dutch tolerance had taken a nosedive.

As Abraham goes on talking, I try to conjure up a picture of his father, the legendary boy, during the Nazi occupation. Abraham's father diverted the Nazi commander in charge of Jewish extermination in Amsterdam, Ferdinand aus der Fünten, from his intention to use the Portuguese Synagogue as an assembly point for the Jewish deportees.

> He talked to aus der Fünten, who visited the Esnoga and wanted to use it for that purpose. My father was only fourteen or fifteen, and was working with the fire brigade to protect the synagogue. My father's story went that he talked to the Nazis about the difficulties of stopping light from coming in through the tall windows, which would have made it a target. He also pointed out the fact that it had no electricity, which prompted aus der Fünten to abandon his second plan to use the building as an army barracks. However, my father

was soon sent to the concentration camp, Buchenwald. My mother ended up in Auschwitz.

Abraham's parents had known each other before the war, and met again after they came back. The once rich and numerous community was reduced to a handful. 107,000 Dutch Jews— 80 per cent of the Jewish population—were sent to camps. Only 5,500 came back. Many moved elsewhere after the war ended, to other European cities, to Palestine, to the USA. Those who came back immediately after the liberation restarted religious services at the still-standing Esnoga, almost straight away. The services have continued to this day. This was a feat of remarkable resilience, says Abraham. It was a major task to keep going, with so much loss, so much pain. There were concerns about the upkeep of the building—a large one in need of constant care, when the community had no resources. So they started fundraising to keep the Esnoga in good shape. To the few thousand returnees of the Holocaust in postwar Holland, the Portuguese Synagogue and the ruins of the Ashkenazi synagogue on the corner of Meijerplein and Mr. Visserplein represented what was left of the Jewish Nation. The fact that the Esnoga remained standing, when most other buildings in the area had been destroyed, seemed like a miracle. The surviving Portuguese Synagogue was an important reminder to the world of the Amsterdam Sephardim's full claim to belonging in the former Dutch Jerusalem.

The postwar generation struggled to put in place an infrastructure for education. There was no curriculum, no books, nothing that could help them to continue with the old Jewish education system. They started Hebrew and religious classes wherever they found a place that could be used as a temporary school. It was just like the early days in the 1600s, when the New Jews were enrolling at ad hoc education centres to learn Hebrew and the Torah. Next, they elected a rabbi, Salomon Rodrigues

Pereira. They started rebuilding and reuniting the *parnassim*. They had just survived a war that had nearly annihilated the entire Dutch Jewry. It became of paramount importance to the Sephardi community to restore its Portuguese identity, and the only way that could be done was by rejigging memory: rewriting what could be salvaged of the rich tradition and rites, and passing that on to the young. Like a phoenix, the symbol of one of the first synagogues in Amsterdam, the lost generations were rising from the ashes of destruction.

The August sun is bright and the morning is luminous; the atmosphere in the outdoor cafe is so relaxed that it seems unnatural to hear about the darkest days in the life of a once glorious community. Abraham Palache has a strange smile on his face, an awkward one, as he goes on talking in a calm, composed voice. "The community was diminished. My mother used to say, the most painful days for the Jews in postwar Amsterdam were the high holidays. Yom Kippur, Simchat Torah. In the Esnoga, she saw all the empty seats around her."

There is a long pause. We hear the buzz of the cafe, the Sunday morning crowd enjoying their breakfast. There is no easy way to deal with what Abraham is describing—"the death of a bustling community"—while sitting in a place that appears to be the exact opposite. The liveliness of the cafe makes this recent, disturbing chapter in the Netherlands' history seem out of place. How was it possible for a whole portion of this society to be ejected overnight, never to return? The Esnoga will have seemed haunted, to Abraham's mother and others who were lucky enough to come home. The rebuilding task was and has been an uphill struggle since. How do you reunite a brutally displaced, demoralised people? Before the very eyes of Abraham and his generation, the *Naçáo* is disappearing from Amsterdam. Can anything be done about that?

Abraham says the Mahamad will never tell youngsters not to move to Israel. But it does hold regular services and celebrate all the festivals at the Esnoga, to engage the younger generation. It is difficult to generate the same kind of interest as the synagogue historically did when it is without its own school, without a systematic approach to spread Jewish Sephardi education. The war broke the continuity, dissolved the elements that constituted the *Nação*.

Some of the community's leaders feel that the only thing they can do now is to try and make the young people learn more about their history by inviting them to take part in Sephardi ceremonies and their accompanying social events, such as bar mitzvahs and circumcisions. Another significant phenomenon determining how the new generation sees its religious and historic affiliation with the *Nação* is the secularism that has swept European society. And this is where the internal strife comes in—how orthodox can the community still afford to be? Shouldn't the *parnassim* make concessions for modern, secular behaviour? Must they not consider the younger generation's need to assimilate, even if it comes at the cost of diluting what is left of the old religion? Yet there are conservative elements that would not offer greater leeway to make community membership more attractive. It is a difficult choice: how would you protect the old religion if you allowed full assimilation? The Amsterdam Sephardim only survived so long—and controlled the course of Sephardi history in early modern times—because they controlled their own affairs and, as we have discussed, assimilation was never fully encouraged by the rabbis.

But now, says Abraham, "we have to survive, and for the sake of survival, we need to be flexible. The internal strife that we have now is all about conservatism versus liberalism." Even in the seventeenth century, there were rabbis who went far enough, and were flexible, even empathetic enough to understand the difficulties that the New Jews were going through. Many of them were still Catholics at heart, while practising as Jews outwardly and socially. The rabbis knew it, but they did not give up. One of the most "cosmopolitan", outward-looking rabbis was Abraham's most celebrated ancestor, Samuel Palache. "I revisit the time often—what I like about it is the environment in which the Jews were living then. I can very clearly see the struggle and how the community tried to survive. I am a biologist, I can understand very well that all they did was to do their best to *survive*—this is the most basic human trait, trying to survive!" Their incredible success story was an unanticipated bonus.

Abraham thinks that much of it—the art of survival—is the same today. But the players have changed; we are living in a different time. This is why he says he keeps going back to his first ancestor in Amsterdam, and Palache's community: the Beth Jacob and Neve Shalom congregations. Because it is not just about history; this is how the New Jews, and other immigrants in other places, settled and developed. Their basic struggle was to protect their communal and religious identity, because it was so very different from what the society they came to represent. Calvinist society was deeply suspicious, if not outwardly hostile, to anyone arriving from Catholic Europe. The New Christians' new Jewish identity was crucial in saving them from the glare of the mainstream Protestant culture.

What happened with the creation of Israel, says Abraham, is that Judaism has ceased to be the identity that its followers struggle to protect. Now that they live in a Jewish State, the identity they are attached to is Israeli. The nature of the Jews' struggle for survival changed drastically after the war. The former Jewish Nation of the Dutch Republic, as well as other diasporic Jews, can feel at home in the modern Jewish State; the religious identities that once linked them to their old "nations" are lost. Is Abraham sad about it? No—he cannot and will not fight against the necessary evolution of societies. "Progress, human history is not about staying still, it is about moving on, about finding new scopes, new breakthroughs." Samuel Palache, and other seventeenth-century Sephardim who came to Amsterdam, understood this recurring pattern. However, the wandering scientist of the twenty-first century has chosen to remain in Amsterdam, when many of his community including members of his family have emigrated to Israel.

Nonetheless, the question that we ponder, sitting on the canalside and watching a superbly well-organised society, is how the Dutch Calvinist–Portuguese Jewish relationship could have created such a remarkable era. I have established throughout Part I of this book that the conditions of acceptance and cooperation were primarily based on self-interest, but there must have been other, uniquely Dutch factors that could not be found elsewhere in Europe. Why here? And why was it in just one city that the Sephardim wanted to be, where they wanted to be reincarnated as the *Nação*? They had successful communities in Venice, Salonica, Fez and other North African cities, but none compared to Amsterdam's Sephardi culture, which flourished during three glorious centuries, excelling in economics, art, philosophy and diplomacy.

I have heard many times that it was a historical accident. What else? "The answer must be in the nature of the Dutch, the way they developed as a people. The Dutch in a way made it possible for it to happen." Abraham is briefly distracted by the waiter asking if we want more coffee. We have long finished our cappuccinos. On a Sunday morning, with clients queuing up for breakfast, we are probably not good for business. We quickly order two more coffees with croissants. The waiter vanishes inside, leaving us with a pleasant enough smile. It is hard to tell if we will still be welcome after we have finished our second cups.

"We—my ancestors—could thrive, because the environment let them thrive. So there was an interest from the locals, the Dutch mentality was such, the need of one group fitted the need of the other." That relationship built on mutual needs survived all these centuries, until the recent unspeakable tragedy. What happened, then? What went wrong in the 1940s, to mark the Netherlands in the history of the Holocaust as the nation to see the second highest number of Jews sent to death camps?

This is a question I probably should not bring up, not with so many happy faces around. But I want to know. I have been impatient all morning to put this to Abraham, as soon as he started talking about the war and his father's role in saving the Esnoga by deterring the Nazis from using it as a deportation point. Although I could not find any historic documents about this episode, others in the community vouched for it. His father's story is a living legend among other wartime stories of heroism and resistance in the Netherlands. Before the hovering waiter offers us more caffeine, I ask Abraham what in his view is the reason that 75 per cent of the Netherlands' Jews were hunted down by the Nazis in the cities and provinces, and assembled in Amsterdam for deportation.

It was due to the Dutch obsession with record-keeping, he tells me. The names and lists of various communities were well documented, and they were readily available in the municipal offices. So when the Nazis came to single out the Jews, although the Dutch Jews looked no different from the Dutch Christians, they could locate every house where Jews lived and every workplace where Jews were employed. An extensive list with personal information on every individual was held by the authorities, and it was a damning register, because every detail of every Dutch person's religious and family background could be found there. I hear a nervous laughter from Abraham. To the others we must have appeared to be enjoying our Sunday breakfast, just like everyone around us, with trivial, social chatter. We were sitting in the sun earlier, but it has moved from us, as the morning has lapsed into noon. In the shade, the breeze from the canal feels cool; I long for the warmth again.

"It was the Dutch mentality of documenting everything and obeying the law that was behind the capture of almost every Jew in the Netherland by the Nazis. There was resistance, certainly there was resistance, but it was amazing that people just let go."

"Let go" of what? Resistance, their resolve, the Dutch tolerance? Were the occupying Nazis synonymous with a "law" that the law-abiding Dutch just could not go against?

"On the other hand," Abraham adds, "it is very dangerous to speculate, but let's say, you didn't get too involved—you were very tolerant, then you just looked the other way. Now I don't know if that is essentially the Dutch mentality, but I think there was something similar that we saw during the war. There was definitely indifference among a large section of our society." There was also order, Abraham says, in the most disorderly of circumstances. The country was under siege, but the trains were running on time. Every week, one particular tram would stop in front of the Hollandsche Schouwburg and it would be loaded with human cargo, bound for Westerbork. "What I find more shocking is the way the Dutch government behaved after the war—which was morally very incorrect, but legally very correct! That is the root cause of many of the problems the Jews faced."

Abraham bursts into full-blown laughter. I look at him, and look up as I try to take in the bitter sarcasm. We are sitting very close to an old, perhaps late-eighteenth- or early-nineteenth-century dockyard crane, with a little chamber attached at the top for the operator. It must be one of the listed structures on Entrepotdok. The former merchants' houses that line the canal are very tall, with smaller windows on the higher floors and huge glass windows at ground level—they must have been shops for retail merchandise, or just storage spaces for goods before they were sold and distributed to retailers. Did any of the buildings belong to the city's Jewish residents?

The glass-fronted living rooms start to show signs of activity among late risers on this weekend morning; some have slid the doors fully to one side, revealing their entire interior. They just go about their chores, putting the kettle on, making coffee, pulling the small breakfast table closer to the pavement so they can take in the happy Sunday atmosphere without having to step outside. I remember reading somewhere that the Dutch would never draw their curtains during the day. Indoor and outdoor lives become one, and I feel struck by guilt at my foreign, voyeuristic impertinence. One is not supposed to look, and yet, during the coming weeks that I shall spend in Amsterdam, on a second-floor flat in one of the tall merchants' buildings just opposite the crane, I will routinely have coffee in the same cafe on the canal, and watch the residents of the lower floors go about their lives in perfect ease, not remotely concerned by whether or not they are being watched.

At the end of Entrepotdok stands the Dutch Resistance museum, where the story of Dutch heroism against the Nazis is well documented. There was indeed very strong resistance from many, against both the Nazi occupation and the gathering of the Jews into the Hollandsche Schouwburg theatre. The Resistance fighters forged Dutch identity papers deleting the word "Jew". There are many hundreds of passes for border crossings in the museum, and other identity papers that helped a small number of Jews evade the system. But the Resistance could not prevent the Nazis from misappropriating the Dutch authorities' meticulous documentation of the country's varied population.

Abraham does not believe that the Jews were welcomed and allowed to stay because the Dutch were an exceptionally empathetic nation. They just believed in total profit, and wanted to be the supreme economic power in Europe. The New Christians who came with liquid capital and international networks helped to fast-forward the wondrous course of prosperity on which the Dutch Republic was already set. But as the centuries went by, the Portuguese merchants were no longer among the richest; they were also outnumbered by their own poor from the wider Sephardi diaspora, and the Ashkenazi Jews who did not have the same success in business, status or financial authority. The Jews were no longer the *Nação* of enormous mercantile potential. They were beginning to look just like any other immigrant population who had strange customs and rites. The curiosity with which the Dutch had once looked at them was long gone. Instead there was indifference and suspicion.

"The trains ran on schedule," Abraham repeats. One by one, tram carriages would stop by the theatre and be loaded with prisoners, who would be ticked off the list in perfect order and transferred to the train station. Packed with Jews—children, women, men—the trains would trundle past crowded neighbourhoods, then through various localities, towns and villages, before delivering the inmates into camps dotted around central Europe. No one tried to intervene, to derail them.

In the pre-war Netherlands, the Jews were no longer part of the rich high society. They were in fact poor. They had become poorer since the mid-nineteenth century. The Dutch miracle was long over, and so was the usefulness of the Jews. It was not like the early seventeenth century, when the city of Alkmaar had tried to entice rich Amsterdam Sephardim by legalising Jewish presence and ownership of property and giving them land for a cemetery that they were then yet to acquire. Amsterdam had moved quickly to make sure it did not lose its rich Portuguese merchants. The cemetery in Ouderkerk was allocated, as were other rights of self-governance. Amsterdam always cared about its economic interests, and it cared about the rich traders who brought in wealth, cash and business skills, and settled within its municipal boundaries.

In the Netherlands just before the war, the Jews—although well-integrated citizens in all areas of society including politics, media, education and law—did not offer anything like what their early Iberian ancestors had given to Dutch economic growth. It was the self-interest of the Dutch that had once allowed rich New Christians to settle amongst them, and an absence of that saw their descendants extracted out of Dutch society, brutally. From Entrepotdok, just across the bridge from where we are sitting, past the Resistance Museum, lies the tramline that carried them away on their last journey. Were the cafe not filled with a cacophony of voices, we would probably hear the trams, the friction of the wheels along the tracks, running north to south and back again.

I have heard a great deal about Dutch traits, the Dutch mentality, Dutch self-interest. Before coming to Amsterdam, I had done extensive online research to understand this, and was intrigued to find a huge amount of electronic space devoted to the subject. It seems that Dutch tolerance somehow goes hand in hand with Dutch indifference: living alongside multiple societies in apparent tolerance, while never really socially interacting with the person next door. Can there truly be a phenomenon as generic as a "Dutch mentality"? I doubt it. But during my months of research in Amsterdam I would hear this phrase mentioned numerous times by outsiders, from Bosnian refugees to Croatian Catholics to third-generation Dutch Indonesians. What was so remarkable about the seventeenth century in the Dutch Republic, was that the segmentation of society had not yet been "set in stone", as Abraham likes to phrase it. Despite a "mentality" that may have been there, a high level of interaction did also happen between the Dutch Reformed Christians and their Iberian business partners, between Hugo de Groot and the leaders of the Mahamad. Between the *stadtholder* Prince Frederik Hendrik and the interfaith negotiator, Menasseh ben Israel. Between Rembrandt and his tronies. Between Dutch regents and wandering Moroccan diplomats.

It was a different story in the twentieth century. The Jews had lost both their wealth and their Iberian identity. "A heart-breaking loss," chuckles Abraham, "We moved from being the first modern Jewish Nation, to a small community of poor Dutch Jews."

* * *

Between us on the table lies a book that I have brought for Abraham to sign, about his ancestor, Samuel Palache: *A Man of Three Worlds*. Abraham's face glows as he reminisces aloud about the Palaches from Morocco. His ancestors remained thoroughly Iberianised, he tells me, both during their long sojourn in the North African Sephardi diaspora and thereafter in the Dutch Republic. Abraham can also trace back his roots in the super-rich Suasso and Paraira families—all from the Iberian nobility. At the launch of the book's Dutch translation, Abraham gave a speech at the Esnoga, where he talked about how his ancestors had forged the birth of the first modern Jews, who became successful yet still kept state and religion separate. "The world they created in Amsterdam was so much more flexible, liberal, enterprising, empathetic, and most importantly, modern, compared to the present times."

Samuel Palache was probably one of its most maverick individuals. Was the wandering diplomat a Moroccan, an Iberian, or was he Dutch? "He was a man of three worlds, an enthusiastic cosmopolitan. He is part of the Sephardi Jews' historic connection to the Netherlands." Abraham says he can feel the spirit of Samuel's "Wandering Jew" flowing in his veins; it has been a guiding light throughout his life as he travels around the world to cure a persistent viral disease. He laughs heartily, adding, "Twenty generations on, I could just walk out of this book!"

The ghost of Samuel Palache? He laughs again.

And if he did have to go on a long sea voyage, fight some pirates along the way, would he do that?

"Probably!"

13

DAVID COHEN PARAIRA

THE LAST COHEN OF THE ESNOGA

"The is the oldest Sefer Torah we have, it was brought to us by the first rabbi, Uri Halevi; he came from Hamburg. This is older than the community here."

David Cohen Paraira walks with me through the Jewish Historical Museum, in the building that once housed the Great Synagogue and three other synagogues belonging to Amsterdam's Ashkenazim. They were plundered during the Nazi occupation; certain wings, windows and items of furniture were vandalised. The complex was rebuilt and the interior of the Great Synagogue recreated from its original model after the war. It has been used as a museum since 1987.

The Torah scroll that I see behind a glass case is sheathed in a beautiful brocade-and-tassels mantle. It is probably the most important historical piece in the museum, dating back to an earlier time before the community's settlement in Amsterdam—probably to the fifteenth century. This very scroll before me gave a lost community back their old faith, their stolen Judaism. Uri Halevi presented it to the New Jewish community when he took over rabbinical duties at Beth Jacob synagogue at the end of the sixteenth century. I walk with David through isles of glass boxes that contain marriage documents, richly embroidered tablecloths and gold-plated washbasins for the Cohens—the priestly class— to wash their hands before addressing the congregation. The one I am looking at has elaborate motifs from Greek myth, the Judgment of Paris. I stop to ask David if that was not a strange choice of art for a Jewish synagogue.

"Not at all. The plate has no Jewish theme, but it was indeed commissioned by the Portuguese Jews of Amsterdam. It proves their love of beautiful things, their appreciation for other cultures." The lower ground floor of the museum preserves the best specimens of the community's remarkable past. Strong in Iberian theme, they present an age of unqualified liberalism in Jewish history. The appreciation of art and popular culture of the time, and the eagerness to accept and be accepted, feature poignantly in all the exhibits. These beautiful and historic objects—which found their place in a building so savagely destroyed that its last timber was pulled out and burnt as firewood in the winter of 1944—remind us of renewal. The myth of the phoenix comes alive again.

Some of the Torah mantles from the early days of the community tell a picturesque story of how Sephardi women and men dressed back then. They are made from the exquisite dresses, cloaks and robes brought with them from Iberia. The rich fabric, with bright crimson roses all over, the leaf motifs, take us back to a time when the New Christians lived in Portugal, and before that in Spain, where they emulated the latest fashions and tried to be Iberian as truly as possible, so that the Inquisition police would stop harassing them. These mantles, just like the washbasin, show no Jewish theme, only the initials of the families that donated the fabric for the synagogue's use. This would have been an honour—the act of offering one's personal clothing for Torah mantles. What could be holier, more satisfying to the worship-per, than seeing the cloth that once draped their body now sheathing the scrolls that contain God's words?

We walk up the stairs to the main floor of the Great Synagogue and stand before one of the centrepieces of the exhi-bition hall: a giant picture of Antonio Lopes Suasso (1614–85), founder of a banking dynasty in Amsterdam. Born in Bordeaux to a Marrano family and baptised as a Roman Catholic, he moved to Amsterdam in 1654, by which time the community was thriv-ing. He married an Iberian former converso from Antwerp, Violenta de Pinto, and settled in Amsterdam as one of the rich-est and best-connected Portuguese merchants of his day. His pragmatism and penchant for diplomacy kept him level-headed throughout his life, as he struck political and financial deals with both the *stadtholders* of his adoptive country and Charles II of Spain, which his family had left fleeing the Inquisition. His Jewish faith was uncompromising. Despite being successful and rich in Bordeaux, this conviction had driven him, as it did many others before him, to join his former compatriots settling in the most promising city for Marranos in the seventeenth century.

In Amsterdam, Suasso's political skills paid off when the pre-viously unimaginable happened. In return for financial help dur-ing one of the continental wars, Charles II rewarded him with a prestigious title, Baron d'Avernas le Gras. His older son, Francisco Lopes Suasso, inherited the title and took over half of the family's estate, including the banking business, after the death of his father in 1685. The estate's shares were primarily invested in the VOC, the Dutch East India Company. Francisco's role in acquiring political influence as well as wealth went further than his father's. He maintained fabulous relations with Dutch *stadtholders* and it would be to Francisco that Stadtholder William of Orange—the future English King William III—would turn in 1688, when he needed funds to invade England under the

Catholic King James II, his father-in-law. In other words, the Glorious Revolution, as that event is known, has historical debts to a certain Sephardi Jewish banker. The legend goes that when William of Orange asked Francisco Lopes Suasso how his loan could be repaid, the banker answered, "If thou art victorious, I know thou wilt return them to me; art thou not victorious, I agree to having lost them!" This account may not be true word for word, but William III, after becoming king of England, did return the loan of 2 million guilders to his friend. Such a huge sum needed a large container, and William apparently delivered a huge chest full of valuables to Lopes Suasso in Amsterdam following his victory.

Looking at the relaxed young man on the cover of this book, with red lips and in flamboyant clothes, in a rich wig of golden coils; vibrant crimson bows on the frills of his sleeves, necktie, hem and heels, it is challenging to trace his political acumen. How did this young man, following in the footsteps of his father Antonio, grasp so adroitly the intercontinental diplomacy needed to preserve the success and establishment his family had gained since fleeing Spain in the late sixteenth century? Suasso's poise and pose in this painting by an unnamed artist; the sumptuous red, yellow, pink and beige drapery on the table where he rests his right elbow; the rich folds of the curtain in the background— it all gives off a deliciously anachronistic Kahloesque motif.

But then, the setting is also so typically Dutch. One just has to take a look at the small slice of distant sky visible through the open window, past the rich drapery. This is the dramatic northern sky, with all its might, mystery and unpredictability, that the Dutch masters and other subsidiary artists of the seventeenth century repeatedly painted and etched in their collective body of work.

Another interesting feature of the painting, to Suasso's left, is the lower half of a single column, similar to those holding up the Portuguese Synagogue. The home environment where the young

Francisco is sitting is strongly juxtaposed with this portion of a huge column and the far-off, unpredictable sky—a theme resonant with the lives and dreams of Jews at the time. The richness of the interior of this merchant house reflects the comfort and stability the Jews enjoyed in their Dutch Jerusalem; the distant sky and base of a pillar, which could have been copied from Rabbi Jacob Judah Leon's drawings of Solomon's Temple, represent the final goal of every Jew: the messianic expectation that even Shabbatai Zvi's downfall could not thwart.

Might the unknown painter have been Jewish? Probably not. Was the artist instructed to immortalise the Portuguese Nation's colossal progress in this vibrant portrayal of one of the richest Dutch Sephardim of the century? It seems to me that, by including the base of the temple-style column, the artist is trying to note another important point: that no matter how comfortable the Dutch Jewry became, the dream of a final salvation, of a messianic return, never left the community. There were of course impediments, and the dramatic sky is perhaps representative of these obstacles, but the dream lived on. All of the interfaith, intercontinental negotiations and liaisons were about one thing: hastening a favourable atmosphere for the quest for Zion.

The Dutch municipal archives hold some of the last wishes of the Jews of the *Nação*. These "last wills" leave instructions for the wealth of these individuals to be distributed to the Sephardi diaspora elsewhere, should a devastating end arrive and should the Jews of the Netherlands find themselves wandering again.[1] But the apocalyptic tragedy of World War II struck too quickly; the Jews were caught totally unprepared. No one could have predicted the enormity of the catastrophe. They had thought Amsterdam was the safest place for the Jews. During the years leading up to the war, at the height of the Nazi hate campaign, many Jews from central Europe and Germany moved to Amsterdam, hoping they would be protected by the authorities there. Many rejected opportunities to flee once the occupation began in 1940. These last wills have unwittingly archived the worst fears of the Jews. In one cataclysmic stroke in the 1940s, all the fears stood out poignantly against the passion for messianic redemption. Francisco Lopes Suasso's resplendent face, the luminous jewels on his clothes may portray a man of great wealth and position in society—but the Temple pillar and the distant clouds, the penetrating eyes, warn of some hidden trepidation. The hope of and the need for Israel were never too far from the Jews.

* * *

This section of paintings and memorabilia, which all belonged to the influential and powerful Suasso family during the Dutch Golden Age, is arranged under "Dutch Nobility". And I am honoured to have been taken on a visit and introduced to the Suassos by none other than their own worthy descendant, David Cohen Paraira. He is right to feel proud that his ancestor played a bit part in England's Glorious Revolution.

"The wife of my great-great-grandfather descended from the Lopes Suasso family. If you search on the internet for important Amsterdam Jews, you'll find an article about my great-great-grandfather, Moses Cohen Paraira."

How did they do it? How did they amass such wealth and exercise a historic political influence on important European nations? The Jews weren't even part of the guilds—how did they go on gaining such influence?

"Well, Jews were excluded from the trade guild, but Christian law doesn't approve of moneylending, so that was good for the Jews." They were always in the proximity of money, initially cast in that role by ill fate and later, by proving they were good, if not excellent, at multiplying the cash they dealt with. Soon, a stereotype was born, linking Jews with finance and greed. Moneylending was one of the most common ways for Jews to gain nobility and affluence in Christian societies, whether they were small-town moneylenders like Shakespeare's Shylock, or rich banking families like the Suassos. This profession made them the most head-hunted and sought after émigrés in continental Europe, who found high places in rich quarters. After all, where else would their skills have been more appreciated than in Amsterdam? This was where the world's first stock exchange, the Amsterdam Bourse, was opened, by the Dutch East India Company in 1602—around the same time as New Christian traders began arriving in the city.

Francisco Lopes Suasso's legendary loan to William of Orange has been well documented. But there were other influential members of the Dutch Sephardi nobility who also contributed generously as William sailed to London in 1688. Just over two decades had passed since the messianic debacle, and three since the Jews had been allowed back into England. The *Nação* was keen to continue the continental entente, in order to firmly establish a Jewish presence in all corners of Europe. The arm outstretched to Protestant England was for long-term peace and cooperation in the Judeo-Christian relationship. If Menasseh ben Israel had been alive in 1688, he would have been very proud of Suasso and his Anglo-Sephardic diplomacy. It is unlikely that ben Israel knew Francisco's father, Antonio, since he had only moved to Amsterdam from Bordeaux in 1654, a year before ben Israel left for London and met Oliver Cromwell, becoming a resident with a stipend in the English Commonwealth. However, it is very likely that Antonio Lopes Suasso was present at ben Israel's extravagant funeral at Ouderkerk in 1657, at which most of Amsterdam's Jewry and a representative of the House of Orange showed up.

David Cohen Paraira points to Constantijn Netscher's painting of five Suasso boys, five of Francisco's seven sons. Looking at their faces, the rich colours on their clothes and the sumptuous setting, the viewer will not find anything in these characters to distinguish their Jewishness. These third-generation children of former Marrano émigrés gaze at me like any other children in contemporary Dutch paintings. Their cherub faces are playful, exuding their parents' wealthy status. The background is idyllic, in what seems like a well-kept garden. The painting catches the viewer's attention by presenting a forced suspension of action: the boys seem to have been called in from a boisterous outdoor game of sticks and strings. They are too impatient to sit for the painter. Another interesting feature, which David Cohen Paraira brings to my attention, is that, from whichever angle you look at the boys' faces, they seem to be staring at the viewer. We change position and walk back and forth, side to side, with the boys' mischievous gaze still fixed on us.

David and I walk out of the Great Synagogue, now the Jewish Historical Museum, and go over to the other side of the tram-line, to the Portuguese Synagogue. Grand and majestic as always, straight out of a de Hooghe etching, it is surrounded by low redbrick buildings of the same era. The main entrance is not visible, because visitors, as in the seventeenth century, have to walk through a gate located in one of the outer buildings, which today is guarded and ticketed. I soon find out from David why this is the case, why the original design required such fortress-like outbuildings to encircle the Esnoga: the only religious build-ings that could have their front doors opening onto the street were the Dutch Reformed Churches. The doors of synagogues, or Catholic churches, were not permitted to face the main road; their worshippers could not be seen coming in or out.

We walk through the main gate, past security, and step into a courtyard. The low buildings on three sides merge onto the grand main entrance. It seems to me that the courtyard is not nearly large enough to hold all the devotees that the synagogue can accommodate. As if David could read my thoughts, he says,

"It is never full, even in those days in the seventeenth century the Esnoga would never be filled to its full capacity."

Why did they build then, such a colossal building? "Bigger and more ostentatious it had to be, than the Ashkenazi synagogue, that was the point," I hear David chuckle to himself. In 1671, when the Great Synagogue was built four years before the Portuguese, the city's Ashkenazi population now greatly outnumbered the Iberian Sephardim, following various central European massacres, pogroms and wars. The non-descript Ashkenazi synagogues in private homes or warehouses were redundant in the face of this influx of eastern refugees.

I take a mental note of the courtyard and the sheer height of the Esnoga—like a church, it dwarfs the visitor standing below. When it was built in 1675, it was unlike any previous synagogues anywhere in the world. Jewish places of worship had traditionally been simple, unremarkable buildings. The Esnoga's huge, tall, high-arched, stained glass windows denote the only ornamentation; there are no graven images, no leaf motifs, no abstract patterns to clutter the geometric simplicity of the vast redbrick building, partly based by its architect Elias Bouman on existing drawings of Solomon's Temple. I am reminded again of the legend: that these windows, through which light flooded the synagogue, were pointed out by a teenage Jewish firefighter to deter the Nazi commander aus der Fünten assembling the Jews here or offering the site to the German garrison.

The interior of the Esnoga maintains the theme and layout of the original Temple drawings of Jacob Judah Leon Templo—the arrangement of the pews, the positioning of the ark and the podium or *teva* for the rabbi, which faces south-east, towards Jerusalem. The Torah ark is made of dark wood, polished so it glimmers. "This is jacaranda wood, from Brazil. It was a gift from one of the richest men in the community, Moses Curiel," David Cohen says. I detect a generous whiff of wonderment, verging on disbelief, that this was where his ancestors gathered for Shabbat, for bar mitzvah, Rosh-ha-Shana, Yom Kippur, Hanukkah. This was where they came for special blessings from the Cohens before setting off for the New World, from where they would bring back more wealth and ornaments for this splendid house of worship that exceeded, in beauty and size, all other Jewish buildings in the world.

I try to visualise Moses Curiel—his plantation in Brazil, and his twice-yearly journeys back and forth across the oceans that the Jews had chartered as well as any other traditional seafaring community in the world. Did he bring all the jacaranda wood needed to make the ark in one load? Was he involved in designing it? Like everything else in the Esnoga, the Torah ark is of a grand scale: its height towers over the worshipper as it stands perfectly aligned with the colossal columns; numerous stained-glass windows line the tall walls, reaching the ceiling. In most synagogues the Torah ark is usually a curtained area behind the *teva*. In the Esnoga, the *teva* and ark are placed at opposite ends, so that when the rabbi delivers his sermon, he's facing the ark. The seating is arranged in a maze-like pattern around the *teva*. The women's galleries above are held up by the massive columns. Did Francisco Lopes Suasso instruct his painter to paint that single column beside him in a deliberate imitation of the Esnoga pillars, to prove his affiliation with the *Nação* and its magnificent house of worship?

After the height of the columns and the impressive arched windows, the most attractive interior ornamentation is the row of huge brass chandeliers. This is still the main source of lighting in the Esnoga in the evening, the candles lit one by one by an appointed person. But, these days, evening services are only reserved for a special occasion: the holiest day of the Jewish calendar, Yom Kippur, the Day of Atonement. "Then a thousand candles are lit in the Esnoga," David tells me. How long does it take to light them? "One hour." I shall soon experience for myself a beautiful Yom Kippur service here, in the autumn of 2017. But on this mild summer's day in August, standing in the central court-yard of the Esnoga, I cannot envisage the interior in candlelight. There seem to be too many chandeliers hanging over the main hall, and more in the women's galleries above, from where I will watch the service—their polished brass shines in the soft rays of sunlight pouring down through the towering windows.

On a dark night, any light inside the Esnoga would likewise shine out through those windows. This historic piece of advice by a Portuguese Jewish teenager to the Nazis probably helped save the Esnoga from Allied bombing. When all other buildings in the vicinity were in ruins, the Portuguese Synagogue stood high in the skyline, like one of the miracles that the Jews had believed in for millennia. It was God's providence. They always came back from the brink of annihilation, there would always be divine intervention in one way or another, and they would rise again from the ashes of destruction. It was this belief in rising with renewed life from the fire of death that had inspired the early settlers in Amsterdam—who started their lives as New Jews after escaping the stake—to choose the phoenix as the emblem of their second congregation, Neve Shalom.

"It was a miracle!" I hear my thoughts spelled out by David Cohen Paraira, who is the Esnoga's only remaining Cohen—a member of the priestly Cohanim superclass. His only son lost his Cohen credentials after marrying a divorcee. I note this down as something I would like to ask David: how the community feels about being governed by the old Mahamad that strives to preserve this ancient tradition. Abraham Palache hinted at the conservatism of the community, which perhaps persuaded him at first to join the Mahamad—to keep the parallel, liberal line of thinking flowing among the 600 or so members of the Esnoga. Could the Mahamad's orthodoxy be one of the reasons why young people are leaving for Israel, which offers a more liberal Jewish society? One where the young can lead whatever life they want to lead, without losing their Jewishness?

These days there is no *herem* in the Esnoga—religious and social ostracism of the kind that excommunicated Uriel da Costa and Baruch Spinoza—but David Cohen's son has been ousted from performing the traditional role of the Cohens, offering the ritual blessing to the congregation. It seems like a modern-day *herem* to me. "It is not!" Michael Minco, the head of the Mahamad, tells me when I put it to him. "There are reasons why we laymen do not understand many things about rabbinical rules." Can the *parnassim* rule out a modern-day *herem*? Minco says that this might still be carried out in response to violent behaviour by an individual. "I can imagine this being invoked in cases of extreme intolerance."[2]

Perhaps I have used too harsh a word in the case of David Cohen's son. But the Mahamad still exercises its power and abides by the decisions of the rabbinate, just as it did in the past. One of the most recent cases of this obeisance to rabbinical rule drew international attention. During a discussion on whether or not the seventeenth-century *herem* against Baruch Spinoza should be lifted, the Sephardi chief rabbi of Amsterdam, Pinchas Toledano, said that there was no reason to revoke the ban, since Spinoza had never repented or retracted his words. Yet ever since the excommunicated Jewish philosopher was recognised and celebrated by the world's intellectuals a century after his death, there has been talk of posthumously lifting the Amsterdam *Nação*'s ban on its most famous son. Israel's first prime minister, David Ben-Gurion, was one the most outspoken campaigners. Minco tells me that a number of renowned professors from the Hebrew University of Jerusalem came to Amsterdam in the 1950s, and pleaded with the rabbis and the *parnassim* to revoke Spinoza's *herem*. He mimics Ben-Gurion's request: "'Hey, Israel

is full of little and big Spinozas, can you do something about it?'"
But the rabbis refused, and the Mahamad upheld its decision, as
it did in 1656.

Something else I hear from Minco is even more puzzling: a
symposium was held in Amsterdam in December 2015, at which
the Amsterdam Mahamad and Jewish intellectuals from around
the world urged the rabbis to reconsider the *herem*, 350 years
after the philosopher was evicted from the Portuguese Jewish
community. This time, too, the rabbis ruled in favour of the ban
remaining in place, supported again by the *parnassim*. My incre-
dulity is mixed with a certain amount of awe as I hear Minco
say, "When a *herem* is imposed, it's generally for thirty days.
Within thirty days the accused has to come and show remorse,
solve the case and pay whatever he has been asked to pay to get
the ban lifted. The chief rabbi of the Amsterdam Sephardim
decided he was unable to lift it because Spinoza did not, could
not, show remorse."

"Well, let alone thirty days, it's been 350 years!" I try to tease
him. But the head of the Amsterdam Mahamad offers me a
standard reply that explains the orthodoxy of the community
since its inception: "The Parnassim can only ask, they cannot
make decisions on how the community members should behave,
that's a rabbinical matter." Without a green light from the rabbis,
in other words, the board of wardens cannot issue or unissue
edicts. But then as now, there is an implicit agreement between
the two. In any case, the ban on Spinoza has been reconfirmed
and the matter dismissed.

David Cohen Paraira would not dream of fighting against his
son's loss of his Cohen duties. He broke an age-old tradition.
The Cohens must remain physically pure: they cannot touch or
be in close proximity to the dead; they have a separate, fenced
burial place in the Jewish cemetery. They cannot marry divorced
women. These are essential commandments by which an ortho-

dox Jewish society must abide. Cohen Paraira, Minco and many others from the community tell me that it is necessary to hold onto what remains of the old Amsterdam Sephardim, and of the Western Sephardim in general. The founding fathers of this community were born at a time of the religious wars in Europe, as persecuted New Christians. Having once been the centre of the orthodox Sephardi Jewish world, the descendants of the *Nação* cannot just submit to acculturation. They have survived so many calamitous setbacks—the exile, the Inquisition, the Holocaust—and each one of them nearly annihilated them. It is the orthodoxy of the community that has worked as a phoenix effect, just as Saul Levi Morteira would have wanted. The belief with which he ruled the *Nação* is still ruling it, centuries later: that renewal always begins with going back to religion and its commandments. The Amsterdam Sephardim have historically paid homage to this miracle of survival, including David Cohen Paraira today:

> The fact that in the mid-seventeenth century, when the Catholics had to pray in secret locations, in attics and warehouses, the Jews could build such an important building that everyone could see from everywhere in the city, it was indeed a miracle. In Italy, there were many nice synagogues at the time, but they were inconspicuous, hidden from view, and here you were, two big synagogues in one square, it was truly amazing.

Making synagogues invisible from outside was definitely a theme maintained in their building throughout the Jews' history in the diaspora. I ponder the seventeenth-century synagogue in Fez, at the end of a dead-end road, non-descript from outside; in fact, the entrance serves as the entrance to both the synagogue and the adjacent house, or complex of houses. This was the Jewish communities' survival mechanism. Hidden from immediate public view, the diasporic synagogues governed their communities like mini-nations, with rigid rabbinical orders. Away from the mainstream gentile influence, these communities were able to preserve their esoteric traditions. When I stepped inside the little synagogue in Fez, I was transported four centuries back. I imagined the argumentative congregants who would sit on the bench by the entrance, I was told, so they could exit quickly if these internal religious debates became overheated.

The benches in the Esnoga are arranged for the members of the community according to their pedigree. The bench immediately behind the *teva*, says David, is reserved for the chief rabbi when he is not delivering a sermon. Services are usually conducted by several *hazzanim* (cantors, prayer song-leaders) and religious leaders, before the sermon is delivered. The benches right by the podium were traditionally reserved for influential members of the community, such as, almost certainly, the Curiel and Lopes Suasso families. David walks with me around the benches and tells me more stories about the Esnoga's miraculous survival. Most of the benches are original. Apparently many of the prayer books, manuscripts and prayer shawls that were left in the under-bench storage boxes also survived the wartime destruction. I lift the lid of one of these individualised benches. What did it mean that, after the Jews were moved to the Hollandsche Schouwburg and the synagogue was left vacant, the Nazis did not lift the lids of the benches? That they did not desecrate the prayer items? The young firefighter, Abraham Palache's father, had long been sent away to Buchenwald—who was there to make sure they were left undamaged? There are only theories, community legends without historical documentation.

As we walk out of the Esnoga's grand entrance into the courtyard, I ask David whether he is sad that the Cohen line will end with him. "Of course not," he replies. "Having a Jewish daughter-in-law and Jewish grandchildren is much more important to me."

Still, it is sad that his son cannot stand in the synagogue and deliver what the Cohens have traditionally delivered. "These rules are not for these times, as you know. So many people ge divorced, everything's changed. People don't stay married al their lives." Does he think these laws should change, evolve? O are they there for a good reason?

There's a long pause while I walk around the courtyard. I finc it perplexing that David is thinking before replying, unlik Abraham, who is firmly against holding onto the orthodoxy o the past.

Directly opposite me, left of the exit, is a staircase going down to the world's oldest Jewish library, Ets Haim, named after th first Jewish yeshiva in western Europe, where young Jewish boy were given lessons on the Talmud. This was where Rabbis Uzie and Morteira taught, and where Menasseh ben Israel, Uriel d Costa and Baruch Spinoza had been students, before the firs became a prominent rabbi, and the latter two were brutall expelled from their community for talking against its orthodoxy I walk back to David, who has now finished thinking. He says "These rules are hard to apply today, but I am not a rabbi, man 'Cohanim' have lost their function. I know several Cohens in thi community who are no longer priests."

While David seems happy to make general comments on th state of the community today, he refuses to talk about his per sonal views on the restrictions that are still in place. We chang the conversation to what the Mahamad was like then, comparec with now. He answers that of course the board was not demo cratic then. The rabbis very much served the rich, who paid higl membership fees to the synagogue to become part of th Mahamad. They were not elected. But, I suggest, they did man age to achieve what was good for them, for their own society what was productive... "No!" exclaims David. "What is good fo the nation is when everyone is satisfied and has a good life. Those days, he adds, the Mahamad pandered to the rich, anc sent away poor members of the community to Brazil, later t Suriname and Curaçao.

This is not the first time I am hearing this. From snippets of conversations with the descendants of the *Nação* and from the documents in Ets Haim Library, it seems to me that the Mahamad had an aversion to poverty. Keeping the community's profile, religious, ceremonial and financial, in top shape to outsiders was a prerogative of the board members. Having initially helped the impoverished Ashkenazi refugees to resettle in Amsterdam, as time went by they did not want to know them; many of the refugees had developed a bad reputation in Dutch society as beggars and vagabonds. The embarrassed Sephardi rich did not want to be associated with the long-bearded, slovenly eastern European peddlers loitering and hawking in the forecourt of the two synagogues, as depicted by many contemporary artists. Religiously, too, the Amsterdam Mahamad wanted to be a world example of the most refined Sephardi Jewry. Any deviation was treated with utmost seriousness. There was no place for da Costa's preposterous rebellion, no place for Spinoza's pantheism. The latter was more damaging than the former: while at least da Costa could be dismissed as deranged, his successor was a level-headed, calm and well-respected philosopher in the Christian world, who was being heralded as the harbinger of the Age of Enlightenment. Even had he shown remorse, the *parnassim* would not have invited him to re-enter the community; he would have continued to be—and indeed does officially continue to be—"cursed by day and cursed by night".

This uncompromising orthodoxy has been the character of the community; without it, it might as well have ceased to exist, been assimilated and acculturated into Dutch society. The religion with its ancient laws would not have survived had it let go of this essential zeal, the community's Jewishness, because its followers had lived during most of their history in the diaspora. Even in Amsterdam, where there was no ghetto, the *Nação* created its own invisible wall separating it from mainstream society. This

was why Spinoza infamously said that the Jews, with their esoteric rites and rituals, would never get their kingdom back. Can
this work in our modern times, typified by the breaking down of
ethnic and religious boundaries?

I have repeatedly been told by what remains of the *Naçāo* that
its orthodoxy has contributed to an increased exodus of youth to
Israel. Contrary to what Spinoza said—and this is the greatest
paradox of all—in the world's only Jewish state, a Jew can live a
very comfortable secular, even apostatic, life. Spinoza would never
have been ostracised by the "kingdom" that the Jews, defying his
bitter conjecture, have created. It appears to me that violation of
the orthodox character of the community is not welcomed by
today's Mahamad. When David Cohen Paraira's only son, Maurice,
wanted to marry a divorcee, and a halachically non-Jew, since his
wife's father but not mother was Jewish, he was forced to go to a
Sephardi rabbi in Israel who would marry them.

There are no hard feelings—this is the sense I get from David
Cohen Paraira. It is understood, now as in the Dutch Golden
Age, that the community has to survive and preserve its continuity as the *Naçāo* in what is now a staunchly secular Amsterdam.
In a way it was easier before, when the Dutch Republic was
Calvinist. The state religion respected and encouraged the mini-
state of the Jews in Vlooienburg. In fact, the Dutch Reformed
Church made sure the Jews were strictly ruled by their law
books, the *halacha*, and the community was left to be policed by
its own religious law enforcement officers, under the Mahamad's
strict orthodox leadership. "The Portuguese Nation's identity is
not religious any more, it's more historical," David explains. "The
world has changed too quickly. I am afraid in one or two generations, there'll be no Jewish life in Europe any more. Perhaps
there'll still be some Jews in London and Paris, but not in
Amsterdam." The modern State of Israel is partly responsible for
this dwindling of European Jewry since World War II, but this

has also happened, David says, because "many of us have lost the tribal zeal for religion." Those who do have it, and want to live among a Jewish nation, can always go to Israel.

We have walked back through the security gate and come out into the forecourt of the two synagogues. Instead of the curious gentiles seen in seventeenth-century art, walking in their best outdoor clothes with the goods- and people-laden boats sailing by on the Amstel, today we see a network of tramlines crisscrossing from north to south and east to west, and the entrance to an underground theme park, Tun Fun. Over the next few weeks, as I sit in Ets Haim carefully leafing through old manuscripts, my concentration will be broken by sudden, muffled noises of children at Tun Fun. The preposterous existence of this raucous adventure playground just outside the Esnoga's main entrance will seem like a blessing only once, when Heide Warncke, the librarian of Ets Haim, suggests that I leave my two children there while working in the library.

David and I head toward the cafe in the basement of the Ashkenazi Great Synagogue, and order *latke*s—traditional Jewish potato cakes. I have not had these since leaving Jerusalem, where I lived for eight years until 2013. I feel nostalgic, as I see other Israeli food items. "Would you follow the young and move to Israel?" I ask David. "It's not for me," he shakes his head. He won't make *aliya*? "No!" David is emphatic: he has no reason to pack up and relocate to Israel in the immediate future. Unlike many others whose children have moved to the Jewish State after finishing college, David's son and daughter continue to live in Amsterdam.

In any case, he says, it is "a lose-lose situation". The Portuguese Jewish identity is at stake amid Amsterdam's virulent secular atmosphere, which is increasingly tempting the young. The old religious and historical identity has also been endangered by mixed marriages. When members of the community move to Israel, it is true that their Jewish identity is preserved and strengthened, but it loses its diasporic history: the tradition of the past 400 years in Dutch Jerusalem, and before that, in Iberia. David is also nostalgic for the linguistic connection to the Peninsula, to Spanish and Portuguese, which was never lost during the four centuries the *Nação* lived in Amsterdam. A small part of the service today is still conducted in Portuguese.

The Portuguese Nation will very soon live only in history books, he states nonchalantly. That's the result of the Holocaust, the greatest Jewish tragedy since the Inquisition. "I am a poor man now, my ancestors were rich bankers!" "Poor" here is also a euphemism for the loss of tradition, of history—the cultural impoverishment of the *Nação*. David Cohen Paraira is just happy that his son and his daughter are some of the few still holding onto their connection to the Portuguese Sephardi Jewry. His son Maurice lives just outside Amsterdam, and is orthodox. He is bringing up his children according to the Portuguese Jewish tradition; they are learning to pray in the old Iberian way. "It's the service that I would miss most, if I ever had to leave my community," David tells me wistfully. For him, it is the beauty of the service in a Portuguese Synagogue that sets the Esnoga and its members apart from other Jewish diasporas.

Perhaps, deep down, David believes that, by living in Amsterdam with his immediate family, the Cohen Parairas continue to preserve the glorious memory of once belonging to the Spanish nobility, with flamboyant ancestors such as the Lopes Suassos, who were stifled by the Spanish Inquisition but, like the phoenix, rose up and made a fortune in Amsterdam. Perhaps it is still possible for them to move through further cycles of life, with the same pride and accomplishment as their ancestors.

* * *

I have decided that I cannot fully tell the story of David Cohen Paraira without speaking to his only son, Maurice Cohen Paraira, who has lost his membership of the priestly class after marrying a divorcee. He lives in Amstelveen, a southern suburb of Amsterdam, in a picturesque, purpose-built house in a block arranged around a quaint, landscaped garden with miniature water features. It is incredibly green here, hence the name— Amstelveen means "Turf on the Amstel". The city of Amsterdam itself is all grey and bricks, its canals reflecting the tall houses in a fabulous symbiosis. The buildings and canals have been integral to one another since the days of *overvloed*, when the canals were first dug out, creating the grey-and-brick city we see today. Even the beauty is controlled: the waterflow in the canals must be centrally maintained—not too much, not too little, that supposedly "very Dutch mentality". If you start walking south from the Esnoga, along a beautiful route beside the Amstel and various canals, you'll reach Amstelveen in one hour and forty minutes. Walking in Amsterdam is a real pleasure. But you must watch out for cyclists, because they believe the road belongs to them.

Maurice welcomes me in perfect English, with a baby in his arms. A truly modern man, I could not help thinking. He puts his baby down and makes coffee for me, juice for my children, who have been mostly reluctantly tagging along with me to my interviews, libraries and museums, in the summer of 2017. Maurice wears a kippa. When he sits down, the baby crawls to him and climbs onto his lap. I hear another child or baby on the upper floor. I don't see his wife; in fact, she never comes down during the hour that I spend with Maurice.

He has spoken to his father and knows that I have been trying to understand what remains of the *Nação* today. "My Portuguese customs, *minhagim*, the community—we're the third generation after World War II—and the way we have prayed for twenty generations in Amsterdam are important to me. I want to pass all to my children." Which is why, Maurice says, he is still here. "Our Judaism is special and it has remained unchanged for centuries, our way is very different from others." He starts to tell me what makes it different. During the reading of some parts of the Torah, the Ashkenazi Jews stand up, but the Portuguese Sephardim do not. This signifies the belief that the whole of the Torah is holy, not just certain bits of it. "We're humans, we can't say this part of God's text is more important than other parts. So what we do is that when the rabbi comes to read, let's say, the Ten Commandments, we stand for the rabbi. These small gestures of our tradition are important to me."

The way Amsterdam's Portuguese Jews read Hebrew is also different from modern Hebrew. Maurice explains how various letters and words have been pronounced since the Iberian days: "We're loud!" The whole congregation joins in and everyone hears everyone. This way of conducting the service is a reflection of how the early New Christian settlers brought the memory of Judaism from Spain and Portugal into Amsterdam—and of how the Sephardi masters from Fez and the Ottoman Empire purged the burgeoning New Jewish community of whatever Ashkenazi customs it might have picked up from its first rabbi, Uri Halevi. Maurice gives me several more examples that set the Portuguese apart from the Ashkenazim. In Portuguese Sephardi tradition, the blessing after the meal is read by one person, and everyone present says, "Amen"; whereas, in Ashkenazi Judaism, everyone has to say the blessing individually. Likewise, the Hanukkah candles are lit by one person only, not by everyone as in the Ashkenazi tradition.

"It feels so uplifting, when I enter the Esnoga!" It is a step back in time, Maurice tells me, and every time he visits the Esnoga he cannot help thinking, "Wow, we were here! We ARE here!" What he means to say is that the community, however small, is still holding tight. He would like to live close by, so he could go there for the Shabbat services too; because Jews cannot use transport on Saturdays, and the walk is too long with the whole family, he does not visit the Esnoga as often as he would like to. Many Portuguese Jews cannot afford to live in the old Jodenbuurt or even in central Amsterdam because of the house prices. This is also one of the reasons why community life is no longer vibrant in the immediate vicinity of the Esnoga. The Jodenbuurt became known as such not because the Jews huddled there obeying a rule requiring them to live within particular boundaries, but because religious Jews must live near a synagogue for Saturday Shabbat services, when they are not allowed to travel in a vehicle. A Jewish community will always grow near or around a synagogue. Vlooienburg became the Jodenbuurt because of the synagogue on the Houtgracht. These days, Shabbat services at the Esnoga are mostly attended by Jewish tourists, many from Israel. They are often conducted in the adjacent, smaller "winter synagogue", next to Ets Haim Library.

A baby cries incessantly upstairs, which is probably why Maurice's wife never comes down. A new arrival, he tells me; there must be just a year between the infant and the beautifully well-behaved baby girl who is now playing with my children. The crying baby upstairs, the signs of a young family with toys and rattles scattered around the living room, allow me to place the question that I have come here to ask: how does it feel to be ousted from his hereditary role as a Cohen?

"It is difficult. Because you're born as a Cohen—I'm still a Cohen—but I can't practise it any more." Did he try to persuade the *parnassim* to allow him to fulfil his Cohen duties, did he try to convince them to overlook his "transgression"? "Of course I did. I still feel a Cohen. But the rabbinate at the Esnoga said if I married this woman, I'd lose my 'Cohanut'. So I decided to marry my wife and lose my Cohanut!" How, I ask, has he taken it? "I'm happy of course that I have married the woman I love. But ... what can I say? It's best for the community to keep the old tradition. But I'm sad I'm deprived of my role."

It is best for the community, he reiterates, because the community must preserve its ancient *minhagim*. This is the only way the last 600 or so members of the Portuguese Jewish community can carry on their ancestors' Judaic practices.

It was not easy for Maurice to get permission to marry a woman who had been married before, and not only that, one with only a Jewish father, not even Jewish from the point of view of religious law. The couple met when Maurice's future wife was studying—in fact, she was going through a Jewish conversion course at the synagogue. She was converted by a rabbi at the Esnoga to the Portuguese Sephardi tradition. But he would not, could not marry them. Maurice travelled to Israel, to a rabbi of Portuguese descent, Nathan Lopes Cardoso, who agreed to marry the couple. The whole process took half a year. He is happy with this "completion", as he calls it. He has two beautiful baby girls, and, he repeats, his love has won out.

But still, there is a sense of loss—there are no Cohens left in the immediate neighbourhood of the Portuguese Synagogue. Maurice's father, David Cohen Paraira, also moved to the suburbs due to Amsterdam's high living cost. They only visit the Esnoga on high holidays such as Yom Kippur. The prayers that are reserved for the Cohens only, the "blessings", are not recited, and "the melody is lost," says Maurice. The Esnoga has been functioning without the passages of the Torah that are meant to be sung only by the Cohens.

Maurice is sad at the disappearance of the remaining Portuguese Jews from Amsterdam. The postwar descendants of the once super-rich Sephardim cannot afford to live near the beautiful seventeenth-century synagogue. Weekly services are mostly attended by tourists, with only bar mitzvahs, weddings, and the main Jewish festivals drawing the native congregation. The Esnoga is too big; it was too big even when it was built, and as we've heard from Maurice's father, David Cohen Paraira, it has never been filled to its full capacity of 3,000 worshippers. This grandeur was a symbol of the *Nação*'s self-importance, not a necessity, as with the nearby Ashkenazi Great Synagogue that had to house central European refugees. Maurice tells me that they have their own little "Esnoga" in Amstelveen, for the Portuguese Jews who live there. In fact, Abraham Palache invited me to attend a Shabbat service there, which I was unable to make. The Portuguese Jews who no longer live in Amsterdam, Palache said, make sure that on the holiest day on the Jewish calendar, they are at the grand Esnoga before and after the fast.

"When will you be going to the Esnoga next?' I ask Maurice, who's now changing his baby girl, having announced a short while ago that she has soiled her nappy. My children are awe-struck; my daughter will later tell me that I am not "cool" enough compared with this man, who has sacrificed a heredi-tary title for love, and who can change his baby's soiled nappy while giving an interview. "I and my family will certainly be there for Yom Kippur," says Maurice, washing his hands in the kitchen corner.

Of course. Not only is Yom Kippur the holiest day, but the Day of Atonement also marked the forging of the community in Amsterdam a little over 400 years ago, with the spied-upon ser-vice of 1603. It is also the day when someone goes around for an hour lighting 1,000 candles in the Portuguese Synagogue. We are only five weeks away from Yom Kippur 2017—I will return for the service in the Esnoga.

I say goodbye to Maurice Cohen Paraira and come out with my children into the pretty green suburb. We start walking along a leafy avenue, following Maurice's direction. We should soon see some kind of a waterway or a canal, and if we walk with the sun setting to the left, we shall hit the Amstel River that will take us back into Amsterdam. But the children do not make it—after an hour or so, they give up, and we take the tram back to Entre-potdok, to our flat near the Resistance Museum.

14

THE CURIOUS CASE OF THE CURIELS

I am on the verge of winding down my summer research to head back home for the start of school, when I have a gripping encounter during a late evening stroll from the Centraal Station. The waterfront could have come straight out of an old etching of the harbour, except that, instead of white sails and wooden ships, there are floating bars and tourist motorboats. I feel more restless than before I came to Amsterdam. Researching the historic dead has probably left me with an unfinished ending. The community that has gone from riches to rags does not have to tell me that its future is uncertain. With just 600 members, most of whom are over forty, the Sephardi congregation of Amsterdam has good reasons to be concerned about its continuation.

I walk back toward my place, past the medieval fortress, the Waag, past Sint Antoniesbreestraat, with Rembrandt and de Pinto's houses, onto Jodenbreestraat. I have taken this route a great many times during my stay here, trying to conjure up the old Jodenbuurt. To my right, Hoogstraat is still narrow and many of the old houses are still standing. I try to imagine the hustle and dirt and smell and festivities of three centuries of incredible birth and unimaginable growth among the Dutch Sephardim, born out of a handful of Iberian, tempest-tossed Catholics.

The tall windows of the Esnoga from the other end of Jodenbreestraat still mesmerise visitors. The Portuguese Synagogue's simple geometric grandeur and magnificence remain a showstopper, and it is still one of the most spellbinding buildings in the city. At the end of Sint Antoniesbreestraat, past Hoogstraat to my right, I arrive at the magical centre of the old Vlooienburg island. Today, tramlines crisscross here with the grand synagogue complex on one side and a flea market on the other, just opposite Waterlooplein Station, where the old Houtgracht synagogue once stood. Wherever I travel from in Amsterdam, I always end up here, on the square that today is called Jonas Daniel Meijerplein.

Outside the Esnoga, I lean against a raised ridge with a row of olive trees—no longer the old scene immortalised in so many etchings and paintings, there are no sailboats on the nearby Amstel; it is no longer a meeting point of the city's residents. Instead there is a gravel park with benches. Incongruously, but to comical effect, here stand the arched metal bars of the children's subterranean adventure playground. It is a weekend evening—I hear laughter and loud voices from the bars that are still open on the other side of the road that separates the Esnoga from the Jewish Historical Museum. I head toward the noise. I have seen these bars before, near the Blauwbrug (Blue Bridge) over the Amstel, across from the impressive Dutch National Opera. I have repeatedly crossed this historic, ornate, sumptuously decorated bridge during my many walks over the past weeks. It is an 1884 replica of an older, seventeenth-century wooden bridge, which was originally painted blue.

Blauwbrug Bar-Cafe appears to be the most interesting of the eateries on the eastern side of the bridge, with an outdoor space with patio heaters. Amsterdam evenings can be cold even in

August. With the river, and the canals that zigzag like main roads alongside pedestrianised walkways, there is always a breeze. I feel chilly and walk in. A friendly barwoman greets me and finds me a warm spot right under one of the heaters, at a table overlooking the bridge and the National Ballet and Opera House. She is Keren, she tells me, when I ask her name. A few minutes later, she brings my plate of *bitterballen*—typical Dutch finger food, croquettes filled with warming veal stew—and a glass of— no, not Amstel, not even Heineken, but Jupiler, a refreshing Belgian draught beer that seems to be popular all over Amsterdam. She lights a cigarette and sits by the entrance. When I look at her and smile, unsure if I want to have a conversation with a barwoman at this hour, she tells me she's on a short break and asks me what brought me to Amsterdam. I tell her I am writing a book on Amsterdam's Jewish past and ask her if she knew that all of this, where we are sitting—the east side of the Blauwbrug—was once part of the Jodenbuurt.

She looks at me through the smokescreen as if I have said something vaguely familiar. She stubs out her cigarette, gets up to go inside, and asks me if I want to meet someone whose family was originally Jewish. "She says her ancestors were Portuguese, who were members of this synagogue," Keren points to her left, which is where I've just walked from. Such coincidences are rare, and when they align, they seem stranger than fiction. A woman comes out and introduces herself as Claudia. "Claudia—what?" I ask her, and realise my question sounded impolite. I spot my journalistic curiosity to sniff out a potential story. I quickly compose myself and tell her that I have been researching seventeenth-century Amsterdam.

"My brother has been obsessed with it too, he has been putting together a family tree," she says. "We are not Jewish though, but we come from a family who were among the first Portuguese emigrants to Amsterdam." I ask what her original family name was.

"It still is—we still carry our old family name, Curiel. I am Claudia Curiel. My brother is Hendrik Jacob Curiel." She means, she and her brother are descendants of the Curiel brothers? The famous Curiel brothers? "You have to speak to my brother, he is the one who's been researching. Would you like to talk to him? I can give you his number. Hold on a second, I'll go get my phone."

Claudia goes inside. Keren has been listening and now she smiles broadly. I am not sure she realises her introduction has led to an astonishing chance encounter that I can barely wait to follow up on. Claudia comes out with her brother on the line. "Here's Harrie, my brother, a Curiel, like me," she says. "We share the same name like those brothers in your research, who came to Amsterdam from Lisbon!" Claudia passes her mobile to me. I stammer over each word I say to Harrie, my thoughts going back to the pages of the article I have recently been reading at Ets Haim, in which the historian Miriam Bodian talks about the Curiels of Lisbon and Coimbra, how they fled the Inquisition and arrived in Amsterdam via France, an escape route often used by Portuguese refugees to the Dutch Republic.

"I have compiled a long article, with a family tree and as many details as I could find in Amsterdam's city archives and the PIG's community documents. Also from the death register of the Portuguese Jewish cemetery in Ouderkerk," Harrie tells me. PIG, rather peculiarly I think, is the Dutch abbreviation for the Portuguese Jewish Congregation. We plan to meet on Sunday evening, at Harrie's flat in a swanky part of south Amsterdam.

Claudia says goodbye; the shift is over. I look out to my left and see the round house of the National Opera, and try to piece together today's events. I have walked into the Blauwbrug area to calm my agitating thoughts as I prepare to return to London. Instead of feeling sated and soothed, I now feel enthralled by this exciting new lead, an introduction into the descendants of a very important Marrano family from Lisbon, who helped found the

Nação, just around the corner. There is a sudden rise in the room's decibel level. I am surprised to see that, at this late hour, so many people in suits and dresses have filled the empty tables and the bar counter, ordering or holding glasses of beer. Keren has gone back behind the bar. I see her pulling the pump; a queue has formed. I realise that these smartly dressed men and women have just come out of the National Ballet and Opera House after a late-night production. I cannot help wondering if it is a mere coincidence that the Opera House is in such close proximity to the old Jewish quarter. The spirit of the theatre-loving New Jews must be very pleased.

* * *

The next day, I walk to a grandiose neighbourhood in the shadow of the Rijksmuseum. In a leafy avenue, on the top floor of a nineteenth-century terraced building, I have come to see Claudia's brother, Hendrik Jacob Curiel.

"This is my grandfather, and this is me. He was also called Hendrik Jacob Curiel." Harrie points to a black-and-white photo of him holding his grandfather's hand. The older man has an interesting, youthful, relaxed face. "When I was fifteen, he was seventy-five. He also named my father Hendrik Jacob." The latest Hendrik wants to be called Harrie, just to be different, and he has not passed his name on to his son. "I cut the line here! I was named after my grandfather's grandfather, a slave bought to freedom by his Jewish plantation worker father."

Pointing to the picture, Harrie says his grandfather was born in Paramaribo, Suriname, in 1897. He lived for over 100 years. His ancestors moved there in the late seventeenth century from Amsterdam. Harrie has long heard that he has "slave blood" in his veins. The story grew more and more intriguing with time, and some years ago he embarked on a painstaking search for his origins. The name "Curiel" was the first clue: why was he called that? He was brought up in a Dutch Reformed family, so where did the Spanish-sounding name come from? He spent long hours in Amsterdam's municipal archives and in Ets Haim Library, leafing through documents, trying to make sense of both his name and the legend of his Jewish slave ancestors in South America.

We have discussed the high position and authority held by one of the founding families of the *Nação*, the Curiels, and particularly by Moses Curiel, who was probably the most famous son of the family. It was he who brought the jacaranda wood from Brazil that was used to make the Torah ark in the new Portuguese Synagogue in 1675. His grave in Ouderkerk's Jewish cemetery features prominently in a famous painting by Jacob van Ruisdael. Obviously, this high status came with the wealth that the Curiels amassed in the New World. But, before meeting Harrie, I had not come across any documents that confirmed the later Curiels' association with Surinamese slaves, let alone any romantic union that produced many children out of wedlock, as Dutch subjects were not allowed to marry slaves until the abolition of slavery in Suriname in 1865.

This is Harrie Curiel's story. His grandfather's grandfather, Hendrik Jacob Curiel, was born in Paramaribo, and was one of seven children born to Moses de Moses Curiel, an Amsterdam Jew, and Elisabeth Christina Nar, a slave woman who belonged to a Dutch slave owner, Anna Hartog Jacobs. Moses de Moses Curiel was the son of Moses de Abraham Curiel—a direct descendant of the founding Curiel family—and Rebecca Polak, apparently from an Ashkenazi family. It is believed he was circumcised on 13 November 1801, in Amsterdam.[1] He supposedly settled in Suriname after the British returned the colony to the Dutch Republic in 1814. Moses de Moses—which basically means Moses, son of Moses—lived in Paramaribo as a merchant, like many other Portuguese Jews before him, alongside his Dutch Reformed compatriots.

THE CURIOUS CASE OF THE CURIELS

It is not clear how he met Elisabeth, but the couple had four children before they could marry, thanks to the new law abolishing slavery. Before their marriage, Moses de Moses had to "buy" Elisabeth and their four children from Anna Hartog Jacobs. The original purchase document, which Harrie shows me, states that Hendrik Jacob Curiel, Harrie's grandfather's grandfather, was nine years old when his father, Moses de Moses Curiel, bought him for 300 guilders. He paid similar amounts for each of his other three offspring. The couple had three more children after marriage. Their marriage certificate shows that Moses de Moses was sixty-two years old in 1864 when he was finally able to marry Elisabeth, the mother of his children, and by doing so, to pass on his family name to the children—but not his religion.

Since Judaism could not be passed to children of a non-Jewish mother, the offspring of Elisabeth and Moses de Moses were brought up in the Christian faith, as members of the Evangelical Lutheran Church. Membership of the Dutch Reformed Church was limited to the white upper classes, so the enslaved and the *mestizos* joined the rural organisation, the Evengelisch-Lutherse Kerk, which was in existence from 1818 till 2004. Elisabeth herself was thought to have been an illegitimate child of a Dutch Jewish merchant from the "Naar" family. Her mother was a slave called Adjuba, whose name is mentioned on the marriage certificate. So, sometime around 1840, when Moses de Moses bought his wife and children, this line of the family ceased to be Jewish.

Hendrik Jacob, the firstborn of Moses de Moses Curiel and Elisabeth Nar, had a son in 1866 called Frederik Adolf Curiel. Adolf married a Dutch woman in Suriname, Betsy Adolphina Abercombie. The couple had a son in 1897 and they named him Hendrik Jacob Curiel. It was to this Hendrik Jacob that Harrie's grandfather was born, given the same name. In another black-and-white photo that Harrie shows me, I see Harrie's grandfather, the great-grandson of a Surinamese slave and a Portuguese

Sephardi Jew from Amsterdam, as a young man. Photographed with his wife and another woman, whose hand he is frivolously holding instead of his wife's, Hendrik Curiel has a sprightly, mischievous face. It seems as if he enjoyed his good fortune, and had a good life in early-twentieth-century Suriname.

To take even a simplified, step-by step journey to trace the Curiels' origins back to Lisbon would be a mammoth task, and is not of massive interest to the reader. However, given the family's important contribution to the Portuguese Jewish community in Amsterdam, the lives of certain Curiels merit elaboration. In particular, those from whom Harrie Curiel says he feels proud to descend, even though he did not grow up with Judaism, are the early members of the *Nação*. As I had tea with him, his Moluccan wife Frida and their son Ruben Zacharias, one evening in August 2017, I felt—though he did not say so in as many words—that he was nostalgic about his Jewish past, that he wished the break from such a rich tradition had not happened in his family. Later, when I searched for documents at Ets Haim, trying to piece together the Curiel family tree, the librarian, Heide Warncke, told me how obsessively Harrie has been trying to pin down his family connection among the Jewish Curiels, before the lineage was broken by the romance between a Jewish plantation owner in Suriname and a slave girl, herself a "half-caste" child of a Jew and a slave

The first Curiels in Amsterdam were immensely influential. Their hardship and courage before the burning stake of the Portuguese Inquisition were legendary. The most prolific historian of "Hebrews of the Portuguese Nation", Miriam Bodian, has written a great amount on the Curiels' origins in Lisbon and their lucky escape. The first Curiels to arrive in Amsterdam were the brothers, Jacob and David—theirs was "one of the richly documented merchant families in Amsterdam."[2] The family originated from Lisbon, then Coimbra, with the name Nunes, and periodically suffered the wrath of the Inquisition. The name Curiel was only adopted by one of the many children of Duarte Nunes, who had fled Portugal to join the Sephardi Jewish community in Syria. Duarte Nunes' fourth son, Jeronimo Nunes Ramires, stayed in Lisbon, and married a woman called Maria da Fonseca, whose family had a strong Marrano tradition. One of Maria's sisters was burned at the stake and her brother was arrested and tortured by the Inquisition police.

Jeronimo and Maria were the parents of David and Jacob. Before their return to Judaism in Amsterdam, the two brothers were called Lopo da Fonseca Ramires and Duarte Nunes da Costa. After the death of her husband, and the arrest of her brother, Maria quickly got out of Lisbon with her sons, the first stop being Madrid. The trio then moved to southern France. As we've seen, it was a well-trodden route of the would-be emigrant to northern Europe. Unfortunately, Maria would never make it to Amsterdam; she died in the French port of Saint-Jean-de-Luz. Her sons brought her remains to Amsterdam, and buried her in Ouderkerk cemetery under a new Jewish name, Sara Curiel.

Lopo da Fonseca Ramires, or David Curiel, would soon become a very important member of Amsterdam's nascent Jewish congregation. His brother spent some years in Amsterdam before settling as a merchant in Hamburg under his Jewish name, Jacob Curiel. Before his move to Germany, the brothers helped form the community's first board of trustees in 1622. The *imposta* board of the early days would subsequently be known as the Mahamad, a powerful body in Portuguese Sephardi tradition made up of selected members, usually four, the *parnassim* (wardens) and the synagogue's treasurer, the *gabay*. Both brothers and their cousin Abraham Curiel—a recent escapee from an *auto-da-fé* in Lisbon—all served as treasurer for several years.

Another interesting aspect of the early Curiels' deep Marrano conviction is their connection to Dr Eliahu Montalto, who was

Saul Levi Morteira's teacher in Venice, and whose body Morteira brought to Amsterdam; his is the oldest gravestone at Ouderkerk. David and Jacob Curiel's aunt was married to Montalto. Both brothers, before they fled Lisbon, were under surveillance by the Inquisition police because of this connection. It was under Montalto's spiritual guidance that the Nunes Ramires family observed crypto-Judaism.

Extraordinarily, after their escape from Lisbon and rebirth as New Jews in Amsterdam, the brothers maintained a staunch allegiance to the Portuguese national identity—not necessarily as Jews, but as Portuguese. Both, within a few years of arriving in Amsterdam, had ended up serving the Portuguese Crown. They became "indispensable" to the Portuguese king and his government, especially when they negotiated the release of the king's brother, Dom Duarte, held hostage by the Spanish in Milan.[3] The Curiels provided momentous assistance in upholding the Portuguese national cause, its independence from Spain. It seems as if they blamed solely the Spanish Inquisition for their family's misfortune. Their collective suffering had its origins in the first displacement, in 1492, when their ancestors had to flee Spain for Portugal because of the Inquisitorial decree. When Portugal followed suit under pressure from Spain and the family had to finally succumb to the Portuguese Inquisition and start a Marrano existence, its deep resentment was aimed at the Spanish, not the Portuguese Crown, which was in a dynastic union with the Spanish Habsburgs. The three generations of the Curiels in Amsterdam would play a vital role in suppressing Spanish authority against Portugal.

With the restoration of an independent Portuguese dynasty in the mid-seventeenth century, the new Portuguese king paid back the family's debt generously. Jacob was knighted by João IV for his services as a royal agent in Hamburg. Meanwhile his eldest son, Moses Curiel, joined the Amsterdam Mahamad and later inherited his father's knighthood. The family's loyalty to its Portuguese identity is also evident in the children's dual names: Jewish and Portuguese. While many other former Marranos had immediately changed their Iberian names for Jewish ones after reaching sanctuary in Amsterdam—including Menasseh ben Israel, Uriel da Costa and Rehuel Jessurun—the Curiels used their Portuguese names as frequently as their Jewish ones.

Moses Curiel's Portuguese name was Jeronimo Nunes da Costa. He served the Portuguese Crown in the Dutch Republic from 1645 to 1697, and rose to become one of the most powerful and enterprising individuals in the *Naçāo*. He was at the head of the Mahamad for six consecutive terms. His phenomenal wealth would enable him to purchase a cornerstone in the brand-new Esnoga built in 1675. He played an influential part in Portugal regaining its independence, using his connections with the Dutch *stadtholders* and rich Sephardi merchants alike to put pressure on Spain, the old enemy of the Seven United Provinces. It was also Moses, son of Jacob, who donated the jacaranda wood for the Esnoga's ark. The father–son team—one in Hamburg and the other in Amsterdam—became the representatives of an important trading company established by the New Christians in Brazil, the Companhia Geral do Comercio do Brasil. With its predominantly Marrano merchants, this company exercised a total monopoly over the import of olive oil, wine, flour and salted fish to Brazil in return for exporting jacaranda to Europe. Moses Curiel almost certainly controlled its supply to the Dutch Republic.

Known to the Christian world as Jeronimo Nunes da Costa, Moses Curiel was probably the most celebrated merchant–diplomat of the Amsterdam Sephardim after Samuel Palache. It was no easy feat for a member of a former Marrano family, long persecuted by Inquisition tribunals, to continue to be loyal to his parents' country, from which they had been driven out by torture, imprisonment, and fear of death.

David, Jacob, Abraham, Moses—these were the best-known Curiels, the builders of the New Jewish community in Amsterdam. Their unconventional characters, idiosyncratic loyalties, business acumen and desire to leave a legacy showed the early signs of what their descendants would become and experience, five generations on. While they contributed significantly to strengthening the Jewish community's wellbeing in Amsterdam, as time went by and the Dutch trade moved to other satellite postings in the colonies, the Curiels were the first to follow suit. It is difficult to ascertain when exactly a branch of the family settled in Suriname, because we know that some of them had sailed to the New World and prospered there as early as the second quarter of the seventeenth century, having tried their entrepreneurial skills in all available trades. The New World presented the Portuguese Jews with unprecedented opportunities. Free from the Amsterdam guilds, they could take on any trade they wanted; so it is hardly surprising that there was a strong presence of Jewish traders in the Americas from early on.

A proper chronology of the Curiel family's arrival and settlement in Suriname is difficult to establish, since various branches of the family spread all over the Sephardi diaspora, including in the New World. Another difficulty in drawing up a clear family tree, as Harrie has experienced during his research in the Amsterdam City Archives and with Ouderkerk's death register, is the similarity of the names of the Curiel descendants. David, Jacob, Moses, Moses de Moses, Duarte, Ramires, Nunes, da Costa, Abraham— the same first and last names go around and around. Still, the Curiel family remains one of the best-documented Portuguese Jewish families in Europe. It is also one of the most dispersed, according to Miriam Bodian: "Along with his brother Jacob Curiel, and other relatives, [David] contributed to creating a far-flung Portuguese Jewish family commercial empire."[4]

Five generations after David and Jacob Curiel arrived and settled in Amsterdam as Jews, we have Moses de Moses Curiel, who moved to Suriname on his own, so far as we know. When he was circumcised in 1801, he must have been around eight days old, in accordance with the Jewish rite. We can safely say, then, that he was in his early twenties when he moved permanently to the Dutch colony of Suriname. In Paramaribo, he would become romantically involved with a slave woman, Elisabeth Nar. Were he permitted to marry his lover, or had it been possible for Elizabeth to convert to Judaism while she was a slave and property of a wealthy Dutch woman, he would almost certainly have passed the Jewish link to his seven children. But even to bequeath his family name to his children prior to the couple's marriage proved difficult—Moses de Moses was only able to give the Curiel name to his eldest son, Hendrik Jacob, after he bought him. By then Hendrik Jacob was a big boy, and had already been brought up with the Protestant faith, the religion of his mother and her owner.

We shall never know why Moses de Moses, after he bought back his first four children and their mother, never tried to convert his family to Judaism. There were many instances even in the early days of the community's settlement when Portuguese Jews in the New World came into contact with African slaves, some of whom were brought back to the Dutch Republic and freed after converting to Judaism. They even had burial spots in the Jewish cemetery. As we know from the story of Spinoza's grandfather, the rules of burial at Ouderkerk were so strict that even uncircumcised Jews could not be laid to rest there. And yet, according to the cemetery's register, a number of slaves—or "black servants" as they were known in Amsterdam, where there was officially no slavery—were buried inside the fence, an area reserved for important members of the community. The best documented of the slaves brought by the Jews to Amsterdam was one we have already met: Eliezer, "the good servant" of the merchant Jacob Israel Belmonte, also known as Diego Dias Querido, "one of the richest merchants in sugar and slaves in Brazil, India, Goa, Cochin and Angola."[5]

Belmonte rose to the same influential status as the Curiel and the Suasso families, but his contribution to the community is more memorable, as he was one of the first founding New Christians to return to official Judaism in Amsterdam. He was also one of the first traders on the African coast, directly dealing with slaves. He used his slaves as interpreters in central African Portuguese sugar plantations, such as those in São Tomé, and as servants in his palatial home in Amsterdam, which was famously etched by de Hooghe. Belmonte taught his slaves basic instruction in the laws of Moses, and also converted some of them to Judaism. These converted "black Jews" were buried inside the fence at Ouderkerk, along with the Jews of Spanish Portuguese descent. Eliezer served Belmonte and became a familiar face in the community. It is extremely likely that he converted to Judaism, as he was almost certainly circumcised—otherwise he would not have been buried within the bounds of the Jewish cemetery.

The reason for this digression into Jews and their slaves is to make a point in connection to Harrie's story: that the *Nação* was well acquainted with African slaves or "servants", as they were called once they reached Amsterdam where there was no law permitting slavery—in fact, under the Union of Utrecht that established the Republic, all men were meant to be treated equally, the reason why the persecuted New Christians had been given sanctuary in Amsterdam in the first place. According to synagogue records, there was constant interaction between Portuguese Jews and their black maids or manservants. This was so prevalent that at one stage the *parnassim* had to seriously look into the situation, to minimise such behaviour. This became a problematic issue for a community so conscious of its public image that even the Ashkenazi peddlers were seen as embarrassing to its social status among the Dutch upper class.

THE CURIOUS CASE OF THE CURIELS

The *parnassim* decided that black, Ashkenazi and occasionally Christian servants should no longer be permitted to crowd at the synagogue entrance before opening hours, to reserve prominent places for their mistresses in the women's gallery. This tradition had been in place from the establishment of the Houtgracht synagogue. The fee-paying male members held reserved places on the main floor, but that was not the case for their wives, mothers and sisters in the gallery above. A rule introduced around 1641 stated that black maids were no longer allowed to "sit in the front rows of the women's gallery, but only on the eighth row or further back."[6] It was also announced in the same year that black circumcised Jews were not to be called to carry out ceremonial acts in the synagogue, such as carrying the Torah scrolls.[7]

The record of such rules proves that, in 1630s and 1640s Amsterdam, the faces of black Africans were not uncommon. There are etchings of African women by Rembrandt, and he could not have painted them from memory of seeing them elsewhere. His black subjects may not have been his sitters, but they were not far off—he just had to look out of his window and capture glimpses of a profile, of the flitting feet of a maid walking behind her mistress, the awkward gait of a young manservant while his master enjoyed a walk with his friends on Breestraat.

In 1647, the Ouderkerk cemetery record shows that blacks and "mulattoes" were allocated a separate, specific place within the cemetery, which many historians see as an indication that Jews were marrying their African acquaintances, who were by then living in Amsterdam in great numbers. The *parnassim* introduced various restrictions throughout the second half of the century to minimise such mixing, but failed to stop it.

Dienke Hondius writes about a fascinating impression, recorded on parchment by a famous calligrapher in 1681, of a certain Isack de Matatia Aboab's "reconciliation" with the *parnassim*, after being granted permission to bury his young mixed-race son at Ouderkerk: "The picture shows a merchant dressed in Dutch fashion with a hat and long wig, holding hands with a small dark-skinned boy, visiting the cemetery."[8]

* * *

Reading this, I try to imagine Harrie's great-great-great-grandfather, Hendrik Jacob, as a young boy, whose father, Moses de Moses Curiel, had to pay to free him from slavery. It seems that, since the time of Eliezer the good servant, Portuguese Jewish society had become more conservative and inward-looking. Over a century after Isack de Matatia Aboab's story, Moses de Moses left Amsterdam, in the early 1800s. It had probably become almost impossible for the children of Jewish–African liaisons to be accepted by the high command of the *Naçāo* in Amsterdam or by its satellites in the colonies. Moses de Moses' children were not only considered non-Jewish, they were hereditary slaves owned by a shrewd Dutch businesswoman, and they were illegitimate. Perhaps Moses de Moses did not even try to make them Jewish.

Although slavery was not permitted in the United Provinces, Moses de Moses did not attempt to bring his children to Amsterdam, where the Curiels were socially well positioned. Maybe precisely for that reason, the Curiels in the colonies stayed put. In Paramaribo, despite the existence of slaves and the slave trade, non-white faces were commonplace; they had their own social network and support system, protected by the Reformed Church. Among the *Naçāo* in Amsterdam, a mixed-race child would have been seen as black, and the Portuguese Jews were not above prejudice against Africans, even those who had converted to Judaism. In fact, Portuguese merchants who went to the colonies and returned home with African servants attempted to start a slave market in Amsterdam, but the city regents did not authorise it.

THE CURIOUS CASE OF THE CURIELS

Outstanding research has been carried out by the Dutch historian Lydia Hagoort into Beth Haim, the Jewish cemetery in Ouderkerk. Hagoort says that many black Africans had found their ways into Portuguese families in Amsterdam and worked as servants. Their status is totally clear in Dutch notarial records, as is their physical description as *swarten*, or "negros". When it came to a proper census of the black Africans on Dutch soil, the authorities, so used to registering people according to their racial and religious affiliations—their "nation"—came up against a solid wall. Due to the legal ban on slavery, those sub-Saharan Africans who arrived in the Dutch Republic from the colonies could be recorded as "*swarten*" or "negroes", but not as "slaves". Many could and did leave their "sponsors"/masters once they realised that they did not need a formal manumission. Yet the attitude of the *Nação* remained tainted by racial prejudices, writes the American historian Jonathan Schorsch. Schorsch also points outs in his book, *Jews and Blacks in the Early Modern World*, that leading rabbis and members of the Mahamad—including famous names such as Morteira, ben Israel and the poet and writer de Barrios—held the view that, even after conversion, "blacks" and "mulattoes" would remain "non-Jews in the eyes of 'whites' in regard to their 'nations'".[9]

The "whites" basically meant the *Nação*. Moses de Moses must have been aware of this, and presumably did not want to further disadvantage his non-white children with a slave woman who, according to available records, was not maltreated by her mistress, Anna Hartog Jacobs. All Moses de Moses could do was to pass on his name to his children. This de-judaised branch of the Curiels lived in Suriname for almost 100 years, until Hendrik Jacob's grandson and namesake decided to move back to Amsterdam in 1927.

* * *

Here, the tale of the Spanish-Portuguese-Dutch-German-Surinamese Curiels takes a fascinating turn. The Curiels have dispersed all around the world, and many have lost the connection to their Dutch family tree. It is a different story for Harrie, born in Amsterdam in the early 1960s. From childhood, he wondered where his name, Hendrik Jacob, came from.

Harrie's grandfather, also Hendrik Jacob, was sixty when he was born. He has fond memories of him, a farmer, in a little town of south-western Holland called Krabbendijke, where he owned a farm with his half-Indonesian wife. The Curiels' tendency to marry out has been a recurrent family trait. After he settled in Amsterdam, Hendrik Jacob married Apalonia Curiel-Jiskoot. Again an illegitimate child of a colonial Dutchman, Jiskoot, Apalonia was brought by her father to Holland, and he helped the newlyweds settle on their farm. Harrie never knew his grandmother, who died before he was born, but he realised from early on that his was not a typical Dutch family. Apart from having a name like Curiel in a Dutch school, his father and uncle, a quarter Indonesian, looked different.

"I visited my grandfather mostly on Sundays. We played chess together. He was always telling nice stories about when he was young in Suriname. He always wore a suit, collected stamps." This well-dressed, kind chess player, however, hid the most unimaginable secret from his immediate family. "Hendrik Jacob Curiel, my grandfather, came back from Suriname in 1927," Harrie tells me, and there's a dramatic pause. We are sitting in his living room on the top floor of a stylish apartment, a stone's throw from the Rijksmuseum. "A few years after he came back, he joined the youth wing of the NSB, the Nationaal-Socialistische Beweging. But he didn't tell anyone after the war ended, I'm not sure even my father knew."

I did not expect this bizarre twist in the Curiel story that has already defied human perceptions of probability. I choose not to say anything, and wait for Harrie to reveal more. Hendrik Jacob's neighbours, who were already members of the NSB, helped him join the nationalist party. It was 1933, and Hendrik Jacob, who was a member of the Lutheran Church, started his new job distributing the party's propaganda newspaper, *De Zeeuwsche Stroom* (The Zealous Stream). In 1939, a year before Hitler's invasion of the Netherlands, the Suriname-born farmer and his half-Indonesian wife had a second son, whom they named Hendrik Jacob. "That was my father." Harrie is smiling and probably enjoying the shock and disbelief on my face. He must have experienced this from strangers ever since he started his research into his family tree and discovered this shocking secret. How can it be possible?

It is true that, under Hitler's law, which considered Jews to be anyone with one Jewish grandparent, Harrie's grandfather was not a Jew. The Jewish line had ended with his great-grandfather, Moses de Moses Curiel. Hendrik Jacob, the NSB member, was the grandson of his namesake, the slave boy of Moses de Moses. But it would not have been difficult for the German officials, who had in their possession an extensive list of the entire Dutch Jewish population, to link anyone in the Dutch Nazi Party called Curiel to the famous noble Sephardi family in Amsterdam. I do not ask the obvious question of how he did it. I search for clues among the papers and documents that Harrie has placed on the dining table where we are sitting. His grandfather must have known about his Jewish link; about his rich, centuries-old heritage; about the dire persecution that had driven his ancestors to flee the Inquisition and settle in Protestant Amsterdam. The question that remains, then, is rather: how could he do it, join the Dutch Nazi Party? Was it the same old Marrano story of adapting and obeying the law, bowing to the authorities to stay alive?

Harrie Curiel says that no one can answer this question. It was perhaps the decision of a weak man with a half-Indonesian wife who struggled to fit in, in a small village. "A majority of the Dutch population hated the NSB. Why my grandfather became a member I really don't understand ... this question will stay with me the rest of my life!"

I look at the picture again, of the young man with three women standing leaning against a front door that opens in two parts, top and bottom—a typical Dutch village house. He has an intense gaze and a frivolous smile through a dark moustache. He wears a black hat and has a shiny belt around his waist with large, round metal disks. The women are wearing typical early-twentieth-century Dutch dresses and bonnets. The woman immediately to his right is very young, in her late teens. To his left stands a beautiful woman on whose hand Hendrik Jacob has placed his own, as if he is trying to coax her into posing for the camera. The third woman, standing slightly apart from the group to Hendrik Jacob's far right, is also wearing fashionable Dutch clothes complete with a bonnet and white lace, but she is not ethnic Dutch. She is his half-Indonesian wife, Apalonia. Hendrik Jacob must have been the most unlikely candidate to join the NSB. But he did, just a few years after he came back from Suriname. What motivated him has been a nagging source of shame and guilt for Harrie. In fact it was the discovery of his grandfather's Nazi allegiances that first prompted Harrie to dig deeper and find out who he was, who his ancestors had been.

The NSB apparently did not ask questions. It needed members, and all potential applicants were considered. In order to make the recruitment process easier, the party, established in 1931 by the Dutch nationalist Anton Adriaan Mussert, essentially copied the German Nazi Party manifesto, but left out the paragraphs referring to Jews. Within six years, the NSB had 52,000 members, and in the Dutch provincial elections of 1935, it won 8 per cent of the country's vote. Much of its support came from the Catholic sector, and the country was stunned by

Mussert's election gain. The Catholic Church and the main political parties expressed strong opposition to the NSB, despite Mussert's insistence that nationalism rather than anti-Semitism was his party's motto. He proved it by inviting everyone, including Jews, to join the NSB. Interestingly, some young Jews did. However, it is generally thought that "extremist elements in his party forced him to change his views. In 1938, Jews were no longer allowed to be NSB members."[10] When Nazi Germany invaded the Netherlands in 1940, many NSB members expressed their support for a campaign to annexe the Netherlands to the Reich. Their leader Mussert, however, was not taken seriously by the Germans.

Our story keeps going back to the Shoah, the Holocaust; and the Dutch role in it remains one of the most perplexing paradoxes of twentieth-century European history. After the war, all the NSB leaders were arrested, tried and imprisoned. Anton Adriaan Mussert was sentenced to death and executed. Harrie's grandfather was also arrested along with his family and put on trial. He was found guilty, but let off lightly. He was kept in an internment camp for one year, before being freed in 1947. "The judge was mild in his verdict. He gave only one year because my grandfather was from Suriname therefore he might not have fully understood the political situation of the time."

As Harrie tells me this, he is still in shock. It is only recently that he has found out about his family's Nazi past, soon after his discovery of his Spanish-Portuguese Jewish ancestry. His extensive research has since created a fascinating family tree. I get the feeling, as I leave Harrie and his family in their bright new apartment, that he did not have an easy time carrying out this research. One reason may have been that the small Portuguese Jewish community, whose life revolves strictly around the Esnoga, did not feel comfortable with a Curiel who was not a Jew; worse, whose grandfather had joined the Nazis.

JERUSALEM ON THE AMSTEL

The journey back from Harrie's flat to Entrepotdok is right across a huge green lawn, past the Rijksmuseum, and along one of the pleasant, though touristy, historic canal walks. The space is covered with people lying down or reclining, enjoying the soft warmth of the setting sun. Many ice cream and waffle kiosks line the walkway leading to the underpass of the Rijks. Buskers with classical instruments are busy with their repertoire of *Für Elise* and *Moonlight Sonata*. How very "Amsterdamish", my children have said—not your usual buskers with backing tracks trying to be Bob Marley. Teenagers and young tourists poke their heads out of the giant "iAmsterdam" letters that stand on the edge of the lawn, in the shadow of the museum. The night guards on the massive billboard showing Rembrandt's *Nightwatch* stare back at you from whichever angle you're looking at them. Under their watchful eyes, I enter the underpass.

After crossing many canals, I hit Herengracht, which then merges into Nieuwe Herengracht, a magnificent walk. On both sides of the canal are palatial, sumptuous, sometimes double-fronted, seventeenth-century houses. Many bear plaques giving a brief history of the rich merchants who once lived at this influential, hip address. Some of these houses belonged to Jews, including the diplomat-merchant Moses Curiel, who lived at no. 49. By the end of the seventeenth century, 2,400 Portuguese Jewish families lived in the United Provinces.

I walk on and arrive at the back of the Esnoga and the Jewish Historical Museum, formerly the Great Synagogue of the Ashkenazim. It was from this angle that Romeyn de Hooghe etched his famous etching of the two synagogues. The tall, narrow, quirky, tilted seventeenth-century houses stand in perfect symbiosis with the Esnoga's high, redbrick structure. Except for a lonely cafe on the ground floor of one of the houses, an old pharmacy, a barber's shop and some dog-walkers, the area between the two synagogues feels eerily empty. I try to imagine what it looked like in the late 1600s, with the dark, narrow houses, the canals and alleyways of a crowded Jodenbuurt.

The road continues on, past the tramlines, all the way to Sint Antoniesbreestraat. But to go home, I must turn right here, toward Artis Zoo. I walk past the low buildings at the front of the Esnoga, and the multicoloured metal arches of the children's adventure park, Tun Fun. I come out onto the street, busy with trams and cafes, hotels and sushi bars, a burger joint called Burghermaster. There it is, the Hollandsche Schouwburg. I cross the street just before the theatre. The bistro outside the Resistance Museum is buzzing as usual. Now that I am nearing the end of my summer in Amsterdam, I shall have to visit the theatre—a memorial to the Dutch Shoah that every Dutchman finds hard to discuss.

15

"THEY CLOSED THE CURTAINS WHEN
THE TRAINS PASSED BY"

The outdoor cafes along the tramline are packed with early evening beer drinkers. The windows of the roadside flats and hotels along the road are wide open, Dutch style; through them I can see people moving about, unaware of being watched by an outsider trying to grasp the city's soul.

I cross the road from outside the Hollandsche Schouwburg. On the other side is the Holocaust Museum. I walk a couple of hundred yards along the main road and enter the Plantage neighbourhood, one of the most picturesque and village-like in Amsterdam. The vibrant evening buzz of Amsterdam is all around me. Even on a Sunday evening, the bistro outside the Resistance Museum, at the heart of this neighbourhood, is teeming with diners all the way to the edge of the pavement. It is a strange coincidence that the two buildings, one memorialising the Dutch Resistance and the other the last days of the Dutch Jewry, are situated so close to each other. But it seems hugely symbolic all the same. I feel, as I slowly walk back to my flat on Entrepotdok, that they are competing against each oth-

er's narratives. One mocks the other, and the other tries to jus-
tify its innocence.

When I get home, I tell my children, "We'll do the Resistance
Museum and the Schouwburg theatre the same day." They reply
that they do not want to visit any more museums; the younger one
says he would rather visit the Artis Zoo just opposite, across the
canal. Every morning when we wake up, we see a herd of elephants
out for an early morning frolic in the sand, before the visitors start
arriving. The sliding glass windows facing the canal open all the
way, the whole width of the building, and when we look out, it is
the picture-postcard Dutch view. Right outside on the edge of the
canal is the nineteenth-century crane that once hoisted goods to
the attics of these hook-fronted tall houses. It stands there as part
of Entrepotdok's, and the city's, conservation project.

The beauty of Amsterdam, its perfectly designed grid of canals
and streets, with manicured green spots thrown in, has continued to enthral visitors. Even those who don't come for research
on World War II or the Dutch Jewish history would still most
probably visit the magnificent Esnoga and the Resistance
Museum. The entry ticket to the Portuguese Synagogue includes
two other sites, the Hollandsche Schouwburg and the Holocaust
Museum. These buildings are nothing as ostentatious as the
Esnoga, and many probably do not go on to visit them. But if
one did, even the most unprepared and unhistorically-minded
would be struck by downright bafflement. How did it happen?
The statistics of deportation and murder of the Dutch Jews in
their home city, historically known as the most welcoming of
nations in Europe, just do not make sense.

How did it happen? The question has been lingering and
glooming over my research. At the end of summer 2017, just
before my return to London, I take the train to Antwerp to see
Ludo Abicht, a political scientist and one of the best-known
writers on the Jews of Antwerp. I have been told by people I've

interviewed for my research, both pundits and descendants of the *Naçāo*, that if anyone can make sense of this baffling epilogue to the Dutch Jewish history, it is Ludo Abicht, an octogenarian professor at Antwerp University.

It is thought that the "decline" of the Jews began soon after the death of William of Orange. But, as we know, that decline was not particularly Jewish; it was part of the general decline of Amsterdam or the Dutch Republic as a centre of mercantilism. England and Germany were fast emerging as world economic powers, pushing to one side the Dutch Golden Age. Post-French Revolution liberalism began to undermine the place of religion. The period of "decline" that started at this time would stretch. over more than a century. 1796 is known for the Emancipation, when the Jews won full rights to citizenship in the Dutch constitution. While that was a victory for humanism and equal rights movements, as we've seen, it truly marked the end of the *parnassim*, the end of rabbinical power over the Jews. As a result, the role of the *Naçāo* was made redundant. It was for this very reason that the rabbis had not been keen to welcome the institutionalised "emancipation" that came much earlier with the 1645 Patenta Onrossa, when the Portuguese Jews had enormous influence on the Dutch *stadtholders* and their foreign policy.

Bart Wallet, Dutch historian and professor at Amsterdam University, says that while volumes of documents are available about Dutch Jewish history in the seventeenth century, there is a gaping hole when it comes to the eighteenth and nineteenth centuries. This is precisely why he chose these centuries as the focus of his research. This was also the time when the Ashkenazi Jews were thrust into the limelight; they became more influential and Yiddish culture became synonymous with Jewish culture. The Portuguese Jews, who were still attached to their old manners and their old glories, found it hard to compete with the rise of Ashkenazi ways. They were also suffering the economic inertia that usually sets in when several past generations have lived with incredible commercial success; this too might have contributed to the *Naçáo's* descent into obscurity as the decades passed by. There were many factors that led to this socio-political decay, which could be expounded over and over with historical and sociological research into volumes of available documents. But that still leaves us with baffling questions about the wartime Dutch-Jewish history. Wallet, who was researching eighteenth- and nineteenth-century Ashkenazi prayer books when I spoke to him, as well as the minuscule bound almanac booklets called *luach*, says that his research into Dutch Jewish history always stops at 1940. It is too painful and ignominious for a country that had once invited and proudly boasted of a carnival of nations.

I board a train to Antwerp, the city where New Christians lived in the early modern period, when it was under Spanish rule, thriving in the businesses of precious stones, dried fruit, and moneylending. There were many Marranos among them. The *Naçáo* was yet to be formed in Amsterdam, but in Antwerp, the former Jews from Iberia were well organised and prosperous, and would remain so until they were pushed out when the Protestant northern provinces declared independence from Spain and became the Dutch Republic. Ludo Abicht's *The Jews of Antwerp* is among the scholarly books on this subject.

The early morning train from Centraal Station goes south via several historic cities: Leiden, Rotterdam, Dordrecht. The train stops briefly in Breda, where many people get off. Just after Breda we cross the River Scheldt, the famous blockades of which moved, shook and transformed the fate of the United Provinces throughout the medieval and early modern periods. In fact the flooding of the Scheldt by William of Orange—often compared to the biblical deluge—finally wiped out the Spanish siege of the 1570s, and William I emerged as a Moses who had led his people across the Dutch Red Sea.

THEY CLOSED THE CURTAINS

The two regions were so interconnected, and at the same time so separated—by Spanish imperial rule, mass revolt, and the emergence of the first European republic. The train moves off from Breda, which was also where the treaty was signed to end the second Anglo-Dutch War, in favour of the latter. I look out of my window. Amidst commuters in black suits, running to and fro with takeaway coffee, I do not see any signs that would link this city to the great Dutch strategic gain over the English. Breda was also host to other important treaties; the English used it several times to resolve their internal political wars.

I arrive in Antwerp at late morning. Before heading for Ludo Abicht's house, I walk around the old diamond market that spreads out right from the doorstep of the ornate station. Once it must have looked like a maze, where the Jews settled in its dark alleys with a lucrative diamond trade, cutting, polishing and selling the precious stones. Today, I see mostly Indians, sitting behind glass boxes under bright florescent lights. It is early for diamond buyers, but many shops are open. I walk through the town, past Rubens' house and the touristy, pedestrianised square, where people are already sitting at outdoor tables with beer that comes in many varieties and different-shaped glasses. One does not need a reminder that this is of course the beer country. Just behind the square is the old Jewish quarter, which is deserted today. There are no Jews living here now, I will be told later. Antwerp's Jews are mostly Ashkenazi, and they live in a different neighbourhood.

From the station, it is a good half hour's walk to Ludo Abicht's fabulous 1960s converted apartment. He leads me to an upper floor and makes coffee. We have already started talking. He teaches Political Science at Antwerp University, but today is his day off. As we know, the Jewish history in the Low Countries began in Antwerp. The city's "Jews" were Marranos living in a province ruled by the same Catholic monarchs whose Inquisition

309

had driven them out of their homeland. Ludo is looking for reference books for me as he talks; I already have a pile on the table to browse through, next to my enormous mug of coffee—I shall have three of these during my conversation with Professor Abicht.

"In fact the Jewish presence in Antwerp is recorded since the twelfth century, we have proof, we have tombstones. But when the Spaniards reconquered the city, more than half the population—including those of the bourgeoisie, intellectuals—left Antwerp and went to Middelburg or Amsterdam. And they took with them the Jews." Amsterdam would have been a different place had these Antwerp New Christians not come to strengthen the *Nação* being formed there from the end of the sixteenth century. Ludo stands before a map, on which he showed me earlier the trade route that the central European Jews had taken to arrive here: along the Rhineland, through Bruges and what is today Brussels. When he said that Antwerp's Jewish presence went back to the twelfth century, that was before the time the New Christians started arriving. The earliest Jews there were Ashkenazi.

There might have been a small-scale Marrano presence among the New Christian business community in Antwerp, but it was never made public. The Iberian merchants led their day-to-day lives like the majority of the city's population, who were Catholics.

"As you know," Ludo explains, "Amsterdam was prospering at a great speed with all the extra tradesmen and intellectuals who arrived from the south." These were the Marranos and other New Christians whom the Antwerp Calvinists took north with them to the new Dutch Republic. However, this view has been long refuted as myth by more contemporary scholarship, which argues that there is no direct connection between the Antwerp New Christians and the birth and success of the Amsterdam Jewish community.

Ludo leaves the wall map of the Low Countries and sits next to me on the sofa. "But that's not what you've come here to ask?"

Well, yes, I tell him. But more importantly, I would like to know his views on what really happened in Amsterdam, the city known as an extraordinary European example of early modern tolerance. Why could it not save its Jews who had been here for four centuries? Ludo sighs. In short, he says, the Jews felt so secure, so safe, so Dutch, that they chose not to leave the Netherlands after the Nazi invasion of 1940, although they had a long time to consider doing so. "That's the tragedy—they really didn't think anything could happen, they were so comfortable, and on an intellectual level, totally assimilated..."

Ludo does not finish his sentence. The last words trail off, before he picks up the thread:

"The other thing is, in Holland, even the Resistance was obsessed with religion." I ask what he means. "In Belgium, we don't have religion on our identity papers, but it wasn't the case in the Netherlands. In Belgium, people weren't and aren't registered according to their religion." In the pre-war Netherlands, on the other hand, everyone's religion was mentioned on their national identity card. Abraham Palache talked about the meticulous Dutch record-keeping, which he believed was partly to blame for the Nazis' separation of the Jews from the gentiles. I ask Ludo why Belgium didn't document its citizens' religion. "Well, Belgium was only founded in 1830, as you know. And there was no unifying language here, and we had no Jews. There are many reasons."

But Belgium is not part of my research, Ludo reminds me. The citizens of the Seven United Provinces were registered according to religion from the early 1800s, after the introduction of the Civil Record by the French. "In Holland, the authorities created and maintained a very good system of registering the whole population," says Ludo. This again takes me back to what Abraham Palache said. It was easy to isolate the Jews from the national register, which the Germans then used to make the infamous Hollerith punch cards, on which an individual's sex, place of residence, marital status and profession were coded. The cards were sorted by the Hollerith machine, an early version of the modern computer. It was invented by a German-American engineer, Herman Hollerith, and during the war it was also used, for the first time, to list each person's race, traced back to his or her grandparents. In pre-war times, the machine was used by the United States and most European countries to record census data. The Hollerith used by the Germans in the lead-up to World War II was devised by the German branch of an American company, which would later make the IBM computers.

Some have argued—though more recent scholarship has significantly nuanced this view—that it was by using the Hollerith technique and the flawless Dutch national data that the Nazis could very quickly put together a Jewish Registry—a claim substantiated by a journalist, Edwin Black. In *IBM and the Holocaust*, he argues that the location and rounding up of Jews all over the Netherlands, within just a year after the start of the war, was made possible by this advanced technology. The meticulously documented personal information and data on religious groups in turn served as an effective tool for social control. Before the world could pause to think, Black asserts, information technology had become a weapon of war, "a roadmap for group destruction."[1] As if out of a dark sci-fi film, the Hollerith acted as "the automaton", with thousands of replicas sent out across German-dominated Europe to transfer the national register for citizens into individual punch cards. Card-sorting operations were set up in major concentration camps, which not only recorded the arrivals of the inmates, but also catalogued their individual exterminations.

Those who have spoken to me about the obsessive Dutch habit of documentation have expressed horror and dismay, all these years on, at the thought of the citizens' register falling into

Nazi hands, village by village, town by town, house by house, in order for the Hollerith to codify people into its punch cards. The mayors of the cities were asked to provide the lists of Jews living in their communities based on the extensive civil records, and most of them did. It was not a difficult task in the Netherlands, unlike in Germany where the assimilated Jews had taken German names. In Amsterdam, the Sephardim in particular had maintained their Portuguese first names and their very distinctive Iberian surnames: Paraira, da Costa, Curiel, de Barrios, Prado, de Pinto, D'Oliveira, Suasso, Palache.

But the question still remains: how did the Nazis get hold of the list of Jews, down to the very last person, in every corner of the Netherlands? Every week, truckloads arrived at Amsterdam's assembly point, the Hollandsche Schouwburg. The 300-capacity theatre hosted 3,000 inmates with just one toilet, while they waited for the next departure day, the tram to the unknown. One of the wardens of the theatre site, now the Holocaust Memorial, said to me that some captives must have been forced to ask which of the two tragedies was more bearable—to wait in the squalor, hunger, ignominy and filth of the theatre hall, or to embark on their train journey of no return? Dutch bounty hunters were selling the Jews to the Nazis, for 7 guilders each. Historians have explained this as a product of the Nazis' superb manipulation skills, with which they presented the removal of the Jews from Dutch mainstream society as a solution to the anti-Semitism that had already existed, unbeknown to the Jewish citizens and to those who became members of the Resistance.

In fact, the Nazis used the old Dutch system of Jewish self-administration and created the scandalous Joodse Raad (Jewish Council) to administer all Jews living in the country. The Council's leaders co-operated with the Dutch Nazis, hoping it would help them gain concessions from the Germans. This has been seen as a peculiar aspect of Dutch Jewry, their eagerness to prove themselves law-abiding citizens viewed in the same vein as their forefathers' compliance with the House of Orange and the subsequent Dutch authorities. What the Jewish Council wanted to achieve was to prove that the Jews in the Netherlands were true Dutch citizens, respectful of Dutch law and authority. "Just like the non-Jewish elite, the Jewish leaders, too, generally came up with a 'co-operative, administratively appropriate, and law-abiding' response, an attitude that was 'in line with the pre-war tradition of self-rule and of regular consultation with the authorities.'"[2]

It is also thought that the Dutch authorities did not outwardly want to be seen to be disobeying the occupying authority, in case that hastened the systematic destruction of the Jews and the Dutch Resistance. The Jewish Council and the Dutch administration were not prepared for the sheer speed at which the Nazis operated in occupied Europe, including in the annihilation of the Jews. Jewish and Dutch historians have tried to pinpoint key reasons why the Jews in the Netherlands nevertheless suffered most during the Nazi occupation of western Europe. These include loyalty of Dutch agencies to the Nazi regime; the Jews' historical image as obedient, dutiful citizens; and their nostalgia about the place, their Dutch Jerusalem that had given them sanctuary from the Inquisition and pogroms. "The fact that the Dutch people as a whole were unable to provide their Jewish compatriots with adequate prediction in time and on a sufficient scale has left its stamp on this catastrophic incident in Dutch history."[3]

Another reason behind the high number of Jewish casualties is that the Netherlands was only liberated in May 1945, while France and Belgium were freed of the Nazi occupation the previous year. Also, 78 per cent Dutch Jews ended up in the death camps, compared with 25 per cent of French Jews and 44 per cent of Belgian Jews.[4] "That's why there are so many trees in Yad Vashem, Dutch trees, to cover up the historic, tragic failure," Ludo Abicht says, adding that he is being "a little cynical". I ask him to be as cynical as he would like. So he goes on talking:

THEY CLOSED THE CURTAINS

It was as if every Dutch non-Jew was hiding an Anne Frank. The Anne Frank story is a great story of course. It's moving. But it's become a bit of a legend. It helps cover up in a way what really happened. I still haven't answered your question, because I don't know what drove those people to hunt down Jews and hand them over to be murdered. Were they resentful? Were the Jews too rich, too famous, too successful, too sexually potent? Was there some hidden resentment that never came out?

Ludo admits that it is true, those who turned in Jews were a tiny group of individuals among Dutch society, and he can put forward lots of different arguments, as other historians have done,[5] to understand what might have happened in Holland in World War II—but as a political scientist, he still does not have simple answers to these questions. The Anne Frank story has somehow helped to counteract the fact that the Netherlands had the highest percentage of Jews deported and killed in western Europe.

Many of them were ransomed: the families that were hiding them started blackmailing their secret guests. Most gentiles in Holland were not like the employees that hid the Franks, Ludo asserts. In World War II, centuries of superficial assimilation came crashing down, leading to the near-extinction of a people. The previous centuries of segmentation of society in the name of tolerance and good governance—which later came to be known as "pillarisation"—meant that the culture of seeing but not touching had been ingrained in the Dutch psyche. Toleration does not mean acceptance and, as Ludo Abicht points out, Dutch society has been experiencing the fallout ever since. The country's immigration system today is struggling to deal with deep-seated prejudices against emigrants who, unlike the Iberian Sephardim 400 years ago, do not arrive with cash, gold or superb knowledge of international trade and diplomacy. "It should not have happened," sighs Ludo, "they looked the other way."

JERUSALEM ON THE AMSTEL

I drink my third mug of coffee. Ludo has gone back to his bookshelf, trying to find something to support his argument. The table in front of us is piled high with papers, maps and books. He is frustrated that I cannot read an important chapter in his book on the Jews of Antwerp, which has not been translated into English. I ask what it is about. "It's about, 'What would we have done without the Jews?'" The anomaly of the Dutch failure to protect Holland's Jews ridicules the other historic oddity: that of Amsterdam, Dutch Jerusalem, which sheltered them for over 300 years. Does the horror of three years cancel out the glory of the previous three centuries?

Ludo seems to be struggling to articulate his answer to this. In the end he states, in a raspy, distant voice, "As the Dutch themselves would say—well, the self-critical Dutch—'they closed the curtains when the trains passed by.'"[6]

Amid the light and buoyancy of late summer, I step out of the Abicht house and head for the train bound for Amsterdam Centraal. It is still light when I get off the tram at the Hollandsche Schouwburg, the old "Jewish Theatre" that hides the darkest reality in Holland's history: the disappearance of what was, until the war, a thriving Jodenbuurt on the banks of the Amstel River. The area today is full of museums, toy stores, a massive branch of the Dutch department store Albert Heijn, shoe shops, old pharmacies, cafes after cafes, bars after bars, waffle kiosks, a flea market, antiquarian bookshops. The houses that still stand today to remind us of the past are those of Rembrandt and de Pinto, the quarrelsome neighbours. We do not know if Rembrandt ever paid up for his share of the cost of reconstructing the party wall; I doubt the bankrupt artist ever did.

The theatre that is now a museum of the inexplicable Dutch Holocaust is closed as I walk past. I have been postposing visiting it, despite its serendipitous proximity to where I am living.

"They loved theatre," was Bart Wallet's enduring comment on the first New Christian settlers in his city 400 years ago. "As soon as they arrived, they bought membership cards to Amsterdam's theatres." They had an insatiable thirst for "theatrical performances and frivolous poetic tournaments."[7] The *parnassim* repeatedly tried to stop these performances, because they feared the shows would perpetuate the New Jews' cultural Catholic nostalgia. As we know, the rabbis forbade in 1632 the staging of plays in the synagogue during Jewish festivals, including those with religious Jewish themes such as *Diálogo dos Montes*. But the theatre-lovers' zeal for the performing arts continued to be satisfied in private venues. "Warehouses were rented to perform plays, and the forbidden *enigmas* (poetic variations on the theme of a riddle) found their illustrious home in the salons of Don Manuel de Belmonte", the richest Jew in Amsterdam.[8] Against someone like Belmonte, who probably paid the highest fee of all to the synagogue and who was also a member of the Mahamad, the rabbis could not proceed further in terms of banning performances in private venues.

Throughout the successive three centuries, the performing arts would continue to play an important role in Jewish cultural life in Amsterdam, albeit within various orthodox parameters. Founded in 1892, the Hollandsche Schouwburg was a Dutch municipal theatre with such a high Jewish membership that it was often referred to as the Jewish Theatre. It was a thriving meeting point for cross-cultural ideas and creative activities— until 1941, when the Nazis moved the Jewish captives here and continued to use it as an assembly point for the Dutch Jews throughout the war.

* * *

I visit the Schouwburg theatre with my children before we return to London. We see the Resistance Museum first. As I expected, there is evidence after evidence, rooms full of documentation of subterfuge activities of Resistance fighters evading the Nazi system to protect the Jews, gaining false papers and passports to assign to those who were lucky. There are examples of families that hid Jews. As we hop from room to room, the disturbing statistics of Dutch wartime history follow us: "Of the total number of victims the war claimed in the Netherlands, the Jews accounted for approximately 50 per cent, though Jews had comprised only 1.57 per cent of the population in 1940."[9]

Across the street, the main hall of the Hollandsche Schouwburg, where 300 people could sit and watch a show, holds a sombre memorial to these victims. It is a hollow space, except for the remains of one of the old walls. A tall black obelisk keeps a single flame burning perpetually. Three sets of six benches face the flame, perhaps to mimic the audience, with the obelisk as the stage and the flame as the drama, perpetually replaying in our consciousness what must not be forgotten. It is the simplest of all Holocaust memorials I have seen around the world, but the Dutch flame in memory of more than 100,000 victims is one of the most powerful.

Of the 107,000 deportees, around 5,500 returned after the war.[10] 24,000 hid with the help of the Resistance, of whom 8,000 were caught. There were several thousands who managed to flee abroad. Nothing could showcase more hauntingly the total loss of a majestic epoch in Dutch–Jewish history than this spartan setting against the ruin of an old wall: the black monolith, the single flame, amidst the hollowness of what was once the audience hall of Amsterdam's vibrant Jewish Theatre.

POSTSCRIPT

"These are the Portuguese Jews who died in Westerbork, and were cremated there. Their ashes were brought here. During the war, there had been regular communication between the Amsterdam Portuguese community and the Portuguese Jews in Westerbork. There had been some travels back and forth."

I am speaking to Tirtsah Levie Bernfeld, a Dutch scholar of the Portuguese Jewish community in Amsterdam, about those of the *Nação* who were sent to the Westerbork transit camp in the north-eastern Netherlands. We are in Beth Haim, the Portuguese Jewish cemetery in Ouderkerk aan de Amstel, standing in front of the war memorial for the Sephardi Jews who perished during World War II. It is made of white marble, simple. I try to read the inscription in Hebrew. I hear Tirtsah say, "The other thing is that they tried to go to Portugal. I've seen letters of people already in Westerbork writing to the Amsterdam Portuguese community at the time, 'Don't forget us, put us on the list to be transported to Portugal.'"

I ask her what this list was about. "The Portuguese community of Amsterdam had contacts with the Portuguese authorities [in Lisbon] to set up a list of Jews of Iberian origin and move them out to Portugal. And Portuguese Jews in Westerbork had already sent in letters to their community leaders in Amsterdam not to forget them and to register them on that list." But did the Portuguese government pay any attention to this plea? "No, no, they had no influence. There are some examples where people fled to Spain, who managed to get Spanish passports, but most of them didn't make it. The Portuguese Jews were sent to camps a bit later than the Ashkenazi Jews, because they tried to prove they were Catholics, and even hired professors of anthropology who made all kinds of studies, to show that they were not 'racially' Jews. You know, you try everything to escape your fate. This was what happened here."

The names of the Westerbork victims are engraved on white marble slabs, arranged in a "U" shape on the ground with the memorial standing at its bend. As my eyes go over them, I pick out the most common, familiar family names from Amsterdam's Jodenbuurt.

ABRAHAM V. NATHAN
JESSURUN CARDOZO
JUDITH RODRIGUES LOPES-D'ANCONA
SALOMON V. MOZES NUNES NABARRO
RACHEL V ARON DA COSTA DA FONSECA
CARA SENOR CORONEL—LOPES CARDOZO
RACHEL V EPHRAIM MORESCO

There are many more. Underneath the names, a similar stone slab reads, "*Urnengraven Westerbork 1943–1944*"—cremated at Westerbork. "This means these Portuguese Jews died in the transit camp, and were cremated there," explains Tirtsah. Their ashes were later brought in urns to this cemetery for burial, probably during the war. She goes back to her theme: "But the Sephardi Jews in the end didn't escape their fate. They were deported like all the others, and this memorial is for all of them." She helps me understand the faded Hebrew on the memorial stone. She is of Ashkenazi background; both of her parents were sent to concentration camps, but were among the lucky few who returned.

POSTSCRIPT

Nochem de Beneditty was a judge and chairman of the Portuguese Jewish community in Amsterdam when the Nazis invaded the Netherlands on 10 March 1940. While the Hollerith machine was busy actively listing on punch cards those whom the Nazis considered to be of the Jewish race, de Beneditty went to see a renowned Dutch anthropologist, C. U. Ariëns Kappers, with two lawyers. Ariëns Kappers had co-authored a book, *Introduction of the Anthropology of the Near East*, in 1934. This work documented extensive research on skull measurements of Sephardi and Ashkenazi Jews and demonstrated that, out of those who took part in the study, 235 Sephardim had a different cephalic index curve from the 233 Ashkenazim. Judge de Beneditty used this and similar studies to argue that, after 200 years of living as New Christians in the Iberian Peninsula and having intermingled with the Old Christian aristocracy there, the New Christians had long ago ceased to be Jews. When they came to Amsterdam, they had maintained a homogenous group for 300 years and had not married out. Therefore, they were still racially not Jews, despite their outward conversion to Judaism.

De Beneditty wanted Ariëns Kappers' help to use this argument to try to save all the registered Portuguese Jews, and his lawyers worked hard. There had already been some individual cases of Sephardi Jews directly writing to the occupying Nazi authorities with this anthropological "evidence" of their non-Jewish racial background. A first report pleading for exemption for the Portuguese Sephardim was compiled, based on Ariëns Kappers' findings that the so-called "Portuguese-Israelites" were actually of Mediterranean origin. Soon afterwards, in the summer of 1943, came a second report by another anthropologist, Arie de Froe, who had sent around requests to the Sephardi Jews in the Netherlands to come and be examined in his laboratory. His nearly 100-page report concluded with photographic evidence that the Portuguese were not Jews at all, that they were in fact of "a different racial" group.[1]

These rescue efforts delayed the deportation of the Dutch Portuguese Jews by a year or so, but ultimately the Nazis carried out their own investigation and did not buy Ariëns Kappers' and de Froe's argument. The Sephardim would soon meet the same fate as their Ashkenazi co-religionists. However, while their petitions were being reviewed, some of the applicants had a chance to go into hiding, and a small section of them did. They survived. In February 1944, a majority of the Portuguese Jews who had chosen to await a favourable reply to such petitions to the Nazi authorities, rather than go into hiding, were rounded up and sent to Westerbork. The SS paraded them in the transit camp and one of the officers issued this statement:

> A sub-human race ... The overall impression does not justify a special treatment by sending them to Spain or Portugal, but they should be treated like all other Jews ... The view of the learned professors, who were apparently lacking in political understanding, cannot be shared.[2]

It was claimed by the SS that the photographic "evidence" collected by the anthropologists to prove the Portuguese Jews' non-Jewish credentials were just "lighting effects". Twenty-two families were sent from Westerbork to the Theresienstadt concentration camp in Czechoslovakia. Most of them were transferred to Auschwitz almost immediately, including Judge de Beneditty and his wife. The last remaining inmates of Westerbork still harboured hope that their petition might yet be considered, or that they would hear back from Portugal, even Spain.

Many Jewish historians after the war were appalled by this story, which they felt was dishonourable, a "shameful" coda to the story of the Portuguese Jews of Holland. A 2015 seminar at Yad Vashem, Jerusalem, entitled "Non-Jewish Jews", tried to explain this uncomfortable chapter in Jewish wartime history. This international workshop discussed, among other things, the so-called *Action Portuguesia*, on which Dutch historian Jaap

POSTSCRIPT

Cohen presented a paper. He discussed fate and identity during World War II in relation to the Portuguese Jews, who tried to prove that they had little "Jewish blood" left after years of intermingling with the Old Christians of Iberia. "Cohen expertly tackled the question of whether the *Action Portuguesia* was a scam for a noble cause, or if the Sephardim really believed in their arguments."[3] However, Cohen's criticism of the *Action Portuguesia* was countered by a poignant reply from Professor Dina Porat, Yad Vashem's chief historian. She said:

> All those that took steps, out of dire necessity, to save themselves, were thinking of better times in which they could return to their former identities and traditions. But in the meantime, these actions caused great difficulties and ruptures within their own hearts. In some cases, the survivors kept their new identities, even after the war ended.[4]

Tirtsah Levie Bernfeld believes that this phenomenon showed the lengths to which victims of an impending genocide would go to save themselves. Some members of the historian's own family managed to escape to Spain. It was a desperate measure by a desperate people. The names on the white marble of this sombre war memorial at Ouderkerk are also a haunting reminder of the New Christians' story of survival under the Inquisition, the centuries-old struggle to escape the burning stake. One is lost for words. How can you express the baffling grief one feels at the inexplicable, recurring tragic history of the Iberian Jews? The repeated "ruptures" in their hearts and faiths?

However, what Tirtsah helps me see is what also survives here, which illustrates once again the glorious days of the *Nação*, one of the most remarkable chapters in the history of the Sephardi Jews, in their Dutch Jerusalem. The richness of their life was memorialised at death with equal flamboyance, pomp and ceremony, the love of high art that the Iberian migrants carried forth to the Dutch Republic. Their "hidden" love of figurative art—an inherent imprint of their former Catholicism—is exhibited nowhere more illustriously than on the exquisite gravestones in Ouderkerk cemetery. An engraved hourglass is the most prevalent theme, as if the community was obsessed with time, or its transience. Tirtsah tells me this is a very seventeenth-century style of popular Dutch art known as *vanitas*, a symbolic work of art that represents figurative motifs, including in funereal art.

At the height of the seventeenth century, the apogee of the *Nação*'s success, the artwork on the tombstones of rich merchants become more and more dramatic. I see elaborate biblical figures in action: Abraham with a dagger over Isaac's small body, about to sacrifice him; Jacob dreaming on a stairway to heaven; Rachel fetching water from the well; a pregnant Rachel dying as she gives birth to Benjamin. Many of the gravestones feature bas-reliefs of the raising of the curtain, with poems or words of eulogy dedicated to the dead.

I cannot help thinking, as I look at the artwork on the gravestones, of the former Marranos' quiet rebellion at death, having lived their lives under the rabbinical orthodoxy of the *Nação*. Did they ever fully forsake their Iberian cultural heritage? Why was there this theatrical need at death to visualise the meaning of dying, even pre-ordering tombstones in many cases, which totally goes against Judaism?

Removing dead leaves from the tombstone of David Rocha, the first grave one comes across entering the cemetery, Tirtsah says, "Look here, look at the motif—it's a theatre. The screen has been lifted, the play has begun." But I see there is no one on stage: the player is dead and lies beneath the stone. Atop the empty stage and the gathered curtains is David, playing the harp. The figure of the biblical harp player appears frequently in the art of the cemetery. It was also a popular theme in mainstream historical paintings by Dutch masters, but King David's repeated appearance on gravestones in Ouderkerk is also because many of the deceased were his namesake. Engraving or carving art evoking the biblical significance of the dead person's name was immensely popular. David Rocha's tomb features several other musical instruments, and from the Portuguese inscription on the stone, it appears he was a musician:

Na terra a Gloria do canto
No ceo o canto da Gloria
(On Earth the glory of song
In Heaven the song of glory)

As we walk around, we see a lot of Mordechais on horseback, Jacobs dreaming on ladders, Leah and Rachel, Rebecca offering a drink to Abraham's good servant Eliezer. But the scene that appears over and over again is the theatre itself, always with its curtains raised. The play has not just begun, but has just finished. On many a gravestone, the skeleton of the angel of death wields a scythe. The cemetery is full of curiously sacrilegious display of graven images. The many musical instruments, from both the European and Eastern worlds, proclaim that the deceased were patrons of music and drama. "Totally un-Jewish, the rabbis would not have approved of it!" says Tirtsah, smiling. "Even God makes an appearance, look here! And his hand, the Hand, is cutting down a tree from the bottom." This is the tree of life and an axe is about to brutally cut it down—a theme repeated on many of the tombstones, in particular those of young people and children.

"Now, look who we have here, the grave of Daniel de Pinto!" I am amazed by its over-the-top decoration. His character is as colourful in death as when he was alive. Is he not the one who fought with Rembrandt, I ask, looking at the beautiful engravings that would throw into disarray any Puritan's view on graven images. "Yes, he was the one." Tirtsah points to the adjacent tombstone, saying, "He is buried next to his son, Moses." Often Amsterdam's Jews prepared these stones for each member of the family before they died, and they reflect the European artistic and architectural ideals of their time, from the Renaissance, to Baroque, to early modern. Through this progression, we see the development of Dutch Jewish culture.

"You see next to the elaborately decorated gravestones we have some very simple ones. They belong to the Sephardi rabbis of the time. This is of Rabbi Saul Levi Morteira." Tirtsah points to a mossy, flat stone, on which the Venetian rabbi's name is barely discernible. Also in this oldest part of the cemetery is Rabbi Isaac Uziel's traditional domed grave, again without any ornamentation. Although Uziel's tombstone, one of the first in Ouderkerk, has no graven images, it is most exquisitely beautiful, its conical shape draped—the artist sculpted the stone to make it appear so. The grave of the Moroccan rabbi reminds me of similar tombs I saw recently in the Fez cemetery.

Along the same spot, I see another beautiful, soothing, man-sized slab of marble with a simple epitaph. This is not the grave of a former Iberian New Christian, that is obvious; but it belongs to a very important member of the *Nação*, Samuel Palache. Along with his fellow Old Sephardim, Morteira and Uziel, Palache instructed the New Jews into the laws of normative Judaism. Under a beautiful tree engraved on alabaster white marble, the poems appear undecipherable to a lay Hebrew speaker. Even when I showed their cryptic language to Hebrew scholars, many struggled to translate it, as they found it hard to understand the underlying enigma:

> This is the grave of a wise man,
> Who was good with man and God,
> Samuel Palache.
> May he rest in honour.
> He was summoned by God on Friday, 17 of Shevat, 5376.
> Let me weep bitterly
> Let him rest in peace

POSTSCRIPT

Those who walk upright, enter peace.
They find rest as they lie in death.[5]

"Here's the cornerstone of the community, and he is laid here in a position so he continues to be the cornerstone of Ouderkerk!" Tirtsah shows me the grave of the longest-serving rabbi of the *Nação*, Isaac Aboab da Fonseca. The epitaph on his grave is touchingly self-complimentary. A tomb nearby belongs to another cornerstone of the community, Menasseh ben Israel. Again it is unadorned, except for an enthusiastic homage by the Jews of Britain, grateful for their re-entry to England—to the base of the marble on this slightly tilted tombstone, they added a memorial inscription in 1960.

The simple graves belong mostly to rabbis, who preached against graven images, but it seems that the former New Christians barely paid attention to this rule, defying in death the strict orthodoxy of their recent life in Amsterdam by paying homage to their old Iberian heritage from "the land of idolatry", as the rabbis and the *parnassim* called it. Other unadorned grave-stones belong to the community's poor—a subject over which Tirtsah Levie Bernfeld exercises unique authority. "This is Spinoza's mother. Hannah Deborah Spinoza." Her husband, Miguel, all of whose wives died before him, is buried not far off, in another plain grave.

We move deeper into the cemetery, into the later period of the seventeenth century. As time progressed, the gravestones became more and more elaborate, decorated with personalised themes of death. Apart from the ubiquitous hourglass, there are skulls and crossbones, the angel of death. "If you go to the Old Church in Amsterdam, you'll see [Christian] graves and you'll see a likeness, a true likeness, because they used the same artist, and the same contemporary style. The Jews were first of all barred from most of the guilds; they were also forbidden by their rabbis to engage in figurative art. So they went to prominent Dutch funeral artists. Here's a grave with a later style, the flowers have strong French influence. Gorgeous. The flowers symbolise the dimensions of transience. Can you see?"

The *vanitas* in the Jewish art corroborated an internal rupture: the former New Christians' nostalgia for a lost home, a lost culture. This recalls to my mind an old Jewish woman from Yemen whom I once interviewed for a BBC programme. She emigrated to Israel, learnt Hebrew, raised a perfect Israeli family. But a few years before her death, she refused to speak Hebrew; she reverted to Arabic, reminisced about her childhood in Sana'a.

My thoughts go back to the statement of Professor Dina Porat of Yad Vashem: of how the mass conversion—under torture and fear of execution—from one identity to another can create ruptures in the hearts of the converts. It seems to me, standing amidst these ostentatiously decorated tombstones, that the *Nação* never quite let go of its colourful Iberian past. Rather than being a domain of the dead, Ouderkerk's Jewish cemetery, Beth Haim, the House of Life, is alive with the celebration of a lost cultural heritage. This makes me reflect that the history of the Jews has been full of improbable destinies. What if the Amsterdam Sephardim could have escaped the Nazi death machine using the research of the two anthropologists showing that they were not "racially Jews"? What if Portugal or Spain had come to their rescue during the war? Would the Portuguese Jews of Amsterdam have gone back to their former Marrano existence, living once again under the cover of Catholicism? Would the Hope of Israel that they nurtured in Amsterdam never have materialised?

NOTES

FOREWORD

1. Edward Kritzler, *Jewish Pirates of the Caribbean*, New York: Anchor Books, 2009.
2. Interview with Bart Wallet, Amsterdam, August 2017.
3. Henry Méchoulan and Gerard Nahon, "Introduction", in Menasseh Ben Israel, *The Hope of Israel* (trans. Moses Wall, 1652; eds Méchoulan and Nahon), The Littman Library of Jewish Civilisation, 2004, p. 11.
4. Rabbi Gavin Michal, "Rabbi Leon of Modena—Gaon, Gambler or Heretic?", *Kotzk Blog*, 18 February 2018, http://kotzkblog.blogspot.co.uk/2018/02/164-rabbi-leon-of-modena-gaon-gambler.html [last accessed 27 July 2018].

INTRODUCTION

1. Union of Utrecht, Article XIII, available in English translation at http://www.constitution.org/cons/dutch/Union_Utrecht_1579.html [last accessed 29 August 2018].
2. Interview with Tirtsah Levie Bernfeld, Amsterdam, August 2017.
3. Cecil Roth, *The Spanish Inquisition*, London: Robert Hale, 1937, p. 21.
4. Ibid., p. 23.
5. Ibid.
6. Ibid, p. 27.
7. Daniel Swetschinski, *Reluctant Cosmopolitans*, The Littman Library of Jewish Civilization, 2004, p. 119.

8. Miriam Bodian, *Hebrews of the Portuguese Nation*, Indianopolis, IN: Indiana University Press, 1999.
9. Interview with Bart Wallet.

1. TEMPEST-TOSSED AND FOUND

1. Rehuel Jessurun, *Diálogo dos Montes* (ed. and trans. Philip Polack), Woodbridge: Tamesis Books, 1975, lines 166–173, p. 13.
2. Mark Mazower, *Salonica: City of Ghosts*, London: HarperPerennial, 2005, p. 50.
3. Ibid.
4. Moses Maimonides, "Logbook of a Physician", in Leo W. Schwarz (ed. and trans.), *Memoirs of My People Through a Thousand Years*, New York, NY: Rinehart & Company, 1943, p. 16.
5. Don Isaac Abravanel, "Twilight of Spanish Glory", in Schwarz (ed.), *Memoirs of My People*, p. 46.
6. Ibid., p. 47.
7. "Life in Lombardy", from the memoir of Leone Da Modena, in Schwarz (ed.), *Memoirs of My People*, p. 75.
8. Jessurun, *Diálogo dos Montes*, "Earth's Prologue" (lines 145–9), p. 11.
9. Abravanel, "Twilight of Spanish Glory", p. 46.
10. Jessurun, *Diálogo dos Montes* (lines 160–165), p. 13.
11. Marc Saperstein, *Exile in Amsterdam: Saul Levi Morteira's Sermons to a Congregation of "New Jews"*, Cincinnati, OH: Hebrew Union College Press, 2005, p. 25.
12. Philip Polack, "Introduction", in Jessurun, *Diálogo dos Montes*, p. 25.
13. Jessurun, *Diálogo dos Montes* (lines 175–180), p. 13.
14. Ibid. (lines 190–191), p. 15.
15. Ibid., "Voice of Sinai".
16. The expression is taken from Saperstein, *Exile in Amsterdam*, quoting Heinrich Graetz, *Influence of Judaism on the Protestant Reformation* (trans. Rev. Simon Tuska), Cincinnati, OH: Bloch & Co, 1867, p. 23.

2. FROM ATONEMENT TO SALVATION

1. This phrase was taken from Saperstein, *Exile in Amsterdam*, p. 23.
2. Miriam Bodian, *Hebrews of the Portuguese Nation*, Bloomington, IN: Indiana University Press, 1999, p. 18.

3. Miriam Bodian, "Introduction", in Bodian, *Hebrews of the Portuguese Nation*, p. 19.

4. Maurice Halbwachs, *The Collective Memory*, 1950, accessed via: http://web.mit.edu/allanmc/www/hawlbachsspace.pdf

5. Miriam Bodian *Hebrews of the Portuguese Nation*, p. 22, quoting from de Barrios.

6. *Encyclopaedia Judaica* (online).

7. Swetschinski, *Reluctant Cosmopolitans*, p. 322.

8. Marc de Wilde, "Offering hospitality to strangers: Hugo Grotius's draft regulations for the Jews", *The Legal History Review*, Vol. 85, Nos 3–4 (2017), p. 410.

9. *Remonstrantie nopende de ordre dije in de landen van Hollandt ende Westvrieslandt dijent gestelt op de joden* (Remonstrance concerning the order to be imposed upon the Jews in the lands of Holland and West-Vriesland). Ets Haim Library, Amsterdam, manuscript no. MS EH 48 A 02.

10. Arend H Huussen, *Dutch Jewry: Its History and Secular Culture (1500–2000)*, ed. by Jonathan Irvine Israel, Salverda Reinier, Leiden: Brill, 2002, p. 33.

11. Ibid., p. 26.

12. The phrase is introduced by Miriam Bodian and is also the title of her book, *The Hebrews of the Portuguese Nation*.

3. A SEA-CHANGE IN SEAFARING

1. Shakespeare, *The Tempest*, Act I: Scene II, (400–403), *The Complete Works of Shakespeare*, London: Harrap & Co., 1926, p. 5.

2. Bodian, *The Hebrews of the Portuguese Nation*, p. 46.

3. Phrase used by Bodian, *The Hebrews of the Portuguese Nation*.

4. The Remonstrant factions of Reformed Protestantism.

5. Shakespeare, The *Merchant of Venice*, Act I: Scene III (lines 18–22), *The Complete Works of Shakespeare*, London: Harrap & Co., 1926, p. 177.

6. Jewish Cultural Quarter of Amsterdam, "Tours: Cemetery Beth Haim", https://jck.nl/en/page/cemetery-beth-haim [last accessed 29 August 2018].

7. Mercedes García-Arenal and Gerard Wiegers, *A Man of Three Worlds:*

Samuel Pallache, a Moroccan Jew in Catholic and Protestant Europe, (trans. Martin Beagles), Baltimore, MD: Johns Hopkins University Press, 2003, p. 58.

8. From the diary of Columbus, quoted by Don Isaac Abravanel, "Twilight of Spanish Glory", in Schwarz (ed.), *Memoirs of My People*, p. 43.

9. Edward Kritzler, *Jewish Pirates of the Carribean*, New York: Anchor Books, 2009, p. 98.

10. Egon E. Kirsch, *Tales from Seven Ghettos*, quoted by Kritzler, *Jewish Pirates of the Caribbean*, p. 101.

11. The Cyrus Cylinder is in the British Museum.

12. Shakespeare, *The Merchant of Venice*, Act 1, Scene 3 (lines 49–53).

13. Julie-Marthe Cohen, *Het getto van Venetië*, Joods Historisch Museum (Amsterdam, Netherlands), SDU Uitgeverij, 1990—History, p. 134.

14. J.A.J. Villiers, "Holland and Some of Her Jews", *Jewish Review* Vol. 7 (1912), pp. 10–12.

15. Kritzler, *Jewish Pirates of the Caribbean*, p. 91.

16. José Saraiva António, *The Marrano Factory, The Portuguese Inquisition and Its New Christians 1536–1765*, first published Lisbon, 1630 (trans. and revised by H.P. Salomon and I.S.D. Sassoon), Leiden: Brill, 2001.

17. Steven Nadler, *Rembrandt's Jews*, Chicago, IL: University of Chicago Press, 2004, p. 18. Quoting from Simon Schama, "A Different Jerusalem: The Jews in Rembrandt's Amsterdam", in Ruth E. Levine and Susan W. Morgenstein (eds), *Jews in the Age of Rembrandt*, Rockville, MD: The Judaic Museum of the Community Centre of Greater Washington, p. 5.

18. BBC Religions, "The Talmud", 13 August 2009, http://www.bbc.co.uk/religion/religions/judaism/texts/talmud.shtml [last accessed 29 August 2018].

19. Edith Wharton, *In Morocco* [first published 1920], Oxford: John Beaufoy, 2016, p. 53. Wharton describes the *mellah* in Sefrou, 30 kilometres south of Fez, in the early twentieth century. It had been totally destroyed during the massacres and pogrom of 1912, and Wharton remarks that "its distinct character, happily for the inhabitants, has disappeared in the rebuilding." However, the Sefrou ghetto "offers a good specimen of a *mellah* before foreign sanitation has lighted up its

dark places." When I spoke to the Sephardi Jewish community in Fez, they told me that Wharton's description would also have been fairly accurate for the Jewish ghetto of earlier centuries.

20. L. Poliakov, *Histoire de Antisemitisme*, Vol. 2, Paris: Calmann-Lévy, 1961, pp. 239, 248.

21. *Newsweek*, "How Muslim Immigration is Exposing Dutch Tolerance", 13 May 2009, https://www.newsweek.com/how-muslim-immigration-exposing-dutch-tolerance-80251 [last accessed 11 September 2018].

4. THE WAR OF THE RABBIS

1. Jewish Cultural Quarter (Amsterdam), "The Ets Haim—Livraria Montezinos Library", https://jck.nl/en/longread/ets-haim-livraria-montezinos-library [last accessed 29 August 2018].

2. Menasseh Ben Israel, *The Hope of Israel* (trans. Moses Wall, 1952; ed. Henry Méchoulan and Gerard Nahon), London: The Littman Library of Jewish Civilisation, 2004, p. 155.

3. Franz Landsberger, *Rembrandt, the Jews and the Bible*, Philadelphia, PA: Jewish Publication Society of America, 1962, p. 19.

4. Méchoulan and Nahon, "Introduction", in ben Israel, *The Hope of Israel*, p. 34.

5. Bodian, *Hebrews of the Portuguese Nation*, p. 49.

6. Barry L. Stiefel, *Jewish Sanctuary in the Atlantic World*: *A Social and Architectural History*, Columbia, SC: University of South Carolina, 2014, p. 3.

7. From Menasseh ben Israel, *De Termino Vitae*, as quoted by Méchoulan and Nahon, "Introduction", p. 37.

8. Ibid.

9. Edward Feld, "Spinoza the Jew", *Modern Judaism*, Vol. 9, No. 1 (Feb. 1989), p. 115.

10. Quoted by Feld in "Spinoza the Jew", p. 106.

11. Interview with Bart Wallet.

5. JUDAISM AS NATIONALITY

1. Rehuel Jessurun, *Diálogo dos Montes* (ed. and trans. Philip Polack), Woodbridge: Tamesis Books, 1975 (lines 178–181), p. 13.

2. Landsberger, *Rembrandt, the Jews and the Bible*, p. 11, quoting from Descartes' letter to Balzac in 1631.

3. C.R. Boxer, *Dutch Seaborne Empire 1600–1800*, London: Pelican Books, 1973, p. 8.

4. Ibid., p. 133.

5. Jessurun, *Diálogo dos Montes*, p. 13.

6. Méchoulan and Nahon, "Introduction", p. 43.

7. Feld, "Spinoza the Jew", p. 107.

8. Declaration by Daniel Levi de Barrios, as quoted from the Portuguese Synagogue documents of 10 Oct. 1665 I n Swetschinski, *Reluctant Cosmopolitans*, p. 241.

9. Barry L. Stiefel, *Jewish Sanctuary in the Atlantic World*: *A Social and Architectural History*, Columbia, SC: University of South Carolina, 2014, p. 2.

10. spinozaweb.org

6. THE DOUBLE LIFE OF URIEL DA COSTA

1. All the quotes by Uriel da Costa in this chapter are taken from his auto-biography, *My Double Life and Excommunication*, translation of *Exemplar Humanae Vitae*, in Schwarz (ed.), *Memoirs of My People*.

2. Ibid., p. 85.

3. Ibid., p. 86.

4. I. Zangwill, *Dreamers of the Ghetto*, London: William Heinemann, 1898, p. 69.

5. Expression used by Zangwill, "Uriel Acosta", in *Dreamers of the Ghetto*.

6. Zangwill, "Uriel Acosta", p. 78.

7. BARUCH SPINOZA: THE HERETIC WITHIN

1. Yosef Kaplan, "On the Burial of Spinoza's Grandfather and Grandmother", *Zutot*, Vol. 13, No. 1, pp. 26–39 (2016).

2. Ibid., p. 8.

3. Cited for the first time by historian Marc Saperstein in *Exile in Amsterdam*.

4. Kaplan, "On the Burial of Spinoza's Grandfather and Grandmother", p. 38.

5. A. Wolf, *The Oldest Biography of Spinoza*, London: Allen & Unwin, 1927, cited by Marc Saperstein, *Exile in Amsterdam*, p. 11.
6. I. Zangwill, "The Maker of Lenses", in *Dreamers of the Ghetto*, p. 169.
7. Many translations are available; this excerpt was taken from I. Zangwill, "The Maker of Lenses", in *Dreamers of the Ghetto*, p. 171.

8. HOPE OF ISRAEL: IN "THE LAND OF MILK AND CHEESE"

1. As quoted by Méchoulan and Nahon, "Introduction", p. 83.
2. Simon Schama, *Belonging: The Story of the Jews*, London: Bodley Head, 2017, p. 166.
3. Melchior Fokkens, "Beschryving", as quoted by Simon Schama in *The Embarrassment of Riches, An Interpretation of Dutch Culture in the Golden Age*, Fontana Press, 1991, p. 301.
4. Schama, *The Embarrassment of Riches*, p. 103.
5. I.S. Emmanuel, "New Light on Early American Jewry", *American Jewish Archives*, Vol. 7 (1955), p. 11, quoted in Kritzler, *Jewish Pirates of the Caribbean*, p. 144.
6. Arnold Wiznitzer, "War of Liberation" in Witnitzer, *Jews in Colonial Brazil*, Austin: University of Texas (1960), p. 100.
7. M. Jacob and C. Secretan, *The Self-Perception of Early Modern Capitalists*, Basingstoke: Palgrave Macmillan (2008), pp. 85–6.
8. Schama, *The Embarrassment of Riches*, pp. 123–4.
9. Méchoulan and Nahon, "Introduction", p. 72.
10. Menasseh ben Israel's retelling of Montezino's tale of the Lost Tribes in *The Hope of Israel*.
11. Ben Israel, *The Hope of Israel*, p. 125.
12. Méchoulan and Nahon, "Introduction", p. 48.
13. Ibid., p. 72.
14. Ibid., p. 68.
15. Interview with Tirtsah Levie Bernfeld.
16. Nahum Sokolow, *History of Zionism 1600–1918*, Vol I, New York: KTAV, 1969, pp. 21–46.

9. THE MESSIAH WHO ALMOST CAME

1. Deuteronomy 28:64.
2. As quoted in David G. Mandelbaum, "The Jewish Way of Life in Cochin", *Jewish Social Studies*, Vol. 1, No. 4 (Oct., 1939), pp. 423–60.
3. Ibid., p. 431.
4. Méchoulan and Nahon, "Introduction", p. 91.
5. Y Tishbi (ed.), *Tsitsat Novel Ha-Tsvi*, Jerusalem: Mosad Bialik, 1954.
6. Jessurun, *Diálogo dos Montes* (lines 1164–1167).
7. Abravanel, "Twilight of Spanish Glory", p. 44.
8. Mélouchan and Nahon, "Introduction", p. 95.

10. REMBRANDT'S NEIGHBOURS

1. Schama, *The Embarrassment of Riches*, p. 587.
2. Nadler, *Rembrandt's Jews*, p. 61.
3. Interview with Mirjam Knotter, Amsterdam, August 2017.
4. Nadler, *Rembrandt's Jews*, p. 16.
5. Ibid., p. 5: "The extant records indicate only one dated painting from that year, the *Aristotle Contemplating the Bust of Homer*, now in the Metropolitan Museum of Art."
6. Nadler quoting from Franz Landsberger, *Rembrandt, the Jews and the Bible*, p. 46.

11. THE *MAKOM*: "THE GLORY OF THE AMSTEL AND ITS SENATE"

1. Jewish Historical Museum, Amsterdam.

12. ABRAHAM PALACHE: STILL A WANDERING JEW

1. Interview with Abraham Palache, Amsterdam, August 2017.
2. Ibid., August 2017 and April 2018.
3. Anna Hájková, "'Poor devils'" of the Camps: Dutch Jews in Teresienstadt, 1943–1945", *Yad Vashem Studies*, Vol. 43, No. 1 (2015), pp. 77–111, p. 81. The author takes the figures (1,157 survivors; over 46,000 deportees) from Hagen Fleischer, "Griechenland", in Wolfgang Benz (ed.),

Dimensionen des Völkermords: Die Zahl der jüdischen Opfer des Nationalsozialis-mus (Munich: Oldenbourg, 1991); Mark Mazower, *Salonica, City of Ghosts* (New York: Knopf, 2005, p. 418).

4. Hájková, "'Poor devils' of the Camps".
5. Jessurun, *Diálogo dos Montes* (lines 1148–1151).

13. DAVID COHEN PARAIRA: THE LAST COHEN OF THE ESNOGA

1. Interview with Tirtsah Levie Bernfeld.
2. Interview with Michael Minco, April 2018.

14. THE CURIOUS CASE OF THE CURIELS

1. Harrie Curiel's note: "The circumcision register mentions the name of the child on that date not as Moses, but Abraham. A mistake of the *mohel*. The names of the children of Moses de Abraham appear correctly in the register of Ouderkerk cemetery. Unfortunately, the children of Moses de Abraham and Rebecca Polak are not registered in the birth register. This was because the PIG (Portuguese Synagogue in Amsterdam) did not want to include marriages between Sephardim and Ashkenazim."
2. Bodian, *Hebrews of the Portuguese Nation*, p. 36.
3. Swetschinski, *Reluctant Cosmopolitans*, p. 119.
4. Bodian, *Hebrews of the Portuguese Nation*, p. 164.
5. Dienke Hondius, "Black Africans in Seventeenth-Century Amsterdam", *Renaissance and Reformation*, Vol. 31, No. 2 (Spring 2008), p. 91 (quoting Hagoort).
6. As above. Lydia Hagoort referring to Jonathan Schorch, *Jews and Blacks in the Early Modern World*, Cambridge: Cambridge University Press, 2004, p. 92.
7. Hondius, "Black Africans in Seventeenth-Century Amsterdam", p. 93.
8. Ibid.
9. Hondius, "Black Africans in Seventeenth-Century Amsterdam", p. 88 (quoting Hagoort).
10. SHOAH Resource centre: yadvashem.org.

15. "THEY CLOSED THE CURTAINS WHEN THE TRAINS PASSED BY"

1. Edward Black, *IBM and the Holocaust. The Strategic Alliance Between Nazi Germany and America's Most Powerful Corporation*, Boston, MA: Little Brown, 2001.
2. P. Romijn, "Vervolging van de Joden in Nederland in internationaal vergelijkend perspectief", *De Gids*, Vol. 150 (1987), p. 148 (quoting Blom).
3. P. Romijn, "The War, 1940–1945", in Blom et al. (eds), *The History of the Jews in the Netherlands*, pp. 334–5.
4. Anna Hájková, "'Poor devils'" of the Camps", pp. 79–80, quoting from Hans Blom's chapter "The Persecution of the Jews in the Netherlands in a Comparative International Perspective", in Jozeph Michman (ed.), *Dutch Jewish History*, vol. 2 (Assen and Maastricht: Van Gorcum, 1989), pp. 273–89.
5. For newer studies, see Pim Griffioen and Ron Zeller, *Jodenvervolging in Nederland, Frankrijk en Belgien 1940–1945: Overeenkomsten, verschillen, oorzaken*, Amsterdam: Boom, 2011.
6. Interview with Ludo Abicht, Antwerp, August and September 2017.
7. Swetschinski, *Reluctant Cosmopolitans*, p. 243.
8. Ibid.
9. Blom, Fuks-Mansfield and Schoffer (eds), *The History of the Jews in the Netherlands*, (trans. Arnold J. Pomerans and Erica Pomerans), Littman Library of Jewish Civilisation, 2007. The quote is from F.C. Brasz, "After the Second World War: From Jewish Church to Cultural Minority", in Blom et al. (eds), *The History of the Jews in the Netherlands*, p. 337.
10. F.C. Brasz, "After the Second World War".

POSTSCRIPT

1. Lawrence A. Zeidman and Jaap Cohen, "Walking A Fine Scientific Line, The Extraordinary Deeds of Dutch Neuroscientist C. U. Ariëns Kappers Before and During World War II", *Journal of the History of the Neurosciences*, Vol. 1, No. 24 (2014), p. 18.

2. As quoted by Zeidman and Cohen, "Walking A Fine Scientific Line", p. 19.
3. Leah Goldstein, "Fate and Identity, Non-Jewish Jews during the Shoah", *Yad Vashem Journal*, Vol. 78 (October 2015).
4. As quoted in ibid., pp. 12–13.
5. Epitaph on Samuel Palache's gravestone, translated by Tehila Jouchovitzky and Yael Lavi-Bleiweiss.

BIBLIOGRAPHY

Books, book chapters, academic papers and old manuscripts

"A letter of Menasseh Ben Israel", *Jewish Quarterly Review*, Vol. 16, No. 3 (April 1904), pp. 562–72.

Abrahams, Israel, *Jewish Life in the Middle Ages*. Macmillan, London, 1919.

———, *Jewish Life in the Middle Ages*. Meridian Books, New York, NY, 1958.

Amler, Jane Frances, *The Fifth Kingdom: A Novel about The Spanish-Portuguese Jews*. iUniverse, Bloomington, IN, 2014.

Anon., *The Amorous convert being a true relation of what happened in Holland*. 1679.

Baigent, Michael and Richard Leigh, *The Inquisition*, Penguin Books, London, 2000.

Ben Israel, Menasseh, *The Hope of Israel* (trans. Moses Wall), 1652. Edited with Introduction and Notes by Henry Méchoulan and Gérard Nahon (trans. Richenda George), Littman Library of Jewish Civilisation, 2004.

Biale, David, *Cultures of the Jews*. Schocken Books, New York, 2002.

Black, Edwin, *IBM and the Holocaust: The Strategic Alliance Between Nazi Germany and America's Most Powerful Corporation*. Little Brown, New York, NY, 2001.

Blom, J.C.H. et al. (eds), *The History of the Jews in the Netherlands* (trans. Arnold J. Pomerans and Erica Pomerans). Littman Library of Jewish Civilisation, 2007.

Bodian, Miriam, *Hebrews of the Portuguese Nation*. Indiana University Press, Bloomington, IN, 1999.

BIBLIOGRAPHY

Bolt, Rodney, *The Xenophobe's Guide to the Dutch*, Xenophobe's Guides, London, 2008.

Bonney, Richard, *The Thirty Years' War, 1618–1648*. Osprey Publishing, Oxford, 2002.

Boxer, C.R., *Dutch Seaborne Empire 1600–1800*, Pelican Books, Harmondsworth, 1973.

Braber, Ben, *This Cannot Happen Here: Integration and Jewish Resistance in the Netherlands, 1940–1945*, Amsterdam University Press, Amsterdam, 2013.

Brasz, F.C., "After the Second World War: From 'Jewish Church' to Cultural Minority", in J.C.H. Blom et al. (eds), *The History of the Jews in the Netherlands* (trans. Arnold J. Pomerans and Erica Pomerans). Littman Library of Jewish Civilisation, 2007.

Brotton, Jerry, *This Orient Isle*. Penguin Books, London, 2017.

Carr, Matthew, *Blood and Faith: The Purging of Muslim Spain, 1492–1614* (2nd edn), Hurst Publishers, London, 2017.

Charlton, H.B., *Shakespearean Comedy*. Methuen, London, 1938, 1966.

Cohen, J.F., *De onontkoombare afkomst van Eli d'Oliveira. Een Portugees-Joodse familiegeschiedenis*, PhD thesis, University of Amsterdam, 2015.

Cohen, Jaap, "In de schaduw van Lombroso: Het Antropologische en Psychologische onderzoek naar Portugese Joden in Wereldoorlog II", in Bert Sliggers et al., *Karakterkoppen: over haviksneuzen en hamsterwangen*, pp. 84–99. Utig. Lannoo N.V., Haarlem, 2014.

Cohen, Mark R., *Under Crescent & Cross: The Jews in the Middle Ages*. Princeton University Press, Princeton, NJ, 2008.

Cohn-Sherbok, Dan, *The Jewish Messiah*, T&T Clark, Edinburgh, 1997.

De Villers, Charles, *An Essay on The Spirit and Influence of the Reformation of Luther* (trans. James Mill), C & R Baldwin, 1805.

De Wilde, Marc, "Offering hospitality to strangers: Hugo Grotius's draft regulations for the Jews", *The Legal History Review*, Vol. 85, Nos 3–4 (2017), pp. 391–433.

Eco, Umberto, *The Name of the Rose* [novel] (trans. William Weaver), Secker and Warburg Ltd., London, 1992.

Feld, Edward, "Spinoza the Jew", *Modern Judaism*, Vol. 9, No. 1 (1989), pp. 101–19.

BIBLIOGRAPHY

Franklin, Burt, *The Contemporary Jew in the Elizabethan Drama*. Burt Franklin, New York, NY, 1925.

García-Arenal, Mercedes and Gerard Wiegers, *A Man of Three Worlds: Samuel Pallache, a Moroccan Jew in Catholic and Protestant Europe* (trans. Martin Beagles). Johns Hopkins University Press, Baltimore, MD, 2003.

Goldstein, Rebecca, *Betraying Spinoza: The Renegade Jew Who Gave Us Modernity* (Jewish Encounters Series). Schocken Books, New York, NY, 2009.

Graetz, Heinrich, *Influence of Judaism on the Protestant Reformation* (trans. Rev. Simon Tuska). Bloch & Co, Cincinnati, OH, 1867.

Gutierrez, Juan Marcos Bejarano, *The Jews of Iberia: A Short History*. CreateSpace Independent Publishing Platform, 2016.

Hájková, Anna, "'Poor Devils' of the Camps: Dutch Jews in Theresienstadt, 1943–1945", *Yad Vashem Studies*, Vol. 43, No. 1 (2015), pp. 77–111.

Halbwachs, Maurice, "4. Space and the Collective Memory: The Group in its Spatial Framework. The Influence of Physical Surroundings", in Maurice Halbwachs, *The Collective Memory*. 1950, available online at http://web.mit.edu/allanmc/www/hawlbachsspace.pdf [last accessed 11 September 2018].

Hoftijzer, Paul G., "The Dutch Republic, Centre of the European Book Trade in the Seventeenth Century". *European History Online*, 23 November 2015, http://ieg-ego.eu/en/threads/backgrounds/the-book-market/paul-g-hoftijzer-the-dutch-republic-centre-of-the-european-book-trade-in-the-17th-century [last accessed 11 September 2018].

Hondius, Dienke, "Black Africans in Seventeenth-Century Amsterdam", *Renaissance and Reformation*, Vol. 31, No. 2 (2008), pp. 87–105.

Hyamson, Albert M., *The Sephardim of England: A History of the Spanish and Portuguese Jewish Community 1492–1951*. Methuen & Co Ltd., London, 1951.

Israel, Jonathan Irvine and Salverda Reinier (eds), *Dutch Jewry: Its History and Secular Culture (1500–2000)*. Brill, Leiden, 2002.

Jacob, M. and C. Secretan, *The Self-Perception of Early Modern Capitalists*, Palgrave Macmillan, Basingstoke, 2008.

Jessurun d'Oliveira, Hans Ulrich, *Ontjoodst door de wetenschap: de weten-*

BIBLIOGRAPHY

schappelijke en menselijke integriteit van Arie de Froe tijdens de bezetting. Amsterdam University Press, Amsterdam, 2015.

Jessurun, Rehuel, *Diálogo dos Montes* , 1624 manuscript held in Ets Haim Library, Amsterdam. Translation of selected verses is of a copy of a seventeenth-century manuscript held in the British Library, London: Jessurun, Rehuel, *Dialogo dos Montes, Edited with an English verse translation* (ed. & trans. Philip Polack), Tamesis Books, London, 1975.

Jewish Historical Museum, *Jewish Life in the Golden Age of Amsterdam, 1592–1796.* Jewish Historical Museum, Amsterdam, 1982.

Josephus, *The Fall of Jerusalem* (trans. G.A. Williamson). Penguin Epics, London, 2006.

Kaplan, Joseph, "Rabbi Saul Levi Morteira's Treatise 'Arguments Against Christian Religion'", in Jozeph Michman (ed.), *Studies on the History of Dutch Jewry.* Magnes, Jerusalem, 1975. Available in English translation by Bruce A. Lorence at http://www.etrfi.info/immanuel/11/ Immanuel_11_095.pdf [last accessed 11 September 2018].

Kaplan, Yosef, "On the Burial of Spinoza's Grandfather and Grandmother", *Zutot*, Vol. 13, No. 1 (2016), pp. 26–39.

————— and Dan Michman (eds), *The Religious Cultures of Dutch Jewry* (Brill's Series in Jewish Studies). Brill, Leiden, 2017.

Kayserling, Meyer, *Christopher Columbus and the Participation of the Jews in the Spanish and Portuguese Discoveries*, 1686. Hubert Allen & Associates edition, 2002.

Kritzler, Edward, *Jewish Pirates of the Caribbean.* Anchor Books, New York, NY, 2009.

Kyd, Thomas, *The Spanish Tragedy*, 1587. Printed by Edward Allde, for Edward White. Kindle edition.

Landsberger, Franz, *Rembrandt, The Jews and The Bible.* Jewish Publication Society of America, Philadelphia, PA, 1962.

Levie Bernfield, Tirtsah, *Poverty and Welfare: Among the Portuguese Jews in Early Modern Amsterdam.* Littman Library of Jewish Civilisation, 2012.

Liss, David, *The Coffee Trader* [novel]. Random House, New York, NY, 2003.

Lloyd, Genevieve, *Spinoza: Routledge Philosophy Guidebook to Spinoza and the Ethics.* Routledge, London, 2002.

BIBLIOGRAPHY

Mandelbaum, David G., "The Jewish Way of Life in Cochin", *Jewish Social Studies*, Vol. 1, No. 4 (Oct. 1939), pp. 423–60.

Mazower, Mark, *Salonica: City of Ghosts*. Harper Perennial, New York, NY, 2005.

Morteira, Saul Levi, *Providencia de Dios con Ysrael*, Saul Levi Morteira, c. 1650s (ed. & trans. Gregory B. Kaplan). Manuscript B 16 of the Ets Haim Library, Portuguese Synagogue, Amsterdam, available online at http://heskaamuna.org/morteiraheskatext.pdf [last accessed 11 September 2018].

Nadler, Steven, "The Excommunication of Spinoza: Trouble and Toleration in the "Dutch Jerusalem", *Shofar*, Vol. 19, No. 4 (2001, Special Issue: Sephardic Studies as an Interdisciplinary Field), pp. 40–52.

———, *Rembrandt's Jews*. University of Chicago Press, Chicago, IL, 2004.

———, *Spinoza's "Ethics": An Itroduction* (Cambridge Introductions to Key Philosophical texts). Cambridge University Press, Cambridge, 2006.

———, *A Book Forged in Hell: Spinoza's Scandalous Treatise and the Birth of the Secular Age*. Princeton University Press, Princeton, NJ, 2011.

Newitt, Malyn, *Emigration and the Sea: An Alternative History of Portugal and the Portuguese*. Hurst Publishers, London, 2015.

Oxford University Press, *The Holy Bible*. Oxford University Press, Oxford, 1966.

Romain, Jonathan A., *The Jews of England*, St Edmundsbury Press, Bury St Edmunds, 1988.

Roth, Cecil, *The Spanish Inquisition*. Robert Hale Limited, London, 1937.

———, *A History of the Jews*. Schocken Books, New York, NY, 1989.

Saperstein, Marc, *Exile in Amsterdam: Saul Levi Morteira's Sermons to a Congregation of "New Jews"*. Hebrew Union College Press, 2005.

Saraiva António José, *The Marrano Factory: The Portuguese Inquisition and Its New Christians 1536–1765* (trans. H. P. Salomon and I. S. D. Sassoon). Brill, Leiden, 2001.

Schama, Simon, *The Embarrassment of Riches: An Interpretation of Dutch Culture in the Golden Age*. Fontana Press, London, 1991.

———, *Rembrandt's Eyes*. Penguin Books, London, 2000.

———, *Belonging: The Story of the Jews*. Bodley Head, London, 2017.

BIBLIOGRAPHY

Schwarz, Leo W., *Memoirs of My People: Through a Thousand Years*. Rinehart & Company, New York, 1943.

Shakespeare, William, *The Tempest*; *The Merchant of Venice*, in *The Complete Works of Shakespeare*, George Harrap & Company, London, 1926.

Sharot, Stephen, *Comparative Perspectives on Judaisms and Jewish Identities*. Wayne State University Press, Detroit, MI, 2010.

Slotki, Judah J., MA, PhD, *Menasseh ben Israel: His Life and Times*. Jewish Religious Educational Publications, London, 1960.

Starkey, David, *Elizabeth*. Chatto and Windus, London, 2001.

Stiefel, Barry L., *Jewish Sanctuary in the Atlantic World: A Social and Architectural History*. University of South Carolina Press, Columbia, SC, 2014.

Stoutenbeek, Jan and Paul Vigeveno, *Jewish Amsterdam*. Jewish Historical Museum, Amsterdam, 2014.

Swetshinski, Daniel M., *Reluctant Cosmopolitans: The Portuguese Jews of Seventeenth Century Amsterdam*. Littman Library of Jewish Civilisation, 2000.

Toynbee, Arnold J., *A Study of History*. Oxford University Press, Oxford, 1962.

Tremlett, Giles, *Ghosts of Spain: Travels Through a Country's Hidden Past*, Faber, London, 2007.

Weber, Max, *The Protestant Ethic and the Spirit of Capitalism*. Unwin University Press, London, 1974.

Wharton, Edith, *In Morocco*, 1920. Stanfords Travel Classics, London, 2016.

White, Christopher, *Rembrandt*. Thames and Hudson, London, 1984.

Witznitzer, Arnold, *Jews in Colonial Brazil*. Columbia University Press, New York, NY, 1960.

Zangwill, I., *Dreamers of the Ghetto*, William Heinemann, London, 1898.

Zeidman, L.A. and J. Cohen, "Walking a fine scientific line: the extraordinary deeds of Dutch neuroscientist C. U. Ariëns Kappers before and during World War II", *Journal of the History of the Neurosciences*, Vol. 23, No. 3 (2014), pp. 252–75.

Zimler, Richard, *The Last Kabbalist of Lisbon*. Arcadia Books, 1999.

BIBLIOGRAPHY

Archival papers

Amsterdam Municipal Archives, various papers.

Ets Haim Library, Amsterdam, various seventeenth-century manuscripts:

EH_47_A_11,"Letter by 24 members of Yeshuot Meshiho to hail Shabtai Tzvi as Messiah", Amsterdam, 1666.

EH_47_E_05, "Kol Tefilah ve-Kol Zimrah [Collection of prayers and poetry recited in the Portuguese synagogues of Amsterdam in 1597 to 1782]", collected and copied by David Franco Mendes, Amsterdam, 1792.

EH_47_E_32, "Collection of Hebrew poetry by Isaac b. Abraham Uziel", Amsterdam, early 17th century.

EH_48_A_05, "Collection of historical documents, 16th, 17th and 18th century".

EH_48_A_17_01, "Dialogo entre dos Hermanos I [Anonymous polemic against Christianity in the form of a dialogue between two brothers]", 18th century copy.

EH_48_A_25, "Reglementen. Dutch translation of the regulations (haskamot) of the Dotar society", Amsterdam, 1838.

EH_48_A_26, "Libro de los acuerdos... [Book containing the regulations as they were stipulated by the Kahal Kadosh of the Talmud Tora congregation in Amsterdam]".

EH_48_C_16, "Certamen Philosophico [Polemical treatise against Johannes Bredenburg and Bento de Spinoza by Isaac Orobio de Castro, translated from the Latin into Spanish by G. de la Torre", copied in The Hague, 1741.

EH_48_D_05, "Fortificacion De la Fee [Spanish translation by Isaac Athias of the Hebrew polemical treatise of Isaac ben Abraham of Troki]", copied by Isaac Senior, Amsterdam, 1663.

EH_48_D_20, "Libro del Alcoran [Spanish translation of the Koran", late 17th century copy.

EH_48_D_26, "De los Judios y la Santa Inquisicion del Reyno de Portugal [Treatise on the Jewish question in Portugal by João Carvalho]", Portugal, 17th century copy.

BIBLIOGRAPHY

Online resources

Encyclopaedia Judaica Online: http://www.bjeindy.org/resources/library/access-to-encyclopedia-judaica/

Green, David B., various articles, *Haaretz* series, "This Day in Jewish History".

SHOAH Resource centre: yadvashem.org

"The Dutch Jerusalem", Erenow.com: https://erenow.com/modern/the-age-of-louis-xiv/101.html [last accessed 11 September 2018].

Interviews with Dutch and Belgian historians, 2017–18:

Abicht, Ludo, University of Antwerp.

Cohen, Julie-Marthe, Jewish Historical Museum, Amsterdam

Knotter, Mirjam, Jewish Historical Museum, Amsterdam

Levie Bernfield, Tirtsah, Selma Stern Zentrum für Jüdische Studien Berlin-Brandenburg

Ten Hove, Okke [email correspondence], Dutch historian and Surinamese slavery specialist.

Wallet, Bart, University of Amsterdam.

Warncke, Heide, Ets Haim Library

Interviews and conversations with rabbis and descendants of the Portuguese Jews, Amsterdam, 2017:

Buning, Olivia

Curiel, Harrie

Minco, Michael (current chairman of the Mahamad)

Navarre, David

Palache, Abraham

Paraira, David Cohen

Paraira, Maurice Cohen

Rosenberg, Abraham (rabbi and former curator of Ets Haim Library; not a descendant)

Spiero, Zwi (rabbi; not a descendant)

INDEX

INDEX

INDEX

INDEX

INDEX

INDEX

burghers, 89, 182, 198, 199, 217, 303

burgomasters, 57, 61, 68, 73, 85, 89

burning at the stake, 2, 8, 101, 142–3, 265, 289, 323

Cairo, 27

Calvin, John, 5

Calvinism, 4, 9, 19, 25, 51, 55, 57, 68, 94–6, 113–18, 134, 195, 215

  and apostasy, 134

  and capitalism, 11, 12, 34, 40, 56, 71, 134

  and Catholicism, 35, 50, 57, 113–17, 216, 246

  and conversion, 215–16

  Hebraists, 95–6, 100, 116–18, 185, 202, 207–16, 218

  iconoclasm, 5, 100, 115–16, 212

  and Inquisition, 216

  and Law of Moses, 6, 51, 117, 207–9

  live and let live, 89, 195, 223

  militancy, 115, 134

  and Old Testament, 5, 35, 38, 51, 95–6, 100, 115–18, 165, 167, 179, 207–9, 214

  and pillarisation, 222

  and predestination, 100–101

  predikanten, 68, 116

  and public synagogues, 55, 70

  and Second Coming, 15, 38, 117, 166, 169, 173–6, 185, 189, 215

  and Spinoza, 159

  Synod of Dordrecht (1618–19), 67, 114–15, 116

  theatres and dancehalls, ban on, 116

  and Twelve Years' Truce agreement (1609), 68, 114

  Van Oldenbarnevelt execution (1619), 115

canals, 6, 87, 88, 112, 139, 157–8, 229, 248, 250, 279, 283, 302–3, 306

  canalside houses, 12, 49, 70, 74, 143, 177, 199, 249, 250, 302, 306

  dykes, xiii, 166, 230

  filling in, 203

  and *overvloed*, 275

capitalism, 34, 56, 105, 250; *see also* trade networks

Caribbean, 14, 24, 71, 113

carnival of nations, xviii, 60, 217, 230, 308

Cartagena, 170

de Castro, Orobio, 102

Catalonia, 5

Catholicism, xvii, 4, 113, 130, 215

  and Calvinists, 35, 50, 57, 113–17, 216, 246

  Christmas, 54

  confession of sins, 128, 129

  Corpus Christi, 41

  in Dutch Republic (1581–

INDEX

INDEX

INDEX

INDEX

INDEX

INDEX

INDEX

INDEX

INDEX

INDEX

INDEX

INDEX

INDEX

INDEX

INDEX

INDEX

374

INDEX

INDEX

INDEX

377

INDEX

INDEX

Pereyra, Abraham, 104
Pernambuco, Brazil, 171, 172
Persia, 75–6
Peru, Viceroyalty of (1542–1824), 14–15, 170–78
phoenix, 265
Piedra gloriosa (Ben Israel), 120, 211–13, 219
PIG, 284, 337
pillarisation, 195, 222–4, 234, 237, 239–40, 315
Pimentel, Manuel, 79
de Pinto, Daniel, 200, 202, 207, 214, 281, 316, 325
de Pinto, Violenta, 257
piracy, 67, 72, 80, 130, 253
Plantage, Amsterdam, 305
Plymouth, England, 80–81
poetry, 83, 84
pogroms, 13, 26, 65, 86, 87, 88, 107, 132, 163, 263, 225, 237, 314
  Germany, 107, 223, 225, 263
  Morocco, 65, 86, 87, 223
  Poland, 107, 183, 223, 225, 263
  Russia, 225
  Thirty Years War (1618–48), 216, 223
Polak, Rebecca, 286, 337
Poland, 49, 107, 183, 187, 223, 225, 263, 232
policing, 104–5, 116
political office, barring from, 76
polyphonic music, xxi
Pope, 4, 11, 116, 121

Porat, Dina, 323, 328
Porto, Portugal, 54, 124–9, 132, 135, 138–9, 140, 143
Portugal
  auto plays, 24, 36, 37, 41
  Ben Israel in, 92
  colonial empire, *see* Portuguese Empire
  da Costa in, 54, 124–9, 132, 135, 138–9, 140, 143
  Curiel family in, 283–5, 288–91
  Edict of Expulsion (1492), 2
  fashion, 256
  Garcês in, 150
  Inquisition, 2, 36, 193, 290
  Marranos, 54, 124, 283–5, 288–91
  Montezinos in, 170
  New Christians, xviii, xxii, 1, 3, 35–6, 45, 46, 54
  Restoration War (1640–68), 290, 291
  and Shoah, 319–20, 322, 328
Portuguese Empire, 3, 59, 70, 80, 190
  Angola (1575–1975), 294
  Brazil (1549–1815), 192, 263–4, 286, 291, 294
  India (1505–1961), 59, 123, 181–2, 294
  São Tomé and Príncipe (1470–1975), 294
Portuguese identity, 35–6, 53, 59, 111, 130, 273–4, 276
Portuguese Jewish Congregation, 284

INDEX

Portuguese language, xx, 9, 50, 58–9, 91, 104, 144, 290

Portuguese Nation, The, xix, 59, 76, 106, 150, 224, 240, 259, 272, 274, 288, 290

Portuguese Synagogue,
Amsterdam, xxii, 16–17, 122, 159, 190–96, 217–18, 241, 262–9, 274, 282
artist's depictions of, 195, 197, 221
benches, 269
Bouman's design, 15, 190, 263
candles, 264–5
chandeliers, 264–5
columns, 258, 264
construction of, 16, 34, 40, 87, 159, 168, 190–92, 217
and Curiels, 301
doors, 262
de Hooghe's etching, 221, 262, 302
inauguration (1675), 192, 194, 221, 237, 263
jacaranda wood, 192, 263–4, 286, 291
Nazi occupation (1940–45), 238, 242–3, 248, 265, 269
postwar period, 243, 244–5
services, 264–5, 269, 276–7, 278
Shabbat services, 276–7
size, 262–3, 278
and Templo's plans, 16, 40, 190, 263

teva, 264, 269
Torah ark, 218, 263, 264, 286, 291
weddings, 278
windows, 238, 242, 263, 264, 265
women's galleries, 265
Yom Kippur services, 264–5, 278, 279

potato cakes, 273
de Prado, Juan, 124, 125
prayer books, xxii, 8, 10, 51, 96, 182, 185, 269, 308
predestination, 100–101
predikanten, 68, 116
printing, 87, 88, 95, 96, 100, 133, 183, 184–5, 187, 221
privateering, 80
professions, 17, 88, 91, 184, 235
prostitution, 57, 74, 108, 204
Protestantism, xvii, 3, 4–5, 6, 9, 25, 57, 60–61, 63, 73, 94, 100, 113
and conversion, 215–16
Dutch Republic independence (1581), 3
and Eighty Years' War (1568–1648), 113, 215
in Germany, 6
Hebraists, 95–6, 100, 116–18, 185, 202, 207–16, 218
Huguenots, xviii, 3, 17, 79, 93, 107, 223
iconoclasm, 5, 100, 115–16, 212

INDEX

and Law of Moses, 6, 51, 117,
207–9

New Christians and, 4–5, 9

and Old Testament, 5, 51, 35,
38, 95–6, 100, 115, 116–18,
165, 167, 179, 207–8, 214

predestination, 100–101

Reformation, xvii, 4, 24, 25,
38, 51, 55, 118, 134, 209, 212

Remonstrants, 115

and Second Coming, 15, 38,
117, 166, 169, 173–6, 185,
189, 215

Synod of Dordrecht (1618–19),
67, 114–15, 116

work ethic, 56, 192

Psalms, 152

Public Notary Office, 202

questioning, culture of, 101–4

Quran, 58

rabbis, *see under* orthodoxy

Rabinowitz, Hyman Reuven, 42

Rachel, 324, 325

Ramadan, 75

rationalism, 18, 136, 148, 152,
160

Rebecca, 325

Recife, Brazil, 99, 167, 177, 189,
192

Reformation, xvii, 4, 24, 25, 38,
51, 55, 118, 134, 209, 212

Reformed Church, *see* Dutch
Reformed Church

Reluctant Cosmopolitans
(Swetschinski), 54

Rembrandt van Rijn, xiii, 13, 34,
73, 108, 118, 182, 197–219,
224, 252, 281

African women, depictions of,
295

Aristotle with a Bust of Homer,
203

Ashkenazim, depictions of,
197, 203, 204, 214, 217, 224

Belshazzar's Feast, 210–12, 213

Hebrew, knowledge of, 207–16,
218

humanism, 200, 204, 205, 207,
208

Jewish Bride, 205

Man in Oriental Costume, 49,
50, 74

*Moses Breaking the Tablets of the
Law*, 207–9, 213, 218

Nightwatch, 302

and Old Testament, 118, 185,
198, 200, 203, 205, 206,
207–19

Pinto, relationship with, 200,
202, 207, 214, 281, 316, 325

Triumph of Mordecai, The, 215

Tronies, 108, 214, 252

Rembrandt, the Jews and the Bible
(Landsberger), 217

Rembrandt's Jews (Nadler),
199–200, 203, 210

Remonstrance (de Groot), 57

Remonstrants, 115

381

INDEX

INDEX

INDEX

INDEX

INDEX

INDEX

World War II (1939–45), *see* Nazi
  Germany; Shoah

Yad Vashem, 314, 322, 328
Yemen, 328
yeshivas, 36, 91, 92, 148, 197, 270
YHVH, 100
Yiddish, 95, 187, 221, 307
Yom Kippur, 47, 48–53, 56, 57,
  59, 78, 156, 244, 264–5, 278,
  279

Zangwill, Israel, 157–8
Zeeland, 1, 66
Zeeuwsche Stroom, De, 299
Zidan Abu Maali, Sultan of
  Morocco, 55, 65, 67–8, 72, 80
Zion, 19, 38, 189, 193, 216, 222,
  225, 259
Zionism, 18–9, 109, 157, 180,
  187, 225, 259
Zur Israel, 189
Zuyderzee, 164